Napoleon

The Man who Shaped Europe

NAPOLEON

THE MAN WHO SHAPED EUROPE

by

Ben Weider

with Emile Gueguen

Translated by Phyllis Aronoff and Howard Scott

SPELLMOUNT
Staplehurst

British Library Cataloguing in Publication Data:
A catalogue record for this book is available
from the British Library

Copyright © Editions Trois-Pistoles 1997
This edition copyright © Editions Trois-Pistoles 2000
English translation © Phyllis Aronoff and Howard Scott

ISBN 1-86227-078-3

First published in the UK in 2000 by
Spellmount Limited
The Old Rectory
Staplehurst
Kent TN12 0AZ

1 3 5 7 9 8 6 4 2

The right of Ben Weider to be identified
as the author of this work has been asserted by him
in accordance with the Copyright, Designs
and Patents Act 1988

Typeset in Palatino by MATS, Southend-on-Sea, Essex
Printed in Great Britain by T J International

Contents

The Authors   xi

Preface   xiii

Foreword   xvii

I.   Slanders and Truths   1

II.   The Question of Napoleon's Birth   9

III.   The Statesman   29

IV.   The Military Leader   105

V.   The Writer and Thinker   153

VI.   Assassination on St Helena   173

VII.   The Judgement of History   189

The legend of Napoleon is like the revelation of St John. Everyone knows there is something hidden there, but nobody knows what it is.
Johann Wolfgang von Goethe

The Authors

Ben Weider CM, PhD is the author of several bestsellers, including *The Strongest Man in History: Louis Cyr, the Amazing Canadian* and *The Murder of Napoleon*, which has been translated into forty languages and was an unprecedented international success. In the former Soviet Union and in modern-day Russia, seven editions were published and over 402,000 copies sold. In the Chinese editions, over 70,000 copies were sold.

Through his lectures all over the world, his historical research and his scholarly papers, Ben Weider has made an enormous contribution to keeping alive the memory of the greatest Western ruler in history. From an early age, he has divided his time between his vocation as a historian and the work of establishing the International Napoleonic Society, which represents historians in more than thirty countries. He is president of the International Napoleonic Society and a Member of the Order of Canada. He also owns one of the largest private collections of Napoleonic artefacts in the world.

Émile Gueguen, a retired colonel in the French army and a Grand Officer of the Légion d'honneur, is a historian who specialises in the Napoleonic era. He assisted Ben Weider with his research, especially regarding the relationship between the Comte de Marbeuf, the governor of Corsica, and Letizia Bonaparte, Napoleon's mother – a love that was as strong as that between Romeo and Juliet, and that changed the world.

Preface

André Malraux, General de Gaulle's Minister of Culture, was a great admirer of Napoleon. He had planned that the summer of 1969 would be devoted to celebrating the bicentenary of the birth of 'the Emperor of the Republic', but unfortunately the General's departure from office forced the cancellation of the planned events. Malraux did, however, leave us excerpts of what he wanted to say in his speeches, including the following: 'Napoleon, unlike monarchs, perfectly represents human rights and civil rights. He brought the Revolution to all of Europe, that is, he established the power of the third estate and he created individualism, he established freedom of religion and brought the Jews out of the ghettos and made them full citizens. All his actions embodied the motto of the French Republic: LIBERTÉ - ÉGALITÉ - FRATERNITÉ.'

At the age of nineteen, after studying at the best military schools in France (he enjoyed the same education as Presidents Eisenhower and de Gaulle), the young lieutenant Napoleon Bonaparte wrote: 'To find happiness for oneself, one has to work for the happiness of others. What a joy to die surrounded by children and to be able to say: I assured the happiness of hundreds of families; I had a laborious and difficult life, but the nation will benefit from my work; I had the concerns, my friends had serenity; I was worried, they were happy; I had the pains and they the joys.' Throughout his life, he put his genius at the service of these principles, working as much as twenty hours a day. He often subjected himself to a regime that involved going to bed at eight o'clock at night and getting up again at midnight.

To appreciate the veneration in which Napoleon was held by the French people, my ancestors (not really so distant: my grandmother, born in 1863, used to tell me stories told to her by her great uncle, who had been at Wagram), we only have to recall:

His return from Elba:
Here is a man who finds himself alone on the sands of Provence, facing the police and armies of the king, and who simply marches on Paris, where he arrives in triumph, cheered by the jubilant populace. Louis XVIII was not waiting for him. Shamefully he had slipped away.

The fervour of the people of Paris on 15 December 1840:
That was the day the victim of St Helena 'returned to the shores of the Seine, among the French people he loved so much'. King Louis-Philippe had entrusted his own son, the Prince de Joinville, with the sacred mission of bringing Napoleon's body back from St Helena. From the port of Courbevoie, the funeral procession, surrounded by the largest crowd ever seen in Paris, made its way to the Arc de Triomphe along l'Avenue de Neuilly, then down the Champs-Elysées to the Place de la Concorde and towards Les Invalides. This had been chosen as his final resting place primarily because there were still many of the old *grognards* there, soldiers from the Old Guard of the Grande Armée, who would thus have the reward of guarding their 'little corporal' as they had done on the battlefield. The king, who waited at attention in the crypt, did not try to hold back his tears when a veteran of Wagram, breaking the respectful silence at the precise moment when the coffin came through the double door, cried out, 'The Emperor!'

The election of Louis Napoleon in 1848:
At the age of 40, a record, Louis Napoleon was elected President of the Republic by universal suffrage, winning 75% of the votes, another record, although the Paris intelligentsia had expected his principal opponent, General Louis Eugene Cavaignac (the other was the poet Lamartine), to win with a crushing majority. Louis Napoleon was not elected on his own merits (which were totally unknown in 1848) but uniquely on his name, that is to say, because of the deep love the French carried in their hearts for the memory of his uncle.

In 1819, while Napoleon was suffering on St Helena, Letizia, in

Rome, declared, 'It will take perhaps two or three centuries before the merits and goodness of my little boy are fully recognised, but believe you me, that time will come.' Indeed! That prophecy is beginning to come true. Throughout 1996 the Italians, with their characteristic enthusiasm, organised ceremonies in more than fifty cities and towns in the north to mark the bicentenary of their liberation by General Bonaparte. In France, the government is planning major events for the year 2000 to celebrate the achievements of the First Consul.

As for Ben Weider, he has put all his energy, which is considerable, into accelerating the process. In 1995, after writing several bestsellers on the life and death of Napoleon – he proved that the Emperor did not die of cancer on St Helena but was murdered – he founded the International Napoleonic Society, which has expanded rapidly and already has branches in thirty countries: Australia, Austria, Belarus, Belgium, Bulgaria, Canada, the Czech Republic, England, France, Georgia, Germany, Hungary, India, Ireland, Israel, Italy, Kazakhstan, Malta, Monaco, Pakistan, Portugal, Romania, Russia, Scotland, Slovakia, South Africa, Spain, Sweden, Switzerland and the United States. Soon we will be able to talk about the UNN – the United Napoleonic Nations. The purpose of the Society is to promote the study and understanding of this man of such great talents who devoted most of his life to improving the lot of humanity, and to hold him up as an example to the youth of every nation.

Now Ben Weider has agreed to revise his masterpiece of 1983, *La Sagesse de Napoléon*, adding some recent discoveries,[1] in particular concerning the birth and the death of the Emperor. In doing so he has provided a resource, a sort of bible, for historians, students and the general public. Readers will have at their disposal a reference book based solely on verified facts, which will allow them to discover more about the man Goethe called 'the most extraordinary man of all time'.

Colonel (retired) Émile Gueguen
Grand Officer of the Légion d'honneur

1. Gilbert Martineau would not have been aware of these additions when he wrote his Foreword.

Foreword

Longwood House
St Helena
South Atlantic

Dear Mr Weider,

Your book is a tremendous achievement. In a few chapters, and in a lively style that reminds us that you yourself are a man of action, you marshal your argument, retracing the life and enumerating the merits of this emperor who won so many battles, shaped modern France, enacted a code of laws, founded a prestigious order of merit, designed a policy of religious freedom, and laid the foundations for a united Europe.

His rise was as rapid as that of Caesar or Alexander – although he was neither from a family of consuls, like the former, nor the son of a king, like the latter – and he may be compared with the emperor Claudius, who made all the peoples of the West naturalised Roman citizens. But a vast empire of men and ideas was not enough for Napoleon. His dream of a Europe swept by a new spirit, under the sway of his law of progress, led eventually to his death on the island of St Helena as the prisoner of a reactionary aristocracy. Thus do great destinies contain the seeds of their own destruction.

From Malmaison and Saint-Cloud to the shack of Longwood, from the chateaus of Île-de-France and 18 Brumaire to the silent shores of death and transfiguration, we follow the tumultuous career and great deeds of the last enlightened despot in history, amazed that a single man was able to accomplish so much in so little time. Emperor at the age of 35, ruler of Europe for ten years, man of action, daring and sensible administrator, impassioned legislator, military leader and statesman, Napoleon comes alive again in your book, with his active intelligence, his vast knowledge, his unflinching reason, and his audacity so admirably served by luck.

Your knowledge of the facts is faultless and you could have written a very scholarly work; you chose to let yourself be guided by your heart, by a passion which, for all its warmth, never blinds you. Doggedly, without ever pausing to catch your breath, like a great athlete you reached the goal you had set yourself, and proved that in the gallery of great men – those who have pushed back the limits of their possibilities and are a credit to humanity – Napoleon occupies one of the most prominent places. You are to be congratulated.

Gilbert Martineau
Consul of France, St Helena

CHAPTER I
Slanders and Truths

Slander . . . Slander . . . Slander . . . some of it will always remain

Josef Goebbels

Laws, institutions, monuments, nations all disappear, but their echo remains and resounds in other generations.

Napoleon

The legend of Napoleon is one of the phenomena of history. What other great man has so inspired the popular imagination and given rise to so much controversy? Caesar and Alexander occupy only the libraries of educated readers, Frederick of Prussia has not often reached beyond his borders, and Charlemagne reigns only in the textbooks. Not so for Napoleon.

'Living he nearly conquered the world; dead he possesses it.' These words by Chateaubriand sum up the formidable attraction Napoleon still exerts nearly two hundred years after his death. Against the legions who promote his worship, praise his deeds, exalt his genius and lament his end, self-appointed critics condemn his tyranny, dispute his talents and deplore his fame. And his fame was considerable, leading Chateaubriand to add, 'After enduring the despotism of his person, we have to endure the despotism of his memory.'

During the Emperor's lifetime, there was already a battle between his admirers and his detractors, but the great man, soldier and legislator, philosopher and builder of the European idea, quietly responded: 'In spite of the attacks, I have no fear for my fame. Posterity will do me justice. The truth will be known and the good I have done will be judged along with my faults.' And: 'My critics? I am destined to be their fodder, but I have little fear of being their victim . . . They are biting granite.'

1

The anti-Napoleon campaign began, as might be expected, in England, where politicians, journalists, writers and caricaturists vied with one other to belittle and ridicule the man they called only 'Buonaparte' or, more familiarly, 'Boney'. When he was still only General Bonaparte and his family name and his unusual first name were first heard in the streets of London, his fame as a strategist and the victor at the siege of Toulon and in Italy and Egypt was mainly associated with the bad reputation of the French Revolution. In 1800, when it came time to make peace, Pitt, an orator who deserves a special place in the anti-Napoleon literature, made a judgement, as did his fellow citizens, on false evidence:

'In the first place, we see, as has been truly stated, a change in the description and form of the sovereign authority; a supreme power is placed at the head of this nominal republic, with a more open avowal of military despotism than at any former period; with a more open and undisguised abandonment of the names and pretences under which that despotism long attempted to conceal itself. The different institutions, republican in their form and appearance, which were before the instruments of that despotism, are now annihilated; they have given way to the absolute power of one man, concentrating in himself all the authority of the state, and differing from other monarchs only in this, that, as my honourable friend [George Canning] truly stated it, he wields a sword instead of a sceptre . . . His hold upon France is the sword, and he has no other. Is he connected with the soil, or with the habits, the affections, or the prejudices of the country? He is a stranger, a foreigner, and usurper; he unites in his own person everything that a pure Republican must detest; everything that an enraged Jacobin has abjured; everything that a sincere and faithful Royalist must feel as an insult. If he is opposed at any time in his career, what is his appeal? *He appeals to his fortune*; in other words, to his army and his sword.'

That was the response of the Prime Minister to Bonaparte's famous letter of 25 December 1799, in which he asked: 'How can the two most enlightened nations of Europe, stronger and more powerful than their safety and their independence require, sacrifice trade, domestic prosperity and the happiness of families to ideas of vain grandeur?' The tone was set, and while Bonaparte, borne on the wings of victory, demonstrated his military genius in his second Italian campaign, England was beginning to wonder who was this puny general who had inspired the great Pitt to make such a powerful pronouncement. They did not yet know that the century that was just beginning would be dominated by the personality of this man who elicited such varied epithets as 'the saviour of liberty' and 'a modern tyrant', and by the torrent of liberal ideas that surged over Europe with the armies of the Republic, the Consulate and the Empire.

In June 1800 Bonaparte defeated the Austrians at Marengo, turning to his advantage the conflict between the young Republic and one of the oldest monarchies on the continent, and the sound of his cannons reached the banks of the Thames, where the young writers of the English Romantic movement, inspired by Jean-Jacques Rousseau, the apostle of nature and truth, trembled in horror. Wordsworth had celebrated the French Revolution, proclaiming, 'Bliss was it in that dawn to be alive, / But to be young was very heaven!'; he had associated the fate of humanity as a whole with the success of the young Republic and hoped for the victory of its troops over those of England. Coleridge and Shelley had also been intoxicated by the new wind that was blowing over men and ideas, but they suddenly attacked this tyrant denounced by Pitt. The politician who feared invasion and the poets who mourned a liberty they believed lost made common cause.

The politicians had to stand together to deal with this Bonaparte and conclude the Treaty of Amiens, which was greatly desired by the people and the merchants. This led to the unlikely spectacle of Lauriston, the First Consul's aide-de-camp, who brought the ratification of the preliminaries of the treaty to London, being carried in triumph to the Foreign Office to cries of 'Vive la République française! Vive Bonaparte!' Windows in the wealthy neighbourhoods were decorated with paper lanterns and hats were festooned with laurels. Busts of 'Boney' were even displayed in shop windows, with the inscription 'Saviour of the world'.

This treaty was one of the first foreign policy initiatives of the Consulate, and when it was broken by the British cabinet – which, in the opinion of historians whose impartiality is unimpeachable,

3

was a way of reopening hostilities – the First Consul was very disappointed. He later stated: 'At Amiens I believed in very good faith that the fate of France, of Europe and of myself was decided, and the war was over. It was the English cabinet that started it all up again. It is to the English cabinet that Europe owes all the scourges that followed; it alone is responsible.'

Even before the treaty was torn up by George III's ministers, Napoleon was already complaining that *The Times*, which was said to reflect the views of the government, was constantly spreading abuse about France: 'Two whole pages out of four every day are devoted to base slanders. The French government is blamed for everything low, vile, evil, miserable that can be imagined.' The French government? Rather the leader France had chosen, that little general with the angular features, the turbulent genius whose deeds and plans frightened His Majesty's ministers, sowed panic in the business community and humiliated John Bull.

In 1803, when hostilities were declared, the campaign became even more virulent and the First Consul railed again: 'It is quite remarkable that in my great struggle with England its government has made such a habit of heaping scorn on my person and on my acts.' In Parliament, in the parlours, in the streets and in the countryside, they talked of nothing but 'the Corsican upstart', 'Bloody Boney', the ogre, the bloody tyrant, the Nero, the scourge of Europe and of mankind, a miserable creature whose small size and gesticulations prompted comparisons with a jack-in-the-box. One only has to glance at the popular imagery, at the caricatures of Gillray, Rowlandson and Cruikshank, to be convinced of the depth of the hatred. Napoleon was depicted after the Austrian marriage, sitting beside a Marie-Louise with a monstrous belly, with the horribly vulgar legend: 'How often, Sire, have we anticipated the pleasure of boasting of your exploits in the field of Venus as well as Mars.' Another caricature showed a shouting Bonaparte and a hideous Josephine, sodden with wine, being served the head of George III, the Bank of England, the Tower of London, and other delicacies.

As is only natural, the tide eventually turned, and at the time of his first setbacks the Emperor began to excite curiosity and sympathy in England. During the Hundred Days, when he had come back from Elba and was living in the Tuileries Palace, all the intellectuals and blue stockings in London rushed to Paris. John Cam Hobhouse, Byron's friend and confidant, managed with a great deal of effort to get into France. He was arrested in Valenciennes because of a package of percale intended for a Parisian marquise, and taken to the garrison, over which the tricolour was already flying. He showed letters of introduction to Talma, the Emperor's favourite actor, and Denon, the director of museums.

'Oh, I see!' said the soldier. 'Monsieur must be a scholar. What will you be doing in Paris?'

'Seeing your Emperor, quite simply.'

'Well, you may continue on your way.'

Hobhouse went to Saint-Quentin and Compiègne – where he admired the princely style of the château which had been completely refurbished and refurnished by Napoleon – and arrived in Paris on the evening of 11 April a little like a pilgrim arriving in Mecca. He loved everything: the street lighting, the tricolour floating over the Vendôme Column, the foreign ambassadors hurriedly packing their bags because war was about to start again. A few days later, his dream was realised. He was presented to Queen Hortense, Josephine's daughter, and attended a review of 30,000 troops at the Place du Carrousel. Two or three white horses were led under the windows of the queen, and the crowd shouted.

Hobhouse describes how he immediately recognised Napoleon by his hat, which was unadorned except for the tricolour cockade. He was wearing the uniform of a colonel in the Guard, with only one badge and a small cross on the chest. Hobhouse was not able to stop himself from waving his hat and cheering with the rest of the crowd. His eyes filled with tears, and he felt himself in the presence of a hero equal to those of Greek and Roman history, even while he was aware that all of Europe was massing its forces to destroy this man he knew was one of the great figures of history.

A few weeks later, after Waterloo, a dreadful lithograph was being sold in the streets of London, showing Napoleon caged, surrounded by threatening harpies brandishing scissors and shouting, 'I'll dock head and I'll dock tail him, I'll cut his ears and I'll cut his . . . I'll make a singing bird of him.' And the caption explained: 'Just caught, a ferocious animal never exhibited before in this country, commonly called the Corsican Tiger or Man Destroyer to be seen for a short time for two pence a piece.'

Slander . . . slander . . ., some of it will always remain. This concerted campaign to destroy the Emperor would not end, even after his exile, even after his death, and throughout the nineteenth century a whole British school of history kept up its attack on the work and character of the man defeated at Waterloo. While it used its formidable maritime and colonial power to establish its hegemony over the continent, England nevertheless claimed that through battles, coalitions and financial sacrifices, it had preserved freedom by cutting down the man who had wanted to put the terrible new spirit in power; it was a way of appearing liberal.

Southey's 'Ode to his Royal Highness the Prince Regent of the United Kingdom of Great Britain and Ireland', 'Ode to his Imperial Majesty, Alexander the First, Emperor of all the Russias' and 'Ode to his Majesty, Frederick William the Fourth, King of Prussia', three poems which together form one long work, would soon be hailed as a masterpiece. And after Waterloo, there was hardly an English poet great or small who did not visit the site of the battle and write a poem in praise of England and its delivery of Europe from the 'tyranny' of Napoleon. Ministers, journalists and satirists were equally unanimous in condemning Napoleon, his undertakings, his genius and his accomplishments, speaking of him as nothing more than 'an obstacle to peace'. One writer described how children were taught to shudder at the name of Bonaparte, the 'new Attila', and how the hatred towards him and his supporters continued even after his fall, as did accusations of poisonings and murders, cowardice and imbecility.

Only the true liberals, including Hobhouse, scoffed at this campaign to belittle an enemy and tear off his halo, asking mockingly why England had had to bleed herself dry to defeat a coward and an incompetent. Once the emotional reactions had subsided, the historians began their campaign, especially in France, where the pros and the antis attacked each other furiously, trying to figure out the complicated workings of this giant of history. The greatest names – Byron,Goethe, Schopenhauer, Hegel, Hugo, Chateaubriand and Tolstoy – were fascinated by this extraordinary individual. Honest historians, from Thiers to Masson, from Albert Sorel to Madelin, painted for all eternity a portrait of an administrator and military genius. It is a pleasure to repeat the statement by the Pole Mickiewicz to the Collège de France: 'He is not only yours, Frenchmen! He is Italian, he is Polish, he is Russian – he belongs to the world.'

Legend exalted him throughout Europe, even among his enemies. It spoke of 'our father Napoleon' and made his death on St Helena a mythic event. This is what Chateaubriand called 'the marvel of the invasion of the century by a single man', and what Stendhal justified by stating that a hero is 'a powerful natural phenomenon'.

However, lies die hard, and if a lot of Americans even today do not have a high opinion of Napoleon, it is solely because their textbooks are full of extravagant slanders. For example, in *A History of the United States* by Boorstin and Kelley, two prominent historians, we read on page 217: 'In January 1798, the nation faced the danger of war with the French dictator Napoleon.' And on page 147: 'The Louisiana Purchase was a triumph in more ways than we can count. It was one of the first modern proofs that in a battle of wits between a dictator and a government of the people the popular government does not need to lose.'

In January 1798 Napoleon Bonaparte was a young general with no power in government. He had just been elected to the Institut de France for his work in science and mathematics. And in 1803, when he sold (we could say gave) Louisiana to the United States, Napoleon was the First Consul of the Republic, venerated by the French to whom he had brought peace and prosperity after ten years of misery. He had a good deal of affection for the United States and had a bust of George Washington prominently displayed in his office. He was also loved by all the peoples of Europe, even the English; let us recall the frenzied welcome given to Lauriston in the streets of London. Furthermore, there was no battle, for the simple reason that Napoleon offered the whole of Louisiana to James Monroe, who had come to ask him only for the city of New Orleans. In all English-language history books, and not only the one cited above, Napoleon is systematically described as a dictator or a tyrant, while the true tyrants, that is, the monarchs who ruled Europe during his time, are always treated with great deference.

Another slander that has been repeated ad infinitum is that Napoleon instigated the *coup d'état* of 18 Brumaire (9 November

1799) in order to seize power. In fact it was the abbé Sieyès, the president of the Directory – of which the other members were Barras, Ducos, Gohier and Moulin – who decided everything and gave the orders. Sieyès felt a strong executive was an absolute necessity in order to counter mounting threats. The Directory, hamstrung by the bankruptcy of the state and threatened both by internal anarchy and by the forces of the second coalition, had proved too divided to be able to make the necessary decisions. Sieyès therefore decided to change the constitution to replace the Directory with a Consulate made up of a leader, the First Consul, and two other consuls, one in charge of domestic affairs and the other responsible for dealing with the threat of external enemies.

He needed a general, because of course he saw himself as First Consul. His initial choice for his 'sword', as he called it, had been General Joubert, but he was killed at the Battle of Novi, in Italy. Sieyès then chose Napoleon, who was 'sent by Providence'. It is absurd to think that Napoleon, just back from Egypt without his army and with few friends in Paris, could in two weeks have prepared and carried out the coup that was to save the Republic.

On 8 November 1799, after appointing Napoleon military governor of Paris, sending Barras under escort to his country property and assigning General Moreau to keep a close watch on Gohier and Moulin, Sieyès gave the order to the deputies and senators to meet the following day at Saint-Cloud, on the pretext that there was a Jacobin plot afoot.

The events of 9 and 10 November 1799 are well known. Afterwards, when the three consuls, Sieyès, Ducos and Bonaparte, met to decide on the most pressing measures to be taken, it was immediately obvious that Bonaparte was head and shoulders above the others in every way. And it was Sieyès himself who insisted that Napoleon become the First Consul, exclaiming with enthusiasm, 'He knows everything, he does everything, he is capable of everything.'

These, then, were the conditions that made Napoleon the leader of France. He did not seize power; it was first entrusted to him by the head of the government and then confirmed in a popular vote the result of which was very eloquent: more than 3,000,000 votes in favour versus 1,562 against.

CHAPTER II

The Question of Napoleon's Birth

It is widely acknowledged today that Louis Charles René de Marbeuf, governor of Corsica under Louis XV and then Louis XVI, played a decisive role in the admission of the young Napoleon Bonaparte to the royal military school in Brienne. Without him, Napoleon would never have become an officer and consequently a general and then emperor.

It is also recognised that it was for the love of Letizia that this noble Breton general remained in Corsica from 1764 until his death in 1786, although he had originally come to the island for only four years; and that Marbeuf was the father of Louis Bonaparte, the future king of Holland, who was born on 2 September 1778 – they looked as alike as two peas in a pod. He was the child's godfather, and he sponsored three days and three nights of celebrations for the whole town of Ajaccio in honour of the baby's birth.

But as soon as it is suggested that Marbeuf might also be the father of Napoleon, there is a general outcry from all those who have never taken the trouble to consult the archives of the period. They will tell you that Marbeuf knew the Bonaparte family well only after the birth of Napoleon, and that his love affair with Letizia did not begin until 1773. They will also say that Napoleon, who was born on 15 August 1769, was conceived in November 1768 and that, since there was a war going on at the time between the French and the Corsicans under Paoli, and since Letizia was in Corte and Marbeuf in Bastia, the two had no chance of meeting.

We do not see why a child should not be proud of his parents even if they are not husband and wife, and since Marbeuf was an honest, upstanding man, whereas Charles Bonaparte was extremely mediocre, we will present the information we have compiled from period documents, in particular letters in the

National Archives in Paris (number 400 AP 115), which we have in the form of microfilms.

In 1764 Corsica was a province of the Republic of Genoa and its inhabitants had been fighting for their independence for thirty-five years. Under the orders of Paoli Pasquale, a general 39 years of age, they were about to drive the Genoese into the sea. They had already freed the whole interior of the island and most of the coast. All that remained to Genoa was four maritime strongholds: Bastia, Calvi, Ajaccio and Bonifacio.

Cornered, the Genoese asked France for help; it was the fifth time they had done so since 1729. Louis XV and his minister, the Duc de Choiseul, accepted, their main concern being to prevent the English from taking over the island as they intended. The year before had seen the end of the disastrous Seven Years' War, the Treaty of Paris and the loss of Canada and the Indies. They could not allow perfidious Albion, their long-standing enemy, to gain a base within reach of the Mediterranean coast as well. General Marbeuf was in command of the French expeditionary force.

Louis Charles René de Marbeuf was born in Rennes on 4 November 1712, the tenth child of Charles de Marbeuf, the president of the Parlement of Brittany, and Jeanne Jacquette de Musillac. The family belonged to the very old Breton high nobility. Already in 1385, a Thibaud de Marbeuf had accompanied the Duc d'Anjou to the Holy Land, and since 1500 the Marbeufs had provided eight successive presidents of the Parlement of Brittany. Louis' grandmother, Louise de Louët, was the lady of Pen-ar-Vern, a château in Sainte-Sève, a commune three kilometres west of Morlaix. She had brought that property into the Marbeuf family as a dowry. Mme de Sévigné was a great friend of hers and often spoke of her in her letters, always in glowing terms.

Louis was groomed for the army, and he had a brilliant career in it. Captain at 20 years of age and colonel at 35, he possessed great strengths as a military leader. He also gained a reputation as a skirt chaser, and in fact he remained unmarried until the age of 40. This aspect of his private life obviously did not prevent him from being a great leader, serious about his work and the missions entrusted to him. He was recognised as a man of dialogue, who preferred persuasion to brute force. In fact this is what made the Duc de Choiseul assign him to Corsica; Choiseul knew that

Corsica would never yield to violence but was very amenable to friendship. Marbeuf was the personification of generosity and nobility of spirit. Physically, he was a solid, stocky man 1.60 metres tall with blue-grey eyes and a steely gaze that could be cajoling or could shoot daggers when he was angry. At the age of 40 he married Éléonore de Quémadec, ten years his senior, who brought him a dowry of lands and domains, including the imposing Château de Callac in Morbihan.

Letizia was born in Ajaccio, a town of three thousand inhabitants, on 24 August 1750. She was the daughter of Jean Jérôme Ramolino, an inspector of bridges and roads for the Genoese – who must have had plenty of free time, because there were no bridges or roads in Corsica – and Angela Maria Pietrasanta, the daughter of a leading citizen of the town. Letizia's father died when she was 5 and she soon had a young stepfather, François Fesch, a Swiss lieutenant in the Genoese military; on 3 January 1763 her half-brother Joseph Fesch, a future cardinal, was born. Letizia's immediate family was all on the side of the Genoese, and therefore in the opposite camp to Paoli's patriots.

Until the age of 13, Letizia was a very pretty little Mediterranean tomboy with jet-black hair and eyes, totally illiterate – she never went to school – who ran barefoot through the streets of the town or on the beach near the citadel. She was not yet 14 when she became pregnant and married her 18-year-old neighbour Charles Bonaparte, a lad 1.78 metres tall, as handsome as Letizia was beautiful, with a similar dark velvety gaze. The baby, a boy, was still-born.

Marbeuf and Letizia fall in love

In June 1765 Charles Bonaparte decided to leave for Rome to try to recover an estate of lands and three houses taken by the Jesuits some decades earlier. Charles's great-grandmother, Virginie Odone, had been stripped of her inheritance as a result of an illicit will made by her brother, Paul-Émile, in favour of the Jesuits, who had demanded this as the price for his entry into heaven.

To go to Rome, Charles needed money and a safe-conduct. He requested and obtained an audience with Marbeuf and went to the Résidence de France accompanied by Letizia, 15 years old, in the beautiful dress she wore to go to mass. While Charles read the long petition he had prepared, Marbeuf, 53 years old, could not take his eyes off Letizia, whose fresh beauty had captivated him, and when Charles concluded with a statement that he would be particularly reassured if Marbeuf would agree to look out for his young wife during his absence, that winner of battles and of hearts granted everything Charles had asked for. 'Leave without fear and obtain restitution from the Jesuits. They are used to it; you are not their first victim. Take your time. I will personally watch over your charming wife. With me, she will be in very good hands,' he added, flashing a tender and penetrating glance at Letizia, who blushed nervously.

Charles left for Rome, and for two months Marbeuf spent several hours a day with Letizia. He did not make her his mistress at this time, however; Marbeuf was a man of honour and he did not want to betray the trust of a husband, even though Bonaparte's attitude had appeared rather ambiguous to him. Furthermore, in his eyes Letizia, although she had already given birth the year before, was still only a little girl. He would have felt he was committing a vile deed against this young woman who had inspired a completely new feeling in him.

For the first time in his life, Marbeuf was in love. He wanted nothing more than to have Letizia close to him, because he was perfectly happy when she was there. He took pleasure in undertaking her education – and she had everything to learn: reading, writing, music, French, dance, parlour games, manners. And he, in turn, wanted to learn Corsican; she would be his teacher. His lion's heart was deeply touched, and Letizia, at first a little surprised by all the attention she was receiving from such an important and distinguished personage (Marbeuf was the representative of King Louis XV in Corsica), slowly melted under the charm of the great seducer. Not without difficulty, he got her to stop calling him 'Monsieur le comte' and call him simply Louis.

In September, when Marbeuf's duties called him back to Bastia, Letizia was very unhappy. Her thoughts were with Louis much more than with Charles, from whom she had heard nothing since his departure for Rome. So it was that the great love between Marbeuf and Letizia was born in the summer of 1765 in Ajaccio – carried by Cupid's arrows, chaste and pure, which would be followed four years later by those of Eros.

In October Charles returned from Rome, where he had led a life of debauchery. In the cafés where he liked to drink, he would boast of his exploits in the Eternal City, and soon all Ajaccio was laughing at him. Then Letizia's grandfather, Joseph Pietrasanta, received a letter from the abbot Celli, a friend of his who lived in the Vatican, saying that Charles had been living with a widow and had got her pregnant. Nothing too serious, he added, she had known what she was getting into. On the other hand, when she discovered that her two daughters of 17 and 19, who lived with her, were also pregnant, she had gone to the authorities, and Charles had only avoided arrest by escaping over the roofs in the middle of the night. Furthermore, on his return to Corsica, Charles had spent a night in Bastia at the home of Marco Franceschi, a friend of Paoli, and nine months later the young maid in the household had died giving birth to a baby boy, a child who, as he grew, showed a resemblance to Charles.

Shortly after Charles's return, Letizia too found herself pregnant. She would give birth to a girl, who would not live any longer than the boy born earlier. There was beginning to be talk of blood incompatibility between Charles and Letizia.

Not long after his return from Rome, Charles made a short trip to the interior of the island and, thinking it would be a good idea to do a little self-promotion, made a written report to Marbeuf, whose personal friend he claimed to be. He expressed his views on the mood of the people and the policies that he would have adopted. Marbeuf's answer, sent from Bastia on 5 November 1765, was as follows[1]: 'Fundamentally this is the concern of the Republic of Genoa and is of no interest at all to me. I can only hope that it approves the conduct you and your fellow citizens have adopted . . .'

Early in 1767 Charles rejoined the independence movement, and he took Letizia to Corte, the fiefdom of Pasquale Paoli. Paoli, 42 years old, was also dazzled by Letizia's beauty. But he did not have much liking for 'this young man with curly hair that smells of the perfumes of the Continent', and he sent him away, giving him some responsibilities in the parish of Talano.

Although she was only 17 years old at this time, Letizia liked pretty clothes and spent a lot of money on them. In a letter to Joseph Pietrasanta from Ajaccio, dated 16 March 1767, the archdeacon Lucien Bonaparte complained bitterly of her extravagance and blamed her mother for failing to give her proper guidance, stating that 'Letizia should have married a prince who gave her the household budget to handle.'[2] In April, for a reception for an ambassador of the Bey of Tunis, Paoli adorned Letizia with all the frills and furbelows of a princess from the *Thousand and One Nights* – puffy trousers,wide belt and silk veils, and a tiara, necklaces and bracelets – making her the belle of the ball and the ideal of Corsican beauty. The ambassador was so impressed that he devoted a whole page to her in his report. After that, Letizia found herself pregnant again. This time the baby was a strong, vigorous boy, Joseph-Nabulion, who was born in Corte on 7 January 1768.

In the period 1764–8 there had been only minor clashes between Marbeuf's French troops and those of Paoli; the two leaders had maintained the *modus vivendi* they had established at a meeting in Casinca early in 1765. This was soon to change.

Louis XV, by the Treaty of Versailles of 15 May 1768, bought Corsica back from Genoa for a few million francs and simply annexed it to the French Crown without even consulting Pasquale Paoli. Marbeuf knew the Corsicans well enough to be aware that it was not in their temperament to let themselves be sold like cattle. He knew that this annexation would lead to war between France and Corsica. He also knew that France, one of the two great world powers, could not lose face to a small nation of 140,000 people. And he knew that after the war there would be a period of peacemaking, organisation and reconciliation. Then he would be able to play an important and interesting role in teaching the Corsicans to love France and participate in its glory and greatness.

Marbeuf himself, in an extension of his love for Letizia, loved Corsica as if he had been born there. He already knew that he would devote the rest of his life to this beautiful island rather than return to the continent like any other soldier at the end of his tour of duty. To preserve his advantage for the future period of peacemaking, he had to avoid getting any Corsican blood on his hands and thus could not act as commander-in-chief in the war. He explained all this to the minister Choiseul, who recognised its pertinence and appointed the Marquis de Chauvelin to lead the operations.

On 29 May 1768, with the arrival of reinforcements from France and the departure of the last Genoese, the French fleur de lys was flown for the first time over the citadel in Ajaccio. But Chauvelin was slow in taking up his duties, and it was Marbeuf who received a letter on policy from Choiseul: '. . . Corsica will be subdued by force or negotiation. If it is by force, we owe no mercy to the inhabitants. If it is it by negotiation, we have decided to accept all just conditions that would accommodate the Corsicans, mainly that they never be returned to the Republic of Genoa. . .' Marbeuf commanded a few limited operations that led to the pacification of the cape north of Bastia.

Then, at the end of August, Chauvelin arrived. He was a marquis in lace, who was accustomed to life at court and had never taken part in the smallest battle. Under his command, the French went from one defeat to another, culminating in their ignominious surrender of the garrison of Borgo. The town was held by five hundred officers and soldiers of the Légion royale under the command of the Chevalier de Ludre, who had arrogantly boasted that he could stand firm against all of Corsica.

During the night of 6 October, Gio Carlo, a young Corsican leader, guided by the local priest, had two hundred of his best soldiers steal into the houses east of the town. Ludre was not able to dislodge the Corsicans, and his communication with Bastia was cut off, even though it was only fifteen kilometres away, because Paoli himself had a large number of troops occupying the surrounding area.

On 8 October Chauvelin, at the head of his army, broke through the encirclement, but he was not able to take Gio Carlo's positions in spite of direct fire from three-inch cannons. The Corsicans repulsed all attacks from what soon was reduced to an expanse of gravel and smashed beams red with the blood of the soldiers from both camps.

Frightened by the spectacle of more than two hundred dead and dying soldiers and by the coming of nightfall, Chauvelin panicked and returned to Bastia, abandoning Ludre to his sad fate. Ludre surrendered on 10 October and was taken prisoner in Corte with his whole garrison.

Marbeuf asked for Chauvelin's recall and received as his replacement a true military man, Marshal de Vaux. At the age of 64, Vaux was one of the most competent and celebrated leaders in the French army. He had distinguished himself in nineteen sieges and fourteen major battles, and had been wounded four times in close combat.

Vaux was quick to act. He landed at Saint-Florent on 9 April 1769 with reinforcements that brought the total French forces up to almost thirty thousand men. On 4 May his army began to prepare to leave Saint-Florent-Bastia to march on Corte. They advanced like a steamroller crushing everything in its path, and the Corsicans, unable to resist, saw their last hopes dashed on 9 May at Ponte Nuovo.

Paoli had to leave Corsica; he would spend twenty years in exile. On 9 May, before his departure from Corte, he sent for Letizia. 'My dear Letizia, there are difficult times ahead for our nation. I know how devoted you are to the Comte de Marbeuf, and I am asking you to use your influence with him to lessen the suffering of our people. I want you to be the Cornelia of the Corsican people.'

The logbooks tell us that Marbeuf, who commanded the eastern division made up of the Soissonnais, La Marche, Buckley and Roscomon regiments, rejoined Vaux at Omessa on 19 May 1769, after having cleared and secured the route from Bastia through Vescovato, Loreto, Penta and Casabianca, to Morosaglia. At Omessa, Vaux entrusted him with restoring order and reinstating the government of Corte, and the command of his division was turned over to his second-in-command, Campenne.

On 21 May in Corte, Marbeuf found Letizia happy and relieved to place herself under his protection again. In fact, contrary to the legend sustained by certain eminent historians such as Alain Decaux, Letizia was no La Pasionaria. For example, in a letter to her grandfather, Joseph Pietrasanta, dated 13 March 1769, she spoke of nothing but money and clothes: 'You will give eight louis d'or for me to Foumbrouge, the bearer of this letter, as well as some gowns, including one in fine Lyon silk . . .'[3] This letter destroys the myth that Letizia travelled with Paoli's soldiers, rifle in hand. It proves that, seven weeks before Ponte-Nuovo, Letizia was most concerned about looking pretty. It also casts doubt on the idea that she was pregnant when it was written, five months before 15 August 1769. A woman who was four months pregnant in the poor conditions prevailing on the island in 1769 would not have been ordering expensive gowns (instead of maternity clothes) of fine Lyon silk.

As for Charles Bonaparte, he left the parish of Talano as soon as he learned of the defeat, and on 25 May he was in Ajaccio, where he proclaimed to anyone who would listen: 'Ewiva el re et suo goberno!' ('Long live the king and his government!'). In other words, he had changed sides. Marbeuf would later give him a title and make him, as Letizia's husband, one of the most important people in Corsica.

Was Marbeuf Napoleon's father?

As we have already seen, if 15 August 1769 is accepted as the date of Napoleon's birth, Marbeuf cannot be his father. However, this date cannot be considered a certainty. In fact, Napoleon's birth was only entered in the Ajaccio baptismal register on 21 July 1771. This two-year delay is unique for the years 1768 to 1771; all other children born during this period were registered on the day of their birth or within a few days. This is a rather strange anomaly, which is made even more interesting by the fact that the priest in Ajaccio categorically refused to baptize the child or even to allow him into the church, and that Marbeuf himself had to send Laurent Giubega, the king's chief prosecutor, to Ajaccio from Calvi with instructions to do whatever was necessary to settle the matter.

Laurent Giubega, although he belonged to neither Letizia's nor Charles's family, decided that he himself would be the godfather. The priest forbade the use of the baptismal font, but that did not stop him. The religious ceremony (not the baptism) took place in the family home; this is stated in the certificate. Napoleon, with his blue-grey eyes and steely gaze that could go from charming to flashing, was very conscious of the absurdity of that certificate, so much so that, when he married Josephine in 1796, he supplied the baptismal certificate of his brother Joseph Nabulion.

That same 21 July 1771 Marbeuf, although he was very busy in Bastia presiding over a session of the Conseil supérieur, whose work he was directing, made a special trip to Ajaccio, where he stayed for only six hours. He wanted to make sure that the orders given to Laurent Giubega were being properly carried out and, especially, he wanted to see Letizia on the day that the existence of Napoleon was finally being granted official recognition.

All this is confirmed by a letter from archdeacon Lucien

17

Bonaparte to Joseph Pietrasanta, Letizia's grandfather, who sat on the Conseil supérieur in Bastia. The following are extracts from that letter:

> Ajaccio, 24 July 1771
> The Comte de Marbeuf – let this remain between us – came to Ajaccio on 21 July for Napoleon's baptism.
> In front of the crowd that filled the house, he at first only sent a message to Letizia with his majordomo, and saved giving her his personal compliments for a little later.
> He stayed for six hours.[4]

Yes, Marbeuf, the governor of Corsica, slipped away from Bastia at a time when his presence was indispensable to go to Ajaccio just to pay his respects to a lady of very modest condition on the baptism day of a little fellow who had eyes that were just like his!

As for Charles Bonaparte's attitude towards his wife's relationship with Marbeuf, he not only accepted it with pride, but he tried to gain advantages from it, as is shown in his letter of 24 August 1771, in Italian, to his grandfather Joseph: 'We must speed up the process of establishing the nobility of our family by making as much as we can of the Comte de Marbeuf's benevolence. It is now or never. In the eight days he just spent in Ajaccio, he came to get Letizia every evening, which aroused much envy in our neighbourhood.'

In conclusion, if Napoleon is Marbeuf's son, he was conceived in Corte at the end of May 1769, and was born in February 1770. And why was 15 August 1769 chosen as his date of birth? Perhaps quite simply because Letizia went on holiday in Brittany with Marbeuf from 26 August 1769 to 7 May 1770, and a date when she was present in Ajaccio was chosen in order to give an appearance of legitimacy.

Marbeuf, Governor of Corsica

Marbeuf returned to Corsica from his holiday on 7 May 1770, vested with full civil and military powers. For three years he devoted himself completely to the demanding tasks of peacemaking and establishing a modern economy in the new province of the kingdom. He was unable to spend as much time as he would have liked with Letizia, but he did not forget her. Already, on 24 December 1768, he had named her grandfather, Joseph Pietrasanta, to the Conseil supérieur of Corsica, which was made up of twelve important citizens. He appointed her husband Charles an assessor in the royal jurisdiction of Ajaccio, with an annual salary of nine hundred pounds, and then gave him one of the very first titles when he decided in 1771 to create a Corsican nobility from scratch. Marbeuf's stratagem was to dig up an ancestor, Jérôme, who had supposedly been given the title Egregium Hieronimum de Bonaparte by the Republic of Genoa in 1560. With this recognition of his blue blood, Charles proudly added the particle to his name immediately.

Marbeuf's return to Letizia took place in 1773. He spent the whole summer with her in Ajaccio. Then, to be better able to play host to her in Bastia, he had a beautiful villa built in the middle of an olive grove. She lived there with him in the summer of 1774, and Lucien was born in the spring of 1775.

In September 1774 Marbeuf went to the court at Versailles to obtain funds and suitably qualified staff for the development of Corsica. Louis XV had died on 10 May 1774, after a reign of fifty-nine years, and Louis XVI, aged 20, sat on the throne of France. General Narbonne served as interim commander during Marbeuf's absence. Narbonne was from the high nobility and had powerful support at court. He was very ambitious and aspired to supplant Marbeuf and apply his own policies. He felt that Corsica would only be subjugated by brutal repression and contemplated genocide without a qualm. He published a decree addressed to the rebels:

'The time for compromises and pardons is over. Henceforth, you have a choice between:
  − surrendering and going into penal servitude
  − dying in combat
  − dying on the wheel.'

Narbonne launched a series of bloody operations that ravaged and terrorised the population. This scorched earth policy was viewed with favour by an influential clique at Versailles, who wanted to eliminate the entire male population of Corsica − after all, there were only 60,000 of them altogether − and bring over the Acadians who had been driven out of Canada by the English; this new population, they reasoned, would be absolutely loyal to the Crown. This was not mere theory, as genocide had been common in the previous two centuries, often on a scale a hundred times greater. At this point, Marbeuf fell ill and was obliged to delay his return. Narbonne started a rumour that Marbeuf would not be coming back.

Meanwhile Charles, who had continued to lead a life of debauchery and was always short of money, had his mother-in-law's furniture seized on the pretext that Letizia's dowry had not been paid in full. He auctioned it off himself from nine o'clock to noon in the Ajaccio market square, while Letizia – who was on the verge of giving birth to Lucien – and her mother remained shut up indoors, mortified.

On 22 May 1775, fortunately, Marbeuf returned with the intendant Bertrand Boucheporn, an excellent administrator who was completely devoted to him. The conflict with Narbonne continued to heat up. Narbonne had removed Marbeuf's supporters from most key posts and replaced them with his own men, who backed him in order to keep the advantages they had won. But Marbeuf had seen this kind of thing before and, sustained by a love that did not let him even consider the possibility of leaving Corsica, he countered his adversary's violence with patience and skill. In the end he defeated Narbonne and forced him to leave. That is how the fate of the Corsican was decided.

Marbeuf's triumph in 1775 marked a true turning point in the history of Corsica, because the issue was much larger than these individuals; what was at stake was nothing less than Corsica itself. With Narbonne, it was destined for genocide. With Marbeuf, there was a consolidation of administrative institutions and participation in the life of France. The victory of the man who had been identified with Corsica since 1764 had a very precise meaning. It meant the end of the uncertainty and turmoil, the restoration of tranquillity and the start of productive work. Everything was conducive to order and clarity; this became a reality in 1775 with the beginning of the new regime, and it could hardly have been achieved any earlier.

Marbeuf's return marked the beginning of a period of prosperity that was to last ten years. After his death in 1786, Corsica was again stirred, this time by the winds of the coming Revolution.

Marbeuf loved and respected by the Corsicans

After the elimination of Narbonne, Marbeuf's position and demeanour in Corsica were those of a viceroy adored by his subjects, and Letizia was almost constantly at his side.

In April 1776 in Bastia, she was at confession before Easter services when she suddenly rushed from the confessional, red with anger, and in front of an audience of stunned penitents shouted: 'Monsieur, you are totally lacking in propriety. I shall never set foot in your confessional again!' Before giving absolution, the priest had apparently asked about the intimate details of her life in the olive grove.

Marie-Anne (Eliza) was born on 13 January 1777. On 24 May 1777 Marbeuf was given the title of marquis and he received, as a gift from Louis XVI, an immense tract of land that covered the communes of Cargese, Paomia, Revinda and Piana. Cargese, where Marbeuf had previously established a Greek colony, was situated on the west coast thirty kilometres north of Ajaccio. The region was especially beautiful, rich and healthy, and Marbeuf decided to build Letizia a château there which would be a larger and more beautiful replica of Pen-ar-Vern.

It was at this time that the deputies of Corsica voted unanimously to place a marble plaque on the facade of the Palace of the Twelve in Bastia in his honour. Its gold letters read: 'To Louis Charles René, Comte de Marbeuf, commander of the Order of Saint-Louis, lieutenant-general of the French troops, governor of Corsica, president of the Estates, well known for his prudence, justice and intelligence and his generous gifts to the whole island. So that the memory of his good deeds will be eternal, all the orders of the island, celebrating the presence of this eminent man at their head for the greater good of Corsica, have had engraved on this marble plaque an expression of the love engraved in their hearts.'

Not to be outdone, the town of Bonifacio wove a banner with a portrait of Marbeuf and the inscription *Lo fece la natura, poi ruppe la stampa* (Nature made him; then she broke the mould). This banner was paraded through the town during processions and received in the church by the priest from his pulpit.

Marbeuf gave big celebrations in Bastia and Ajaccio, always in honour of Letizia, which did not please everyone, at least not Colonel de Laric, who wrote to his father:

Bastia, 16 June 1778
The commanding general, Marbeuf, left last night for a long stay in Ajaccio. His heart is taken there by Madame Letizia Bonaparte. He brought her to Bastia last winter, and all the parties he gave were in honour of that woman. All the other ladies would pay homage to the idol, even the wife of the intendant, who in her position should be above that, who fawned on her in the most servile manner. That is what keeps this gallant man in Corsica and what keeps him from leaving the country. He will leave his bones here, leading such a life.[5]

Another letter from Bastia, dated 11 July 1778:

I had the honour to inform you that Monsieur de Marbeuf was in Ajaccio until November. He is now tied to his mistress's apron strings and no one can tear him away for any business, or even see him. He is completely absorbed in Letizia and he is now making her an apartment in his house adjoining his quarters; we have never seen anything like this. This way of living will lead to the grave sooner than to the [marshal's] baton!'[6]

Louis, the father of Napoleon III and the future king of Holland, was born on 2 September 1778. He was the image of Marbeuf, who was his godfather; the wife of the intendant Boucheporn was his godmother. At the baptism, the bells rang out for three hours, and Marbeuf held a big celebration for the entire town of Ajaccio, lasting three days and three nights. This is a long way from the time when the priest refused to allow Napoleon to enter the church.

Towards the Empire

The year 1778 marked a turning point not only for Corsica but for all of Europe. Marbeuf arranged and paid for the admission of Joseph to Autun, of Napoleon to the royal military school in Brienne, and of Joseph Fesch, Letizia's half-brother and a future cardinal, to the seminary in Aix. Admission to Brienne required four degrees of high nobility, and without Marbeuf it is obvious that Napoleon did not have the remotest chance of getting in.

Marbeuf also had Lucien admitted to Autun and later to Brienne. In 1799 Lucien, at the age of 24, was president of the Council of Five Hundred in Paris. He was responsible for the success of the *coup d'état* organised by Sieyès on 18 Brumaire in Saint-Cloud. Marbeuf also got Eliza admitted to the École de Saint-Cyr, where she made friends with the daughters of France's highest nobility. If he had lived long enough, he undoubtedly would also have given Louis, Pauline, Caroline and Jérôme the benefit of the best schools in the kingdom. And we should not forget that if Letizia, who had become 'Madame Mère', impressed the greatest princes of Europe with her class and distinction, it was solely due to the education Marbeuf had given her.

After this digression, let us return to 1780. The château in Cargèse was finished, and Louis and Letizia would live there for the next few years, a time of unblemished happiness in a setting worthy of their great love. Paoletta (Pauline) was born on 20 October 1780. Maria Annunziata (Caroline) was born on 24 March 1782.

The Château of Cargèse

Perched on a hillside west of the town, the château had a southern exposure and was set among superb gardens covering an area of six hectares, 300 metres long and 200 metres wide.The flower beds, lawns, pools with fountains, and groves of mulberry, olive and fruit trees were irrigated with water from two mountain springs.

The entrance to the main building was through a courtyard lined with orange trees. Two huge rooms in the basement were used as servants' quarters and the dining room, the servants' refectory and the kitchens, with roasting ovens, pastry kitchen and bread oven, were on the ground floor. The second floor, which was reached by a wide stairway, was the master's domain, comprising a large drawing room and four bedrooms, each with a dressing room and wardrobe. There were two luxurious marble bathrooms designed by an Italian artist, with alcoves and pozzolana bathtubs. From the wide balcony overlooking the Gulf of Sagone, you could see as far as Capo di Feno and the western point of the biggest of the Sanguinaires Islands at the entrance to the Gulf of Ajaccio. On the third floor were the chapel and ten bedrooms. The attic was divided into six rooms. Above the pediment of the main entrance was carved Marbeuf's coat of arms, 'azure with two crossed silver swords with gold hilts and guards, points down, shield placed on the cross of the Holy Ghost', and the crown of a marquis, a title granted to him by Louis XVI 'in recognition of his great achievements on the island of Corsica'.

The diary of Charles Bonaparte

The dates when Letizia was in Cargèse with Marbeuf can be found in Charles Bonaparte's diary among the statements of accounts and wages paid to the family's employees and the records of favourable dates for planting. Every year Letizia went to Cargèse with her children; she did so in December 1780, August 1781, May 1782 and February 1783. It should be noted that in February 1783, with Joseph and Napoleon on the mainland, Letizia's children were Lucien, 8 years old; Eliza, 6; Louis, 4; Pauline, 2, and Caroline, 10 months. Who would believe that Marbeuf, at 71 with full responsibility for Corsica, would have wanted to have this screaming, demanding brood with him day and night for months on end if they were not his own children?

Charles also noted in detail the gifts he received from Marbeuf – tons of lumber, furniture, expensive fabrics – as well as work done by soldiers on properties he had received from Marbeuf, in particular a mulberry nursery, totalling thousands of days of labour.

In 1783 a little drama took place following the death of Éléonore de Quémadec, Marbeuf's elderly wife, in Paris. Marbeuf could not accept the idea of dying without leaving any official descendants. In noble families this is a serious failing. He must have wished more than anything that he could have married Letizia and acknowledged his children. Alas! this was impossible, since Letizia was already married. At 72 years of age, Marbeuf therefore decided to marry Catherine Gayardon de Fenoyl, aged 18.

Catherine s arrival in Cargèse in no way prevented Letizia from staying there. The two women become the best of friends, and gossips reported that Marbeuf was leading the luxurious life of a sultan. At any rate, the two friends found themselves pregnant at the same time. Letizia, who had seniority, was the first to give birth; her son Jérôme, was born on 15 November 1784. Catherine gave birth to Alexandrine de Marbeuf on 29 December.

In 1785 Charles, ill, went to the mainland for treatment; he died in Montpellier, at the age of 39, on 24 February 1785. Fewer than ten people attended his funeral.

Laurent de Marbeuf, Catherine's second child, was born on 26 May 1786.

Napoleon returned to Corsica as a young ensign of 16 on 15 September 1786, after eight years' absence. Five days later Marbeuf died at the age of 74. He was given a lavish funeral in Bastia, in which the entire grieving population took part. He was buried, as he had wished, in a vault in the Saint-Jean-Baptiste Church, in order that, as he had stated, 'a link would be established under the protection of St John between the Brittany that witnessed my birth and the Corsica that adopted me and witnessed my death'. (Saint-Jean-du-Doigt near Morlaix is a pilgrimage site devoted to the cult of St John the Baptist.)

Impartiality, integrity, graciousness and justice were the qualities that governed Marbeuf's life. The Corsicans liked him and the French appreciated his firmness, his discernment and his administrative skills. 'He is a very honourable, humane, kindly man, without malice, if anything too good and too approachable for a man of his position with the high responsibilities he has,' it was said. Commander Bertrand noted in 1817, that is after the Empire, when Napoleon was on St Helena, that the name of Marbeuf was still revered in Corsica.

Epilogue: Napoleon

It seems that as soon as he returned to Corsica in 1786, Napoleon knew Marbeuf was his father, and that he knew it because Letizia told him. Thus, immediately after Marbeuf's death, he went to the beach with his mother to gather seashells, which he used to spell out 'Vive Marbeuf' over the door of their house in Ajaccio. The lettering was still there several years later, as noted by the Comtesse de Boigné, née d'Osmond, in her *Memoirs*.

Gaspard Monge, the famous mathematician, wrote that on the ship that brought them back from the Egyptian campaign in 1799, Napoleon had confided in him about his birth. In 1802 the mayor of Montpellier, remembering that Charles was buried in his city, wrote to the First Consul to inform him of his plan to build a monument and garden in his honour. Napoleon's answer was blunt: 'I forbid you to do anything for him.' In 1804, when he had just been made Emperor, he replied to someone who was boasting that he had been born on the same day: 'How can you claim to know my true age?'

In 1810, before Napoleon's marriage to Marie-Louise, the emperor of Austria told him that genealogical research showed that the Bonapartes had been princes in Italy in the thirteenth century, and that Napoleon had therefore merely regained the legitimate rights of his family. Napoleon replied, 'I have nothing to do with those Bonapartes, and I prefer to be the Rudolf I of my dynasty', referring to the founding monarch of the house of Habsburg, who carved out an empire with his sword.

On the other hand, Napoleon showed himself to be very attached to the Marbeufs. For example, he made Catherine Gayardon-Marbeuf a baroness of the Empire, with an allowance of 15,000 livres. Her daughter, Alexandrine, had married the Comte d'Ambrugeac, who had emigrated and was serving with the British uhlans; Napoleon brought Ambrugeac back to France and made him a general in the Grande Armée. Laurent de Marbeuf (1786-1812) was given friendship, affection and solicitude by the Emperor (his half-brother?). Napoleon got him admitted to the military school in Fontainebleau and gave him a life annuity of 6,000 francs from the Treasury and an allowance of 12,000 francs from his own purse. Then, to keep him at his side, he made him his aide-de-camp. He arranged for him to marry a wealthy heiress from Lyon, Mademoiselle Marie d'Églat de la Tour Dubost, and as a wedding present gave him the Hôtel Montesson, one of the most beautiful mansions on rue Mont-Blanc. He appointed him, at the age of 25, colonel of the Sixth Regiment of light calvary and baron of the Empire. Laurent died of wounds he received at Krasnoy (1812) after leading his cavalry to victory over a formation of Russian infantry. Napoleon never recovered from the loss. It affected him very deeply, and from then on his unshakeable optimism gave way to periodic melancholy.

Letizia

Letizia was only 36 when Marbeuf died, and for a very long time she kept all the charm of her youth. Comte Beugnot, who met her at the baths in Aix-la-Chapelle in 1809 when she was 59, expressed his admiration as follows: 'Madame Mère possesses all the beauty of which a woman is capable, and if Raphael had known her when he painted his admirable picture of the holy family, he would have looked no further for the model for St Anne.'

Letizia had many suitors in the fifty years that remained of her life, but she was absolutely faithful to the memory of her beloved Louis. She had a large portrait of Marbeuf, which was her most precious possession. In 1791 it was prudent not to draw attention to one's close links with the nobility, and Napoleon wrote from Paris to Joseph, who had remained in Ajaccio: 'Remove the portrait of Marbeuf from the drawing room.' Letizia replied: 'I would rather tear out my heart. That portrait will remain where it is.'

In 1793 Paoli, who had regained control in Corsica, asked Letizia to come to him in Corte. Her refusal, combined with actions against him by Napoleon and, especially, Lucien made him decide to capture Letizia by force in Ajaccio. On the night of 24 May, warned by a friend, Costa de Bastelica, only a few hours before the arrival of the commando sent by Paoli, Letizia escaped with her half-brother Fesch, Eliza, Louis, Pauline – and the portrait of Marbeuf, although it was of substantial size. Fleeing first towards the Milelli, then to the coast, where Napoleon would come to rescue her, Letizia spent several days and nights in the scrub-covered hills. She would not leave the picture behind, and kept it with her on all her wanderings, even on the mainland, to Toulon, La Valette, Bausset, Mionnac and Marseille, in spite of the fact that anyone with any relationship to the highest French nobility was being beheaded on the guillotine. Today that portrait of Marbeuf again hangs in the place of honour in the drawing room of the Napoleon house in Ajaccio.

After Marbeuf's death, Letizia, with her fierce pride, devoted herself entirely to her children, who adored her, and earned the well-deserved title of saintly woman, which cannot be dissociated from that of 'Madame Mère'. Let us remember the words of Paoli, who in 1769 had called on her to be the Cornelia of the Corsican people. She was that; indeed, she may aptly be called the mother of the Corsicans of today. Had it not been for her love, Marbeuf would have yielded to the formidable pressure of Narbonne, and the island would have been populated by Acadians; there would no longer have been any Corsicans. The love of Marbeuf and Letizia in its luminous purity changed the face of the world, and when we think of the great lovers of history and legend – Philemon and Baucis, Tristan and Isolde, Abélard and Héloïse, Romeo and Juliet – we must not forget Louis and Letizia.

NOTES

1. National Archives, Paris, No. 400 AP 115. This letter proves that Marbeuf knew the Bonapartes in 1765.
2. ibid.
3. ibid.
4. ibid.
5. Quoted in *Les Makis de la résistance corse* by Christine Roux (Editions France-Empire, 1984).
6. ibid.

CHAPTER III

The Statesman

The heart of a statesman must be in his head.

Napoleon

Although Napoleon was imaginative and a political visionary, he nonetheless stated: 'I am the product of circumstances: I have always worked with them. My policy is to govern men as the greatest number want to be governed.' That sums up the art of governing, of which he was a past master, putting his genius at the service of the problems of the day. His political genius was such that he dominated his century, the most important figure since Charlemagne, to whom he often, quite appropriately, compared himself.

After ruling Milan as a victorious general, Napoleon made his start in public life in the eventful period of the Consulate. Some people promote the simplistic view that success came easily to him, that all he had to do was appear, crowned with the glory of his campaigns, for the country to obey him. This could hardly be further from the truth. The task was huge, and this 30-year-old general who carried the hopes of so many had only two advantages: his intelligence and his formidable energy.

Everything had to be rebuilt. France was on the brink of civil war and was at war with Austria and England; the treasury was empty; the administration was impotent; and the central power was threatened from within by royalist insurrections. What the French desired, Napoleon achieved. He re-established order and prosperity, made laws, reduced political divisions and even restored religious peace. For four and a half years he worked like an ox, as he himself said, informing himself and learning, and he displayed his extraordinary gifts in his choice of men, methods and solutions. It was in the years of the Consulate that the institutions originated which for so long exemplified modern France.

29

The budget was balanced again, the Council of State and the Bank of France were created, and paper money was replaced by gold and silver coins. The laws of the Revolution were combined with Roman law and common law to form the Civil Code; Napoleon presided over fifty-five out of one hundred and seven meetings of the Council of State and wrote the text himself. The Concordat with the Vatican brought God back to France. The royalist émigrés returned in substantial numbers. The Treaty of Amiens brought an end – only temporarily, alas – to a state of war that had lasted for three centuries. The First Consul became president of the Italian Republic, imposed a regime on Holland and, already passionately interested in the organisation of Europe, helped Switzerland become a federal state. And then, through the Final Recess of 1803, he put an end to the continental ambitions of Austria, which had been defeated at Marengo – aptly described by one historian as Napoleon's 'baptism in personal power'.

Authority and order were the watchwords of the Emperor who was emerging within the First Consul. 'The weakness of supreme power is the most horrible calamity of people,' he said, '. . . The love of peoples is only esteem.' And results were not long in coming, because this formidable thinking machine lacked neither imagination, judgement nor method. 'Work is my element,' he would say, 'I was born and made for work.' His incessant activity and extraordinary abilities allowed him to develop infallible tactics because there was no minute of life he left unused. He summed up his tactics as follows: 'The maximum of consequences always follow events.' His method may be described in a few words – 'What is it? Why? How? How much?' and his mind was filled with briefs, statistics and notes. His constant concern was to foresee everything that could happen, never relying on luck, and he was always ready to take action. Such superhuman activity dazzled even the least enthusiastic of men, the pessimistic philosopher Schopenhauer, who called Napoleon 'the most beautiful manifestation of human will'.

He was far from being an ideologue, however, for in him reigned supreme the three great qualities of the statesman: realism, common sense and imagination. He applied his vast genius to the most mundane questions. 'To each day its pain, to each circumstance its law, to each man his nature.' His realism enabled him to get the most out of people, and he could measure and judge them at a glance. He invited the young royalist leaders fighting him in the Vendée to join with him, promising that his government would be one of youth and spirit. And he constantly drew his collaborators, both civilian and military, into a flurry of work. In the wee hours of the morning, after deliberations lasting eight hours, his ministers would be collapsing with fatigue and he would walk behind their chairs and shake them by the shoulders, saying 'Come, citizens, it's only two o'clock. We have to earn the money France gives us.' He was often heard to murmur, as if to convince his entourage, 'The days are centuries!'

He put the interests of the state ahead of everything else, by necessity as much as by inclination, exercising power not only with unflagging energy but also with a meticulous attention to detail. This is shown in his daily schedule as Emperor. Rising at dawn, he attended to his private mail and the newspapers in his dressing gown, received his doctor, architects or librarian during his toilet, and had urgent dispatches read to him in the bath. He dressed and left his quarters at nine o'clock, and received his officers, members of his family or dignitaries. These were work meetings, to which he would summon anyone, civilian and military, he wanted to answer questions. He then granted brief audiences, for like Goethe he knew the value of time and often his blue eyes would turn almost black with impatience when someone talked too long. At nine thirty he was supposed to eat, but the audiences often went on for so long that he only got to the table at about eleven o'clock. He found eating a bother, so he got it over with in seven or eight minutes and used the time to receive artists or scholars, bombarding them with questions. After a moment of rest in the Empress's quarters, he went back to his office and immersed himself in the work of administering an empire of eighty-three million inhabitants spread over half of Europe. The adjoining map room was filled with maps, plans, statements and statistics, so that information was always at his fingertips.

He would throw his hat and sword on a chair and begin dictating to his secretary, pacing back and forth. His writing shows the effects of this nervous walk: the sentences are well constructed but simple, because only ideas held his attention. Only rarely would he stop to leaf through a report or a letter; the subjects of his dictations were all stored in the drawers of his memory. While the secretary transformed his verbal torrent into dispatches, Napoleon opened the portfolios sent by his ministers and read all the files, skipping no detail, sparing no comment, annotating almost every document. Then he signed orders, commissions and dispatches that would make the pleasure or displeasure of the Emperor known in the four corners of Europe.What sovereign has ever paid so much attention to so many details? Nothing escaped him, not even the privy purse: 'Receipts of 44,800; expenditures of 39,800; leaves 5,000; plus 15,000 from March, which makes 20,000. March 30. N.' He still found time to write articles for *Le Moniteur*, to preside over the Council of State and to write in his own hand to his family. When the clock in his office struck six, dinnertime, the Empress, ravishingly beautiful, superbly groomed and stunningly dressed, was waiting with their guests. Some evenings the clock struck seven, eight, nine, even eleven – absorbed in his work, the Emperor had forgotten dinner. When he sat down at the table for a short quarter-hour, it was again to give orders to his grand marshal or receive urgent dispatches or have excerpts from the press read to him. After coffee, he went back up to his office, leaving Josephine to attend to the guests, and resumed his dictation or reading. In bed at ten o'clock, he was up again in the middle of the night reading reports and, especially, studying the state of his armies, filing in his memory the movements of regiments, the stages of a difficult march or the number of batteries as well as the daily situation of the treasury and the finance department. Often the secretary would be awakened and the dictation begin again.

The same activity took place during campaigns, between battles, wherever he had set up camp. After Eylau, quartered in Finkenstein Castle thousands of kilometres from his ministers, he governed with as much assurance, calm and punctuality as he had from his office in the Tuileries; there are 310 letters in his correspondence for this five-week period. According to his minister, Roederer, Napoleon worked about eighteen hours a day.

His unrelenting realism was coupled with lucid common sense. 'High-level policy,' he would say, 'is only common sense applied to big things.' To govern according to the wishes of the majority, who were disgusted by the excesses of the Revolution, he adopted the ideas of his time, for he knew better than anyone that ideas rule the world. 'Walk at their head,' he reasoned, 'and they follow you; walk behind them, and they drag you with them; walk against them, and they knock you down.' Which forced him to acknowledge in the same breath: 'I am sometimes a fox and sometimes a lion. The whole secret of government consists of knowing when you have to be one and when the other.'

He also exercised common sense in the execution of orders, which often depends on simple details. His correspondence provides ample evidence of this. For example, there is a marching order for an army, which entailed the organisation of a huge, carefully regulated migration across the mountains and plains of Europe; it concludes with the following words in the same handwriting: '6,000 beds have been requested; this is too much; 3,000 will suffice.'

Coleridge described imagination as 'the living power and prime agent of all human perception', and a philosopher-historian said imagination is the leaven of genius. Napoleon was guided as much by imagination as by common sense. But his imagination did not consist of mere fantasies; rather it was the result of long and profound meditation. It worked like a computer on the masses of data filed in it.

Napoleon combined his exceptional abilities with an innate sense of order in both private and public life. Apart from a few short-lived adventures, his private life was above reproach. When Lucien, his younger brother, formed a relationship with a divorced woman of loose morals,the master of France said: 'The French people are moral. Its leaders must be too.' He was often heard to speak sternly against 'depravity of the heart, licentiousness of the spirit, immorality'.

He was equally meticulous in his private finances. Just as he had once managed to house, feed and educate his brother, Louis, on his second lieutenant's pay, the Emperor of the French and King of Italy supervised the use of his enormous civil list – some twenty-five million – and when members of his household wasted his funds, he would lose his temper, saying that a captain's pay would have been enough for him. At lunch, he would sometimes lash out at his grand marshal, stiff in his handsome embroidered suit, asking where he had purchased the clothing and how much it had cost. The officer would answer as best he could, since such details are beneath a great ruler, and Napoleon would say, 'When I was a second lieutenant, it cost less. I do not want to pay more than others.'

Napoleon's love of order was also evident in the material organistion of his work. His desk, decorated with gilded bronzes, was equipped with a sliding cover that could be closed without disturbing the papers. In the map room, there were no frills – only tables covered with maps and files that were updated on a daily basis. In every official residence he lived in, he had his household set up the same way. He would root out the slightest irregularity; he liked to say that the discovery of a disloyal accountant was a victory for administration.

It was this love of order that led him to legislate and codify, to find the most qualified man for each job, to insist on the observance of strict etiquette in his presence and, above all, to combat injustice. Indeed, it was his desire for order that was the basis of his whole system of government, a system that made him one of the great forces in history and that brought him, in the words of Daru, 'more glory, grandeur and power than any man before him'.

Because of this implacable sense of order, he has been accused of being inhuman, selfish, violent, irascible and unfair. It is indeed impossible to ignore his outbursts of fury. He once called Talleyrand 'a silk stocking filled with shit'. He told a cardinal legate, 'I will crush your Church.' As for his having kicked the scholar Volney, that has been disputed. But we must make allowances for the nervous reactions of a man who was carrying the weight of crushing responsibility on his shoulders. Furthermore, when he regained his equilibrium, he had the courage to write to one of his ministers: 'Once the anger has passed, there is nothing left. I hope therefore that you will not hold a grudge against me.'

Napoleon's outbursts must be balanced against the actions and words that demonstrate his essential goodness, generosity, understanding and patience. As he himself said: 'Do not believe I do not have a sensitive heart like other men. I am even quite a good man, but in my earliest youth I strove to silence that part of me, and now nothing plays on my heartstrings.' This is the sad fate of a sovereign for whom being moved meant yielding to the demands of others. He was good nevertheless, kind to his mother and brothers, to Josephine and Marie-Louise, to his friends and his soldiers, and he closed his eyes to their avarice, extravagance or ingratitude. He was generous to his enemies, and once he even tried to save from the scaffold a royalist leader who had tried to assassinate him.

The Napoleonic doctrine

What is the Napoleonic doctrine? It can best be explained in Napoleon's own words, first as a young First Consul, then as Emperor of Europe and finally as an exile on a barren rock. We will thus be able to witness the development and exercise of a form of government that has marked Europe.

'When deplorable weakness and constant vacillation become evident in councils or in power; when, yielding to the influence of opposing parties, one after another, and living from day to day with no set plan, no solid method, the full extent of its inadequacy is revealed and the citizens are forced to admit that the State is not governed; when, finally, the administration adds to its inner emptiness the most serious wrong it can commit in the eyes of a proud people, I mean outer degradation; then a vague unease spreads through the society and, moved by the need for self-preservation, it takes a look at itself and seems to seek a man who can save it.'

This is the theory of the providential man, the eternal truth of which is proven by the history of democracies, in peacetime as in war.

'I too am fundamentally and naturally in favour of moderate government. You do not believe it? Why not? Is it because my actions do not seem to agree with my words? How little you know of things and men! Does the necessity of the moment count for nothing in your eyes? I would only have to loosen the reins, and there would be a fine mess.'

Speaking to his Irish doctor on St Helena, he justified his military policy in the following terms: 'The nation needed a strong government. As long as I was the head of government, France was in the same state Rome was in when it needed a dictator to save the Republic. The nations of Europe, seduced by your gold and your hatreds, formed one coalition after another against my power. It was therefore urgent that the head of the

35

State, constantly threatened and attacked, gather all the strength and all the resources of the country to resist or vanquish. I never made conquests except while defending myself. Europe kept on fighting France because of its principles. I was forced to kill or be killed.'

This doctrine, based on the history of Rome, imposed by the needs of the time and fashioned by a mind gifted with almost all human virtues, was the source of all the deeds of the Consulate and the Empire.

The Constitution of the Year VIII

The Constitution of the Year VIII arose out of political necessity. One contemporary wrote that it was created in such a way that authority would come from above and confidence from below. It was written in one month under the impetus of Bonaparte, provisional consul of the Republic. The plan had been to put the second and third consuls in charge of internal and external affairs, but Bonaparte, on the strength of his popularity as a victorious general, and wishing to give himself powers that would allow him to act, declared bluntly that he refused the role of 'fatted pig' that had been reserved for him, and revised the text himself. It was signed in December 1799 and ratified in a plebiscite in February 1800, with more than 3,000,000 votes in favour and 1,562 against. Universal suffrage was introduced, legislative power given to two chambers, and executive power exercised by three consuls and the Council of State; but in fact the First Consul held the real power, since his two colleagues only had an advisory role.

'What's in the Constitution?' asked a wag.

'Bonaparte.'

And that had to be enough, because the people were tired of the revolutionary assemblies of the regime and the parties; they wanted peace and order.

Was this government of the 30-year-old First Consul a dictatorship? No, because although this all-powerful dignitary had the power to propose legislation, it was the specialised sections of the Council of State that wrote them: finance, legislation, war, navy, interior. There was no secrecy; the ministers attended the meetings and the consuls' approval was required to enact a law. And what a sense of human relations the

First Consul showed as he participated in the meetings of the Council, asking questions and encouraging discussion! In what democracy today do we find the head of state discussing and arguing about the country's affairs with the citizens' elite in this way?

The result was stunning. The foundations of the national and local administration were laid very rapidly, in accordance with the First Consul's wishes. The great social vision of the Revolution was preserved, but the country was governed with a unity of direction and action that reflected the dominating personality of the new leader of the State. The verbal torrents of the revolutionary assemblies had made him so suspicious of all-powerful elected representatives that he refused to tolerate 'talkers and ideologues' and instead favoured the establishment of chambers 'of order and public utility' – without power to propose legislation.

Another political necessity was the Constitution of the Year XII, which established the Empire. This was a normal development of a strong regime; as the Emperor became more sure of himself, he showed less and less tolerance towards people who 'talk but do not do anything' and became increasingly authoritarian. The legislative assembly became a mere recording chamber and the Senate was filled with people devoted to the sovereign. This was a logical consequence of the enormous powers that the Nation, by a substantial majority, gave the only man who could save it. 'The Nation threw itself at my feet when I arrived in government,' Napoleon said. 'I took less authority than I was asked to take.' The liberal Additional Act proclaimed on his return from Elba, which restored the system of assemblies, was also a political necessity.

In every period of his career, he adapted to the necessities of the time, legislating only in accordance with events; but to impose his views on the assemblies, the ministers and the Council of State, he constantly repeated that 'men have no rights other than to be governed', that is, well governed. Thus the administrative centralisation, instituted by the Constitution of the Year VIII, sanctioned by victories and military conquests and reinforced by the Constitution of the Year XII, the beginning of the prestigious imperial regime, became stronger and stronger. But before crying dictatorship and condemning out of hand an authoritarianism that partially muzzled the democratic system of universal suffrage – which did not in fact exist in any European country at the time – it is important to go back to the role of the important Council of State, the basis of the legislative system. The council members, senior officials, and auditors constituted an extraordinary body, surprising in its worth and technical skill. It dealt with all bills, gave its opinions, and ruled on appeals addressed to the Emperor. Twice a week the Emperor chaired the meetings, assisted by the arch-chancellor. The presence of this sovereign whose law ruled from the Atlantic to the plains of Poland did not inhibit those attending. On the contrary, the legislative policy of France was enacted there without the least absolutism, and in a way, it was the entire government. Stendhal spent a short time in that great body of the State and had a marvellous memory of it. 'Napoleon had assembled in his Council of State the fifty least stupid Frenchmen,' he wrote with savage humour.

The administration

The administration bequeathed by the Revolution and the short-lived regimes that followed it was incapable of functioning, since it was made up of elected bodies that were beyond the control of the central power and were thus completely subject to the will of the people who had elected them. 'I hope that in a month France will finally be an organised State,' wrote Napoleon early in 1800, that is, three months after taking power.

He was true to his word. Decisions followed quickly one after another, sweeping away the past. An administration that slavishly represented the voters was replaced by one that represented the central power – that *was* the central power. At the head of each department was a prefect, the *praefectus* of the Romans, whose powers may be summed up in a few words: he was in sole charge of the administration. Napoleon's struggle was not only against disorder, but also against the slowness of decision making – it took three days to go from Paris to Bordeaux – and thus the prefects were omnipotent. 'A hundred leagues from the capital, they have more power than I do,' the Emperor once observed with satisfaction.

However, since there was no question of delivering the entire population of a department into arbitrary power, the prefect was assisted by a council that was in charge of relations with the citizens and a general council in charge of financial management – bodies that still exist today! Four hundred and twenty sub-prefects set up in the *arrondissements* saw to it that power was felt in the most isolated communes.

The 36,000 communes of France, which Bonaparte humour-ously called France's seduced and abandoned daughters, were provided with mayors who were not elected but appointed by the prefect. This was a draconian measure, but it too was necessary in order to put an end to the disorder resulting from the conflict between the administrations of the communes and the depart-ments since the Revolution. The mayors were thus put under the control of the prefects and sub-prefects, and the minister of the interior was soon able to tell the First Consul that orders and laws were being transmitted 'at the speed of an electric current'.

The legislator

Napoleon's ideas on justice can be summed up in a few succinct sentences.

'The greatest instrument of a government is justice . . . I do not know what it means to say a woman is very honourable. She has slept with her lover, or she has not. Justice is like honour.'

'Justice is an island surrounded by steep cliffs. One cannot enter it from outside.'

'I know no half-justice . . . A very strict judicial order must be established if you do not want tyranny.'

His name is indissolubly associated with the Civil Code, a work of law in clear, concise language, whose form, as Stendhal said, was a model for almost all the jurists of the nineteenth century. Written in four months, examined by the courts and tribunals of the country and then by the Council of State – including the First Consul, who chaired more than half the meetings and surprised the members with the breadth of his knowledge and the accuracy of his observations – it comprised thirty-six laws and 2,281 sections and came into force in March 1804, on the eve of the proclamation of the Empire. In 1807 it officially became the *Napoleonic Code*. It covered the law of persons, the law of things, and the methods of acquiring rights. None of the social advances of the Revolution were eliminated and, although it was designed for a conservative society, the Code guaranteed equality among citizens, separation of church and state, freedom of conscience and of work, and the right to divorce. A glance at the social organisation of the great nations of Europe in this period is sufficient to show the boldness of this new document.

'My true glory is not in having won sixty battle,' Napoleon stated on St Helena. 'What will live forever is my Civil Code.' He was not mistaken. In creating that monumental work, he had once again been driven by ideas, and he had enshrined the liberal, individualist ideas of the Revolution. He was so successful that the Civil Code was not modified until a century later, when a new society, one no longer founded on equality on the basis of property ownership, demanded new laws.

The legal apparatus set up by the Revolution was bound to arouse the indignation of a man of order. The magistrates, who were elected by the people, were at the mercy of the voters and were concerned less with justice than with partisan interests. As for the system of the *ancien régime*, with magistrates who owned their offices, the nation wanted no more of it, even though it had been famous for its great names and had enjoyed the admiration and envy of almost all Europe.

The judges of the Consulate were therefore appointed for life by the government, with their security of tenure the guarantee of their independence vis-à-vis the central power. And what logic there was in the construction of the judicial pyramid! In the cantons, there were justices of the peace; in the *arrondissements*, magistrates' courts; in the departments, a criminal court; for three or four departments, an appeal court. The highest court of appeal was in Paris; its first presiding judge had the prestigious title of First Magistrate of France and its members were named by the Senate. Alongside this, a whole apparatus of judicial investigation was created, with various levels of public prosecutors. A law society safeguarded the independence, dignity, competence and ethics of the legal profession.

The system was a work of perfect logic and order which ensured maximum guarantees to the accused. It was introduced at the beginning of 1800, only six months after Bonaparte was named First Consul.

Our consideration of Napoleon's legal and judicial reforms would not be complete if we failed to mention the Code of Civil

Procedure, instituted in 1806, which protected the parties in a lawsuit, and which remained unchanged until 1959, and the Commercial Code of 1807, which governed trade on land and sea.

Napoleonic society

In 1799, when General Bonaparte suddenly came to the forefront of events, disorder reigned supreme in French society. There was hatred between social classes, political and religious divisions led to violence, the workers were producing little and the peasants would not readily exchange their produce for *assignats*, the paper money issued by the Revolutionary government on the security of expropriated lands. In his own words, 'France was reaching the limit of general disorganisation', and he did not intend to build his work on these shifting sands.'The government is like the sun at the centre of a society: the various institutions must revolve around it without ever deviating from their orbits. The government must therefore regulate their activities so that they all work together towards general harmony,' explained the First Consul to his minister, Mollien.

The first investigators sent around the country by the government of the Consulate confirmed the inescapable preliminary observations that excesses, dishonesty, insecurity and economic stagnation had sown discord everywhere and had destroyed the national will. Bonaparte himself immediately set to work clearing the debris of the Revolution, and did not stop until 1815, with the job still not finished. No one was excluded; he employed any man of talent, wherever he came from: 'I am national. I use all those who have the ability and the will to follow me . . . I will have honest people of every stripe.'

One hundred and fifty thousand royalists, the élite of old France, had emigrated, fleeing the excesses of the Revolution. He brought half of them back, gave them amnesty, used them and often made them part of his new 'democratic nobility', the Légion d'honneur, which soon became the organisation of the nobility of the Empire, with titles given in recognition of services rendered. Ministers, senators and members of the Council of State were counts; top-ranking officials and mayors, barons; high dignitaries and marshals, princes. What was original in this creation of a new élite closely tied to the regime was that the title was only transmissible to the eldest son; it therefore rewarded the individual and not the family. And any talented man could set his sights on a coat of arms, just as every soldier could aspire to a marshal's baton. The principle was truly 'career open to talent', without distinction as to birth or fortune. To those who criticise the restoration of a titled aristocracy, it may be pointed out that about sixty per cent of the titles in the Empire were granted to men from the bourgeoisie and twenty per cent to men from the lower classes. 'The men who surround me obtained their titles on the field of honour,' stated Napoleon. 'They have demonstrated their abilities.'

The high bourgeoisie had got through the turmoil of the Revolution without suffering much. It consolidated its position during the Consulate and the Empire, taking control of the Chambers of Commerce and regional councils, and the Emperor, who watched it all, often rewarded bankers or industrialists by naming them to the Légion d'honneur or by giving them titles. And he recruited the sons of this social class eager to enter the corridors of power to the administration or the judiciary. 'The men of the regime should be chosen from important families,' he recommended, 'but especially the good families that belonged to what was formerly called the Third Estate, the healthiest part of the population and the one with the most and the closest ties to the government.' Later, he looked back on this formidable attempt to mix the social classes, this concern to bring the nation together, and he summarised it in one of those statements he had a gift for: 'I wrapped them all up in my Consul's toga.'

The propertied class, made up of those who had bought the rural property of the émigrés or the Church, also needed his protection, because they lived in constant fear of the return of the former owners or of reprisals by organised groups of royalists.

The situation of the artisans and merchants was not enviable. Some of them had become involved in political clubs and neglected their livelihood, while others had been ruined by the war. The Revolutionary anarchy which had allowed the road network and port facilities to deteriorate had done the rest.

As for the peasants, who had become the owners of small plots of land thanks to the laws of the Revolution, they were as frightened as the petite bourgeoisie, because they wondered if these *biens nationaux* (national lands), paid for with *assignats*, might not be taken back from them one day by the true owners. Living in this insecurity since the Directory, and burdened with heavy taxes, they produced no more than the strict minimum they needed to survive.

None of these problems and anxieties escaped the new master of France, who published a proclamation as soon as he took office. In it he exhorted, 'Let us bring to the workshops, to agriculture and to the arts that fervour, that constancy, that patience which astounded Europe in difficult circumstances.' The results were quick in coming. What brings together men of every segment of a society headed for disaster is confidence. But confidence is only given to someone who has proven himself, whose ideas are those of the nation and whose character guarantees success, who promises peace both within and without and who is capable of imposing it. Bonaparte achieved the miracle of the Year VIII only by speaking a language the country wanted to hear: 'Our only concern must be the future. We need to draw on all the available talent and all the French.' We might add 'and everyone's energies', because he knew how to elicit them and rally them to his cause. As Stendhal observed: 'The most lowly chemist's boy working in the back of his master's shop was stirred by the idea that if he made a great discovery he would get the cross. Glory was the true legislation of the French.'

The Légion d'honneur

Napoleon created the Order of the Légion d'honneur on 19 May 1802, as a reward for civil or military service by the best citizens of the Republic: 'Members of the Légion d'honneur will be military personnel who have been awarded coats of arms. They may also be military personnel who have rendered major services to the State in the struggle for freedom: citizens who, through their knowledge, talents and virtues, have helped establish or defend the principles of the Republic or have promoted love and respect for justice or the public administration.'

A decree of 1 July 1804 established the form of the decoration: a star with five double points, enamelled in white, on a red moiré ribbon, with the words '*République française*' on the front and '*Honneur et Patrie*' on the back, in silver for legionnaires and in gold for officers, commanders and grand officers. These were the four original ranks of the Légion d'honneur. Today, it has three ranks – *chevalier* or knight, officer and commander – and two dignities – grand officer and grand cross. The Grand Chancellery of the Légion d'honneur administers the awarding of the decorations and the associated grants as well as support services for the legionnaires: nursing homes for disabled persons, retirement homes and schools. The first Grand Chancellor was a civilian, Bernard de la Ville, Comte de Lacépède (1756-1825), an illustrious naturalist, member of the Institute and senator. Lacépède would have preferred to continue his scientific research, but he dedicated his life to the order and developed it into an important organisation.

The Grand Chancellery was located in the Hôtel de Salm, a beautiful building on the banks of the Seine opposite the Tuileries. It is still there today. As chance would have it, Prince Frédéric de Salm, who built the building, was guillotined on 22 July 1794 with his friend General Alexandre de Beauharnais, the husband of the future Empress Josephine.

In addition to wearing the emblem, legionnaires enjoyed various privileges, including a stipend for each rank: legionnaire, 250 francs; officer, 1,000 francs; commander, 2,000 francs; grand officer, 5,000 francs. They were entitled to carry hunting weapons and could, under certain conditions, enter the nobility. Special schools were set up for the daughters of the less well-to-do members. But the legionnaires also had to comply with certain rules; for example, they could not exercise the trade of domestic or innkeeper.

One of Napoleon's first appearances as Emperor was at the majestic first presentations of the Légion d'honneur on 15 July 1804, in the courtyard of Les Invalides, the same place where the President of the Republic today decorates those named grand officers and grand crosses. Napoleon would have liked the ceremony to take place on 14 July, the anniversary of the storming of the Bastille and a national holiday, but that year 14 July fell on a Saturday. The Emperor, on horseback, was welcomed by Cardinal de Belloy, the Archbishop of Paris, in the presence of most of the important dignitaries of the Empire, who were seated in tiers. Josephine and Hortense occupied a special platform draped with cloth of empire green with gold bees.Cardinal Caprara, the papal legate, said a mass, then the grand chancellor called on the recipients to come forward one by one to receive the emblem of their rank from Napoleon's hands.

The procession included the marshals; Generals Oudinot, Macdonald and Marmont; and officers and soldiers, among them Jean Roch Coignet, who was to become one of the most famous *grognards* of the Guard, with which he took part in every battle Napoleon fought, from Marengo to Waterloo. Then came Cardinal Fesch, Cambacérès, Talleyrand, Monge, Laplace, Prony, Cuvier, Montgolfier, Fontanes, Denon, David, Mehul and Bernardin de Saint-Pierre. A *Te Deum* composed by Desvignes concluded the ceremony, and the imperial procession made its way back to the Tuileries through a jubilant Paris.

The splendour of the ceremony at Les Invalides was surpassed by the presentation of decorations on 16 August of the same year in Boulogne, where 200,000 men were encamped in preparation for a landing in England. The place chosen was the valley of Terlincthum. It was set up in the form of an amphitheatre, with a corps of 100,000 men forming a semi-circle facing the imperial platform at the centre.

Napoleon arrived at noon, wearing his uniform as colonel in the chasseurs of the Garde. After a speech by Lacépède, the presentations began in order of rank in the Légion d'honneur and alphabetical order; a simple soldier could thus be called before his general. The Emperor pinned the decoration on each legionnaire with his own hands and exchanged a few words with him. That day marked the Légion d'honneur's true entry into the heart of the nation. Its repercussions were universal, and they have continued to this day. By bringing together all the fighting men under the banner of sacrifice of life for the nation, the 'red', as the soldiers called it, completed the transformation of the traditional army of the *ancien régime* into a cohesive force that reflected the whole nation.

Two monuments mark the memory of 16 August 1804: a marble pyramid placed exactly at the spot where Napoleon stood and the column of the Grande Armée, topped with Houdon's statue of the Emperor. The column was seriously damaged in 1944 and restored in 1962, with a new statue by P. Stenne.

In writing the basic documents, Napoleon had personally seen to it that the Légion d'honneur put into practice the principle of mutual aid and solidarity. This reinforced the traditional aspect of the new institution in a way that could only meet with general approval, while helping bring the legionnaires closer together. On 15 December 1805, thirteen days after the Battle of Austerlitz, a decree signed at Schönbrunn created schools for the daughters of legionnaires. The first was established in 1807 at the Château d'Écouen under Marie-Antoinette's former lady-in-waiting, Mme Campan, who was famous for her extraordinary talents as a teacher. The second school was opened in 1810 in the former Abbey of Saint-Denis with Mme de Bouzet as Principal. The Emperor's visits are legendary in the history of these institutions. Starting in 1810, homes for girls orphaned by the war – whether or not they were daughters of legionnaires – were also opened under the auspices of the Légion d'honneur.

In spite of all the vicissitudes France has experienced since 1804, the Légion d'honneur has remained the most important French order of merit. Its prestige is such that almost all the orders of merit created since on every continent are proud to take it as a model.[1]

Diplomacy

At the beginning of the Consulate, France was in its seventh year of war. As Consul and then as Emperor, General Bonaparte hardly had a chance to put his sword back in the scabbard, because, as one of his ministers told a British diplomat, France only expanded as a result of the repeated efforts to suppress it. In a Europe made up of oligarchies hostile to the system born of the Revolution, Napoleonic diplomacy could not be separated from the art of war, and the Emperor was forced to impose his diplomatic views through victories and conquests.

On 22 November 1799 the Ministry of External Affairs was entrusted to the crafty Talleyrand, the 'prince of diplomats', who remained in the position for seven and a half years under the direct authority of the First Consul and then the Emperor. This was a strange relationship but an excellent one, because the two men respected each other. The minister brought to it the manners, experience and traditions of the *ancien régime*, and Bonaparte brought boldness, energy and imagination.

The first act of the Consulate was to write to the British sovereign and the German emperor to suggest a reconciliation.

Napoleon asked George III, 'How can the two most enlightened nations of Europe sacrifice trade, domestic prosperity and the happiness of families to vain ideas of grandeur?' To Emperor Francis II he wrote, 'I am a stranger to all feelings of vainglory, and my first wish is to put an end to the bloodshed.' These two sentences clearly show the true nature of the greatest conqueror in history in international relations: putting trade, prosperity and human happiness ahead of the glory of conquests, and going to war only when forced to.

From London came a curt reply by a minister stating that there would be no peace without the restoration of France's old dynasty and its former territory. Restoring the borders of the *ancien régime* would have made France smaller than its natural borders, the Rhine and the Alps, which had been established by the armies of the Revolution. The First Consul resigned himself to war.

Even Napoleon's enemies could attest to his preference for negotiation over brute force. As commanding general of the army of Italy, he offered peace to the conquered Austrians against the wishes of the Directory, which wanted to continue a successful campaign. The young conqueror stated this forcefully and unequivocally: 'The brave soldiers make war and desire peace . . . Have we killed enough people and inflicted enough pain on poor humanity? . . . If the overture I have the honour of making to you can save the life of a single man, I will be prouder of that civic crown than of the sad glory which may come from military success.'

In 1800 Napoleon also made overtures to Prussia, but in vain. After Marengo he also made an appeal to Emperor Francis II, begging him 'to listen to the cry of humanity and not to allow a generation of two brave and powerful nations to slit each other's throats for interests that are foreign to them'. But his efforts for peace were fruitless! Europe already feared him too much to listen to him.

Thanks to Napoleon, in the two and a half years from 18 Brumaire to March 1802, when a peace treaty was signed with England, France rose from domestic anarchy to become the major power of the continent. The Swiss confederation entered into an alliance with it, Spain ceded Louisiana back to it, and the Two Sicilies, Portugal and the Ottoman Empire established friendly relations with it. Ignoring the enduring hatred of the Prussian sovereigns for everything to do with the Revolution, he once again took the first step and wrote to them: 'My fondest wish is to see Prussia and France move closer and through their union lay a solid foundation for peace on the continent.' The Recess of the German Empire in 1803 as a consequence of the Treaty of Luneville crowned this vigorous diplomatic campaign by the Consulate. The negotiations that took place in Paris to compensate the losses suffered by the German princes on the left bank of the Rhine marked the end of the German Holy Roman Empire, and Austria's influence in Germany was replaced by that of France.

But there was still England! Throughout the duration of the Peace of Amiens, from March 1802 to May 1803, the First Consul made every effort to avoid a renewal of hostilities. He fulfilled the clauses of the treaty, whereas England, eight months later, still occupied Malta, from which it had agreed to withdraw. The British government made no secret of the fact that it considered the peace nothing more than a truce which, as Addington said, allowed it to wait for an opportunity to resume fighting under better conditions. As justification, England accused France of ceding Louisiana to the United States in April 1803, a matter that was totally out of its jurisdiction and concerned only the two countries directly involved. England also objected strongly to France's mediation in the creation of a Swiss confederation. And it objected most strongly to France's annexation of Piedmont, a reprehensible deed to be sure, but one which could have been a matter for diplomatic negotiations, during which Talleyrand could have invoked the fact that General Bonaparte had become president of the Italian Republic in the most normal way.

The real reason why England broke the treaty and resumed the war was the anger of British financial circles at the inevitable prospect of French hegemony in Europe. Bonaparte was a dangerous man, so dangerous even at this date that, if we are to believe a statement by Wellington to Stanhope, they were already dreaming of sending him to end his days on a South Atlantic island called St Helena.

The First Consul did everything possible to avoid the worst. He went so far as to request the intervention of the czar and the king of Prussia. 'England has taken off its mask,' he wrote to the czar, 'and has informed me that it wishes to keep Malta for seven years.

I ask Your Majesty to intervene, which seems necessary in order to keep the peace at sea, in which you have always taken an interest.' And he wrote to the king of Prussia: 'War is an evil I cannot deplore enough, and I would desire that Your Majesty, having been appealed to by England to guarantee the Knights Hospitalers of Malta, take some interest in seeing that this article of the treaty is carried out.' He even proposed European negotiations: 'As soon as the current disputes are settled, whether by arbitration or by a direct arrangement with England, I am ready to call on a general congress of the principal powers such as Russia, Austria, England and Prussia, and I am willing to make all kinds of contributions and even concessions to help establish in a more stable manner the tranquillity of Europe in general and the independence of each State in particular.'

Just before the treaty was broken, he made another overture, proposing that England keep Malta for ten years on condition that France occupy Otranto and a few places in the kingdom of Naples for the same period. He even made efforts to dissuade George III's ambassador from returning home. 'It is hard to see how a great, powerful, sensible nation would want to undertake a war that would lead to such great misfortune for such a small cause, just a miserable rock,' he said. This is a further sign of his determination to find ways to avoid war and his willingness to pay the price to do so.

But reason did not prevail, because the English were eager to resume the war, considering the Treaty of Amiens a mistake because it was not shameful for France. Such was Bonaparte's view, and such was also the view of more than one British businessman. And when Pitt announced the declaration of war in the House of Commons, Fox, the leader of the opposition, asked sarcastically whether this meant that anything France did outside its borders, or even within them, would be cause for war.

The first cannon shot had not yet been fired when the British admiralty seized 1,200 French and Dutch trading ships and imprisoned the crews. But the First Consul still sought an accommodation. Speaking to the Russian ambassador on 12 June 1803, he stated frankly: 'I would like Russia and Prussia to save me. If both demand my withdrawal from Holland, Switzerland, the kingdom of Naples and the Empire – everything that has been asked of me – but at the same time ask England to fulfil the essential conditions of the treaty, surrendering Malta either to the Hospitalers or to Russia, I am prepared to accept your conditions.'

England would hear nothing of this, and in July it secretly informed the czar that if Russia, Prussia and Austria wanted to take up arms against France, it would make a commitment to provide funds. Two months earlier Bonaparte had written to the pope: 'Your Holiness will see from the copy of the last note from the English ambassador, which I enclose for you alone, that I have been pushed to the limit . . . I would be glad to learn that Your Holiness judged that I am not the cause of the war or of the misfortunes that could result from it, and that I was in all of this constrained and obliged.' How could he be accused of pushing England to the limit when in January 1805, a month after his coronation, he still spoke to the enemy and did so directly: 'Sire, my brother,' he wrote to George III, 'called to the throne of France by Providence and by the votes of the Senate, the people and the army, my first feeling is a desire for peace. France and England are eroding their prosperity. They could fight for centuries. But are their governments properly fulfilling their most sacred of duties? . . . I attach no disgrace to taking the first step . . . I beseech Your Majesty not to deny himself the happiness of personally bringing peace to the world . . . Your Majesty has won more in the last ten years, in territories and in wealth, than the whole extent of Europe. His nation is at the height of prosperity. What can it hope for from war?' Is this the letter of a troublemaker? Consider what such a gesture must have cost a man who had just demonstrated his military genius! To the French deputies, Napoleon acknowledged without false modesty: 'When I resolved to write to the king of England, I renounced the most legitimate resentments and the most honourable passions.

What condemned him to constant war was the preservation of the natural borders because Europe intended to retake the left bank of the Rhine and the defence of the country's economic growth against an England determined to maintain its political hegemony through trading power. As the exile of St Helena stated in a few bitter words, 'I have never vanquished and conquered except in my own defence . . . This is a truth that time demonstrates more and more each day.'

Let us return briefly to the machinations of the European coalitions against Napoleon – that is, against the conquests of the

Revolution – which kept the war going and obstructed the basically peaceful diplomacy of the Empire. The first coalition had been organised by England in 1793 against Revolutionary France and the second in 1799 against the France of the Directory. Between 1793 and 1815 England initiated seven coalitions against France.

The third coalition was the work of the czar, who claimed to be acting as mediator between France and England while making sure he had Prussia's and Austria's support against France, and who in London in April 1805 signed a treaty 'to restore to Europe the peace of which it has been deprived by the inordinate ambition of the French government'. England would of course cover part of the costs of the war.

'I will not let the Austrians and the Russians join together. I will strike them before they form an alliance,' Napoleon decided. This was a defensive measure. Within a few days he beat the Austrian troops and then he turned to the Russians, against whom he won the greatest victory of the Empire, at Austerlitz. Napoleon had done everything possible to avoid that battle, even seeking to talk to the czar the day before. He had written to Talleyrand: 'There will probably be a major battle tomorrow that will be very serious for the Russians. I have done everything to avoid it, because it will be blood needlessly shed . . . Do not be alarmed; I am in a strong position. I regret what it will cost and for almost no purpose.'

The next day he was the victor, and he rewarded his soldiers with the famous proclamation: 'Soldiers, I am proud of you.' The Emperor of Austria requested an interview and received this reply from his conqueror: 'You have made me commit a great wrong. It is not after the battles that conferences should be held. I should only be a soldier today and I do not hide the fact that, as such, I should only pursue victory and not listen to words of peace.' He did listen to them, however, and took leave of Emperor Francis asking him amicably, 'So, Your Majesty promises not to start the war again?' Francis answered that he would swear it and that he would keep his word, and they even embraced before parting. He also made that commitment on behalf of the czar, who had almost been taken prisoner on the battlefield the day before, for Napoleon had added in the same breath: 'The Russian army is encircled . . . But I wish to do something for Czar Alexander. I will let the Russian army go if Your Majesty promises me that it will return to Russia and withdraw from Germany and Poland.' To prove his peaceful intentions, he even sent back the men of the Russian Imperial Guard who had been taken prisoner.

Soon he made further goodwill overtures to England. Pitt died and was succeeded by the Whigs Grenville, Grey and Fox – Fox who had deplored the breaking of the Treaty of Amiens. Napoleon immediately let it be known that he would abandon Malta and the colony of Cape of Good Hope to the English government and that he would even surrender Hanover to achieve a rapprochement. This plan was being discussed in Paris with Lord Lauderdale, the British envoy, when Fox died. 'The death of Mr Fox,' Napoleon said on St Helena, 'was one of the misfortunes of my career. If he had lived, we would have made peace.' The peace he wanted so much! The negotiations broke down, and Prussia – to which Napoleon had just offered Hanover – took advantage of this to declare war.

Napoleon had to return to the battlefield, but he did so without hatred. This was far from the case for his adversaries. 'Napoleon is a monster out of the mire!' said Queen Louise of Prussia. The czar was burning 'to bring respite to Europe', that is, to crush the French and the man he called 'the troublemaker of the world'. The king of Prussia believed himself strong enough to demand that Napoleon withdraw from Germany. Napoleon hesitated once again before engaging in hostilities, and proposed negotiation: 'Let Prussia disarm,' he suggested, 'and the French will go back across the Rhine, but not before.' War against a state he admired and an army he considered the best in Europe seemed to him 'a true monstrosity'. Prussia replied with the demand that France withdraw by 8 October 1806, and Prussian officers came symbolically to sharpen their sabres on the steps of the French embassy.

'Fine, tomorrow I will be in Saxony,' Napoleon grumbled. But at the last moment, he again hesitated, and wrote to the king of Prussia: 'Believe me, Your Majesty, I have forces such that all your forces will not be able to stave off victory for long. But why shed so much blood? To what end? I will speak to Your Majesty in the same language I used with Czar Alexander two days before Austerlitz . . . Why let our subjects be massacred? I do not value a victory purchased with the lives of so many of my children. I beseech Your Majesty to see in this letter only my desire to spare the blood of men.' Who then was thirsting for military glory? The man who wrote these lines or the man who refused to read them?

When the die was cast, Napoleon moved into action. On the 13th he was in Jena. He took his position at the head of his troops during the night, personally inspected the positions holding a lantern, examined the encampments of the enemy, and slept a few hours. Then, with his 92,000 French troops, he crushed 120,000 Prussians, taking 20,000 prisoners. Prussia collapsed and he entered Berlin. There, more than one child of that wealthy city must have watched him pass with the same admiring eyes as little Heinrich Heine did in Düsseldorf: 'The Emperor wore his simple green uniform and historic hat. He rode a small white horse that walked so proudly, so calmly, so certainly, with such dignity . . . If I had been the royal prince of Prussia, I would have envied the lot of that little horse.'

The Russian warmongers refused to learn from the fate of Prussia, and Alexander attempted to bring a hesitant Austria back into his camp. Francis II started secretly re-arming, all the while loudly protesting his neutrality and his prudence: 'If I declare myself, I can expect to have to contend with all Bonaparte's forces.'

So there were further clashes. The Russians were displeased by the resurrection of Poland, which Napoleon had decided to make a buffer between Europe and the Russian giant. The arrival of the French Emperor, the liberator of the territory, was greeted with fervour by the Poles – and with fury in St Petersburg.

It was the Russian commander in chief, Bennigsen, reinforced with what was left of the Prussian army, who resumed the hostilities, which ended at Eylau with 54,000 French against 80,000 Russians, a horrendous slaughter. The man who had fought the battle against his will wrote to Empress Josephine: 'The soul is oppressed at the sight of so many victims . . . Such a spectacle can only inspire a love of peace and a horror of war.'

The French army set up its winter quarters in Poland, from which the Emperor controlled the operations of his huge Empire. Behind his back, Prussia was stirring again and Austria was pursuing its preparations for war while trying to gain time by hypocritically offering to mediate with Russia. The czar obtained further assistance from England amounting to a million pounds and 20,000 soldiers, and ordered his troops to attack the French in their camp. They were on the verge of winning when Napoleon arrived in Friedland on 14 June, judged the situation in a glance and ordered an attack at the end of the afternoon. The marshals objected that it was late. 'You don't surprise an enemy in such a mistake twice,' was Napoleon's reply.

At ten o'clock in the evening the Battle of Friedland was won and Napoleon, exhausted but happy, went to bed among his soldiers in the field. Two days later he informed Europe, through the bulletin of the Grande Armée: 'Blood has again been shed, but at least France is innocent. There has been no political overture that the Emperor has not responded to, no proposal he has delayed in answering, no trap laid by the warmongers that he has not listened to.'

A few days later he met with the vanquished 'autocrat of the North', who declared at the outset, 'If you bear a grudge against England and only against her, we will easily be in agreement, for I have as much to complain about on that score as you do.' Napoleon showed generosity towards the man he had described as 'a handsome, good, young Emperor'. He sacrificed to the vanquished enemy – that is, to the cause of peace – Turkey and Sweden, and even Finland, which would soon be carved up by the Russians, and gave up on creating a kingdom of Poland. Alexander was jubilant. He wrote to his sister Catherine: 'God has saved us. Instead of sacrifices, we come out of the fight with some honour. But what do you say of all these events? Me spending my days with Bonaparte? Spending hours at a time with him!' And he wrote to his mother: 'France must be able to believe that its interest can be joined with that of Russia.'

Which of the two emperors was more treacherous? And whose diplomacy was the more tortuous? Which was the more worthy of the two, the benevolent winner or the loser telling lies?

Tilsit was the high point of the great European empire and the triumph of peace imposed on all its adversaries other than England, but it also signalled the coming together of forces secretly hostile to Napoleon and his diplomacy. The czar, whose entourage were fierce anglophiles, began a mediation process in London between France and England, but the successors of Pitt and Canning in the Foreign Office and Castlereagh in the War Office would hear nothing of it; the decree from Berlin on the Continental System left them no choice but to fight so as not to be suffocated.

In September 1807 a British squadron bombarded Copenhagen in an effort to terrorise the continental powers that were complying with the Napoleonic policy. This aggressive action aroused indignation, and the countries of Europe did an about-face and rallied to the cause of France, with the exception of Portugal, whose regent was controlled by London. 'If Portugal does not do as I want,' Napoleon stormed, 'the House of Braganca will no longer be on the throne two months from now.'

Europe approved, and Spain even offered troops to help subdue its neighbour, on the condition that it be allowed to annex a part of the Portuguese territory. At the end of 1807 French soldiers occupied Lisbon, but again with no offensive purpose and with the approval of almost the whole continent – simply to counter London's manoeuvres.

The situation was the same at the time of the decree of Milan, in December 1807. Napoleon has been criticised for dealing in enemy vessels and declaring any ship submitting to British regulations fair game, but has anyone taken the trouble to look at the details of those regulations? One prohibited neutral ships from entering the harbours of the continent unless they had paid customs duties to Great Britain. And does anyone remember that one year earlier, in 1806, England had declared a blockade of French ports, inspecting neutral ships and confiscating any goods bound for French ports?

Napoleon certainly made diplomatic errors, the worst being his conflict with the Holy See, which lost him the support of Catholics, and the Peninsular War, which slowly wore him down. But here again, excuses can be found for him.

Did not the pope refuse to close his ports to British vessels as the Austrians, the Russians, the Prussians and the Danes had? And was not Napoleon justified, as king of Italy, in demanding that the Holy See conform to the policy of the majority of the continent and expel the enemies of the Empire from its states? Playing the role of spiritual sovereign to protect his temporal interests, the pope set himself up as a martyr. 'French soldiers will have to trample me under their feet if they want to violate my authority,' he declared. This was quite a masquerade, since the papal administration was anything but spiritual. One need only read Stendhal's description of his term as French consul in the Papal States to discover the rapacity of that administration run by clergymen: 'They were judges, lawyers, professors, notaries, writers, diplomats and museum and library curators. The government of Rome belongs to the administration of the Papal States.' Napoleon was equally critical: 'No personal interest should hinder spiritual matters. And how could it not hinder them when the pope as sovereign and the pope as spiritual leader can have contrary interests?' A hundred years later history would bear him out, and after the Lateran Treaty in 1929, the papacy had to be content with the mere appearance of worldly power.

Was Napoleon alone responsible for the Peninsular War? The memory of it haunted him to the end of his days because it was his first experience of defeat. It started with an appeal for his arbitration by King Charles IV, a degenerate Bourbon dominated by his wife and her lover, Godoy, who was Prime Minister. There was the influence of Talleyrand, who favoured the expulsion of the Bourbons from all thrones and the accession of a prince from the Bonaparte family to the Spanish throne. There was also the irritation of a sovereign who was engaged in a struggle to the death for his security and who realised that there was a door on the Iberian Peninsula still open to trade with the British. The only real mistake he made was misjudging the Spanish people, so proud, so noble, so independent, prepared to make any sacrifice and to rise up as one against any foreign interference. Events moved so quickly that once hostilities had begun it was impossible to change policy.

Madrid revolted, and the people, drunk with fury, seized Godoy, threatening to kill him. Charles IV abdicated in favour of his son, and then retracted his abdication. Napoleon then had to decide between the king and the son as they exchanged insults in front of him in Bayonne. Charles IV named Murat lieutenant general of the kingdom but, learning of a new uprising in Madrid, abdicated definitively in favour of 'the great Napoleon' after a nasty scene with his wife and his son, and received in exchange a civil list and a residence in France. Joseph Bonaparte was named king of Spain, but receiving a throne as a promotion and occupying the throne – when the throne was that of Spain – were two different things! Spain in revolt appealed to England, and London jumped at the opportunity to attack the imperial troops from the rear. The 80,000 French soldiers were involved in a guerilla war of hair-raising brutality; both sides mutilated, tortured, burned people alive and pillaged. Joseph entered his capital after a narrow military victory in July 1808, but had to flee after a 'reign' of only ten days. He explained to his brother: 'It would take 200,000 Frenchmen to conquer Spain and 100,000 scaffolds to keep the prince condemned to reign over it on the throne. No, Sire, we do not know this people . . . not one Spaniard will be for me if we make the conquest.'

Wisdom demanded a reversal of the decision, especially since the British, under Wellesley, had landed in Portugal and beaten the imperial troops. It was, alas, impossible for the Emperor of Europe to accept a defeat, to tolerate the permanent threat of an invasion in his rear. Pushed to intransigence by England's intervention, Napoleon was from that day no longer able to impose his European diplomacy.

Prussia was stirring, and in order to contain it he imposed on it, with some difficulty, an agreement limiting its military forces to 42,000 men. Catholic Austria, moved by the fate of the pope confined in the Quirinal Palace and by the somewhat forced abdication of the Bourbons in Spain, was furiously re-arming and preparing to raise 700,000 men. To support his position as European mediator, Napoleon absolutely needed Russia, and all his diplomatic efforts were directed to forming an effective alliance with Alexander. The following letter of 2 February 1808, the letter of a visionary far ahead of his time, is famous:

'Your Majesty will have seen the last speeches of the Parliament of England and the decision to push the war to the limit . . . We can only achieve peace and consolidate our system through great and far-reaching measures . . . An army of 50,000 men – Russian, French, maybe even a few Austrians – going by way of Constantinople into Asia would make England tremble and bring it to its knees before the continent before it got as far as the Euphrates . . . A month after we agreed to it, the army could be on the Bosphorus. The repercussions would reach as far as India, and England would be subjugated . . . The English, threatened in India, expelled from the Levant, will be crushed under the weight of events. Your Majesty and I would have preferred the sweetness of peace and spending our lives in the middle of our vast empires, occupied with giving them new life and making them happy through the arts and the benefits of administration; the enemies of the world will not have it.'

Alexander was struck by this global vision and he told the French ambassador, 'Tell the Emperor that I am devoted to him for life, that my Empire, my armies, everything is at his disposal.'

Things had changed since Tilsit, however, and as a result of his reversals in Spain and his quarrel with the pope, Napoleon was now the petitioner, and Alexander, as wily as he was realistic, took advantage of this to seize Finland and make exorbitant claims on the Ottoman Empire even before the new meeting at Erfurt. Napoleon came to the appointment, which was to be the last great spectacle of the European empire, surrounded by his vassals, the kings of Saxony, Bavaria, Württemberg and Westphalia, as well as the grand duke of Baden and representatives of Austria and Prussia. Before going he had revealed his plans to Talleyrand: 'We are going to Erfurt. I want to come back free to do what I want in Spain, I want to be sure that Austria will be anxious and restrained, and I do not want to be committed in a specific way to Russia with respect to matters in the Levant.'

Well rewarded by Austria, shamelessly betraying the man who had showered him with favours, Talleyrand, 'the lame devil', sabotaged this plan by intervening directly with the czar. 'Sire,' he whispered in his ear, 'what are you doing here? It is up to you to save Europe, and you will only achieve this by standing up to Napoleon. The French are a civilised people; their sovereign is not. The sovereign of Russia is civilised and his people are not. It is therefore up to the sovereign of Russia to be the ally of the French people. The Rhine, the Alps, the Pyrenees are France's conquests. The rest is the Emperor's conquest. France does not want it.'

Thus warned, Alexander was from the outset not as easy as at Tilsit, while Napoleon, eager to send troops from Germany to Spain, insisted that Russia exert pressure to dissuade Austria from taking up arms. To Alexander, the maintenance of Austrian power represented the guarantee of peace in Europe; to Napoleon, it represented the threat of a second front at any moment. They could not therefore reach agreement, at least not completely, and Erfurt was a partial diplomatic failure. France and Russia offered peace to England, which haughtily rejected it. Joseph was recognised as king of Spain. Alexander kept Finland. And if Austria broke with France or Russia, the czar and the Emperor would join forces.

These poor results were Talleyrand's fault, but they did allow Napoleon to gain time to deal with the real threat: the inevitable Austrian attack. So he rushed back to Spain, where as always his presence influenced events in his favour. He won three victories, and on 2 December 1808 he entered Madrid. From there he intended to drive into Portugal, where 30,000 British troops were advancing along the roads under the command of John Moore. Bad news from Paris, where his ministers Talleyrand and Fouché were plotting against him, forced Napoleon to renounce this plan and return as quickly as possible to the Tuileries. The Spanish structure collapsed, the first failure for Europe-wide diplomacy – and Napoleon's marshals retreated one step ahead of Wellesley, who had adopted Napoleon's theories.

Would Austria attack? Napoleon had no doubt it would, but he still tried to negotiate. He gave Vienna a warning: 'It appears that it is the waters of the Lethe, and not the Danube, that flow to Vienna; they have forgotten the lessons of experience. They will need another lesson; they will get it, and it will be terrible . . . All my attention was focused on the battlefield England had chosen – Spain. Austria, who saved the English in 1805, when I was about to cross the Strait of Dover, has saved them again by stopping me when I was going to pursue them to La Coruña. It will pay dearly for this. Either it will disarm immediately or it will have to endure a war of destruction.'

Austria felt that Napoleon was no longer capable of imposing his diplomacy through war because his best troops were immobilized in Spain while the Austrians had half a million men, the German states were in turmoil and England was generously loosening its purse strings.[2] Without declaring war, the Austrians entered Bavaria on 10 April 1809. Leaving Paris on the 13th, Napoleon was in the field on the 17th, and in three days he concluded the Bavarian campaign, which opened the gates to Vienna for him.

His victory at Wagram allowed him to set himself up at Schönbrunn Palace as the victor, where once again diplomatic tasks distracted him from his military responsibilities. He tried first to resolve the conflict with the Holy See by uniting the Papal States with the French empire, leaving the pope with sovereignty only over the Vatican, but over-zealous subordinates botched things by arresting the pontiff and imprisoning him in Grenoble.

Napoleon was furious, but what could he do from so far away? Furthermore, the military situation in Spain was deteriorating and the British had landed near the estuary of the Schelde. The treaty with vanquished Austria was badly handled. Eager to return to Paris, Napoleon gradually reduced his demands and instead of dismantling the empire of the Habsburgs as he had intended, he accepted an indemnity and a reduction in the Austrian armed forces. This was bad diplomacy by a conqueror in a hurry to settle things in order to deal with a threat on another front! And the Illyrian Provinces, with which he enlarged the French empire, infuriating the Russians, were a bad acquisition. The Treaty of Schönbrunn of 14 October 1809 sowed the seeds of the end of Napoleon's supremacy in Europe.

Was the Emperor, who was still all-powerful, aware of this? Did he sense it? England was plotting more actively than ever. Prussia was waiting for its chance. The czar remained aloof. With everyone expecting a brutal outcome, Napoleon's diplomatic master stroke came with the Austrian marriage, a spectacular reversal of alliances, which united the fate of the child to be born – and the Empire that would be his inheritance – with that of the most ancient and illustrious house of Europe. This was more subtle diplomacy, certainly, than that of Austria, which gave the eldest daughter of Emperor Francis to the victor of Wagram in return for an accommodation in the peace treaty.

It was the apogee of Napoleon's reign, the zenith for this poor officer who in ten years had become Emperor of the French, King of Italy, Mediator of Switzerland, Protector of the Confederation of the Rhine, master of almost all the kings of Europe and successor to Charlemagne, with an Empire comprising 132 departments stretching from the Ebro to the Elbe, with eighty million inhabitants.

As the sun sets on empires, it rises on reputations. From 1812 on, the diplomats of Europe, led by Metternich, the Austrian chancellor, wove a veritable spider's web around France and its sovereign, made of forced pacts and secret communications. Sensing danger from the Russians, Napoleon negotiated with Prussia to allow French troops to cross its territory and with Austria to supply a contingent of troops, but the Prussians and Austrians secretly informed St Petersburg that they had only agreed to these things under constraint.

The break with Russia and the terrible campaign that followed were Alexander's fault. He opened a breach in the continental system by letting in English merchandise, he massed troops on the Polish border and he tried to form a coalition with Austria, Prussia and Sweden. Never was diplomacy exercised on behalf of such a mediocre sovereign of no military talent, who resented his position as the second most important person in Europe and nursed the dream of being the first. Napoleon refused to yield to his intimidation. He set out to muster in Germany the largest military force of modern times, the Grande Armée, consisting of 423,000 men, half of them French, and close to 1,200 artillery pieces.

In April, when the czar, assured of the support of the English and Swedes, sent an ultimatum demanding that the French withdraw from all of Germany, Napoleon once again tried in good faith to negotiate. Knowing that England had thrown the whole weight of its influence and its financial resources into the balance in favour of war, he first dictated a letter to Lord Castlereagh, the British foreign secretary, which was filled with conciliatory proposals. Napoleon wrote: 'Many changes have taken place in Europe in the last ten years; they were the necessary consequences of the war between France and England . . . The Treaty of Amiens, if it had been maintained, would have prevented many upheavals.' He proposed that the integrity of Spain and Portugal be guaranteed and that French and English troops be withdrawn from those territories and Sicily. These proposals were dictated solely by 'concern for the interests of humanity and the peace of the people', he stated. 'If this fourth attempt should be without success, like those preceding it, France will at least have the consolation of knowing that the blood that may again flow will be completely on England's hands.'

He also wrote to Alexander, 'friend of Tilsit and of Erfurt', after Alexander had refused to receive the French envoy who had been sent to make a final attempt at conciliation: 'I marched on the Niemen with the profound feeling of having done everything possible to spare humanity these new ills and to reconcile everything with my own honour and that of my peoples and the sanctity of treaties . . . War is therefore declared between us. God Himself cannot undo what has been done. But my ears always will be open to peace overtures.'

He received no answer, but he did not give up hope, and from Moscow, conquered and in flames, he made another attempt: 'I have waged war against Your Majesty with no animosity; a note from Your Majesty before or after the last battle would have halted the march and I would have been willing to give up the advantage of entering Moscow.'

Returning to Paris in December 1812, beaten for the first time, not by arms but by 'General Winter', Napoleon had to face an insoluble diplomatic situation. Prussia openly allied itself with Russia in February 1813, and Austria was only waiting for the French troops to experience a setback to change camps. This was wartime diplomacy if ever there was! Working wonders with his 200,000 men, mostly conscripts with no experience in battle, Napoleon again won victories over the Prussians and the Russians, who, frightened, appealed through the Austrian chancellor for a suspension of military operations and suggested that a diplomatic meeting be held.

This was the Congress of Prague, thrown together by Metternich to allow the coalition members to gain time by offering Napoleon unacceptable conditions, such as a reduction of the borders of the French Empire. Everything went as planned, and on 11 August, the day after the congress had been dissolved, Vienna declared war. During the truce, Austria, Prussia and Russia had had time to assemble close to 500,000 men, who charged the dispersed French forces. Napoleon had to retreat and was unable to prevent the invasion of the national territory. His diplomacy was now no longer capable of fending off Metternich's attacks. To put the responsibility for the continuation of the war on the Emperor of the French and turn French public opinion against Napoleon, Metternich offered a peace based on guaranteeing the preservation of France's natural borders: the Rhine, the Alps and the Pyrenees. Pushed by his entourage, Napoleon decided to accept, but the Machiavellian coalition members withdrew their offer and proclaimed that they were not at war against France but against Napoleon himself – an action that had nothing to do with diplomacy.

Napoleon's last communications with the foreign chancelleries took place not through notes or treaties but through messengers. When the allies, who were rushing along the roads to Paris, offered him a return to the borders of 1791, he flatly refused, saying he would never leave France smaller than he had found it.

Then, suddenly, there were the victories of Champaubert and Montmirail over the Russians and the Prussians, followed by other victories over the Russians, the Württembergers and the Austrians – seven in one week – the last time fate would smile on Napoleon. Europe held its breath. Would this amazing man manage to turn the situation around once again? No!

Meeting at Chaumont, Napoleon's enemies listened to Lord Castlereagh's suggestion that the four allies – Austria, Great Britain, Prussia and Russia – form a twenty-year alliance, with London supplying financing of a million pounds a year.

A month later Paris was under the control of enemy troops, and on 6 April Napoleon abdicated. He negotiated the Treaty of Fontainebleau, which would decide his fate and that of his family, through Caulaincourt, the minister of external affairs. It was his last diplomatic 'negotiation'. 'I will need nothing. Defend the interests of France,' he ordered his representative.

'Think of my wife and son, and care nothing for the rest . . . A soldier does not need a lot of room to die.'

These words give the true measure of the man – quick to negotiate, engaged with reality, caring little for his own interests or his own glory but sincerely attached to the French people who had made his fortune and among whom he wanted to sleep for eternity. A skilful diplomat, unbending, sometimes brutal, but respectful of treaties and sincere – one might even be tempted to say 'naively' sincere – when dealing with men such as Alexander, Talleyrand and Castlereagh, who were great men and shrewd diplomats thanks only to Napoleon's downfall.

The family

'I am a very honest man; I am fool enough to believe in the sanctity of family ties,' Napoleon said on St Helena. Perhaps he wanted to emphasise the bad conduct of his father-in-law, the very Catholic Emperor Francis of Austria, and of sanctimonious England, who together delivered his wife to the intrigues of her faithful admirers and deprived him of his son. In any case, he certainly intended to recall the principles he had always upheld, which he had learned in early childhood. He still had the same respect for the authority of parents and the ardent devotion to a mother who had raised him very strictly. When as a legislator he turned his attention to the problem of the family, he quite naturally thought of re-establishing the authority of the father, the Roman *pater familias*, while guaranteeing the rights of the children, for this man who has so often been called hard and insensitive had great humanity and was driven by a profound desire to protect those the laws of nature exposed to injustice: women and children.

His sense of family was demonstrated a hundred times in the course of his career both as a poor officer and as all-powerful Emperor. His brother Louis shared his stipend and his room when he was a poorly paid second lieutenant. He was most generous with his mother. His brothers and sisters, who were so often ungrateful, benefited greatly from his fortune, and his nephews and nieces brightened his rare hours of leisure. But as soon as he looked at the problem, he returned to his basic principle and legislated explicitly: 'In any society, there must be a leader; in the family, the leader is the husband.'

He was horrified by the depraved society of the Directory, with its extravagant styles, its gambling dens, its speculators, its loose morals – obvious proof of the destruction of the family – and his government of the Year VIII was from the outset determined to create a new society based on order, greatness and morality to replace the debauchery, apathy, ignorance and coarseness that prevailed in the government and in the home. But establishing a new mentality would take more than getting rid of the memory of corruption, ease and depravity. To provide an example, the First Consul began by closing the doors of the Tuileries to the fashionable young women who had been known in the time of the Directory as the *merveilleuses*, who dressed too lightly for his taste and whose free and easy ways recalled an era of which he wanted to obliterate every trace. 'Do you not see,' he asked Josephine in public one day, 'that your friends are naked?'He taught them a lesson.

He next went after divorced women and irregular households and berated his friends and collaborators who lived in such situations, including Talleyrand himself, the former bishop of Autun. This inspired one woman of wit to joke that 'Bonaparte wants everyone to get married – bishops, cardinals, etc.'

When he started work on the *Civil Code*, in particular the articles on marriage, he reminded the legislators of the need 'to mark the solidity of the contracted link in an imposing way' and 'its sacred character' as a 'serious and solemn thing', and he personally attended many of the discussions, never missing a chance to stress the binding and solemn nature of marriage and rail against divorce: 'It would be a great misfortune if it became part of our mores! What is a dissolved family? What are spouses who, after having lived in the closest relationship, suddenly become strangers to one another, yet are unable to forget each other?' While he acknowledged the necessity of divorce – perhaps contemplating his own – he wanted at least to make it difficult by subjecting it to restrictions. His concern was for the children of parents who separated: 'What are children who no longer have a father, who cannot join in one embrace the separated authors of their lives!'

His *Civil Code* thus reinforced the authority of the husband over the wife, perhaps because his own wife, Josephine, flippant, carefree and extravagant, had instilled in him the idea of women as perpetual children. He stated: 'Women must learn that in leaving the guardianship of their family they come under that of their husband.' Was this too harsh? Not at all, for Roman law was hardly gentle to women, and Jean-Jacques Rousseau had helped spread the image of women as overgrown children.

Napoleon insisted that women be given guardianship of orphans, against the legislators who felt women were incapable of administration. Against Roman law, which gave the *pater familias* the right of life and death over the members of his family and the right to dispose of threequarters of his estate as he saw fit, he maintained that the son had a vested interest in the goods of the father, and allowed the father to do as he wished with only one quarter of his estate.

Since the family was the reflection of society, the émigrés had to be brought back, because their old-fashioned manners would counter the Revolutionary moral laxity. He signed a Concordat with the Vatican 'to rebuild the altars' and support Christian morality. He created the Légion d'honneur, whose members were to be models of virtue. He reformed public education and founded a university that would produce pure, strong, upright men.

Napoleon also dealt with the problem of the birth rate, which no other sovereign of the time was concerned with, and made fertility the fashion. When a lady was introduced to him, his first question was, 'How many children do you have?' and he was never satisfied with the answer. There is a story of a lady from the south of France who answered him proudly, because it was true, 'Twenty-four, Sire,' To which Napoleon replied, 'When are you expecting the twenty-fifth?' So strong was his authority that the lady lost her composure and stammered, 'Sire, whenever Your Majesty desires.'

Religion

'Man, thrown into life, wonders, Where did I come from? Who am I? These are mysterious questions that lead us to religion. We rush towards it, our natural penchant carries us there; but then comes education, which stops us. Education and history are the enemies of true religion, which has been disfigured by the imperfections of men,' Napoleon expounded in the solitude of exile.

Was he himself religious? His declarations on the subject are many and varied, and often contradictory. For example, he said, 'I do not believe in religions, but in the existence of God . . . Who made all this?' And, 'The honest man never doubts the existence of God, for if reason does not suffice to understand it, the soul accepts it.' But he also said, 'Everything is only matter . . . I know very well that death is the end of everything.' And, 'Priests have always slipped fraud and lies into everything.' But he concluded: 'Remission of sins is a very beautiful idea; that is what makes religion beautiful and why it will not perish. No one can say he does not believe in it and will not believe in it one day.'

On St Helena, as the hour of truth drew near, he sometimes regretted that he had not really been a believer, but he denied that he was an atheist and meticulously prepared the religious formalities of his death and funeral, and the first sentence of his will stated that he had died in the Catholic religion, apostolic and Roman. The persistent problem of the existence of God preoccupied his active, curious mind and irritated him because there was no rational solution, but he nevertheless declared himself faithful to Catholicism, 'which surely and infallibly reveals the principle of man and his ultimate end'. He was definitely a theist, then, with a respect for the sacred, but he was also undoubtedly, as a philosopher said, a 'fatalistic spiritualist'.

But of what importance are the private beliefs of the First Consul, for his official decisions were dictated by political necessity? When he took power, he observed that most of the French wanted freedom of religion and a reconciliation with the good priests, and since religious peace was important for the accomplishment of his grand political design, he reinstated religion within two years. His favourite argument was that the practice of faith contributed to the restoration of order. 'As soon as I had the power,' he stated, 'I re-established religion. I used it as a base and a root. It was in my eyes the foundation of good morality, true principles and good morals.' As early as June 1800, he said to the priests of Milan, 'No society can exist without morals; there is no good morality without religion; so only religion can provide a firm and lasting foundation for the State. A society without religion is like a ship without a compass.'

The restoration of religion was not easy, however, in a country where the ideas of the philosophers of the *Encyclopédie*, Diderot, Voltaire and Rousseau, were widespread and the deeply anticlerical entourage of the new head of state, especially one of the most loyal members, described all religion as 'sermonising'. Moreover, the royalists, who felt the Church should bolster the legitimacy of Bourbon claims to the throne, expressed the same loathing for the pope and the First Consul. Nevertheless, Napoleon, logical, obstinate, driven solely by the wishes of the majority of the French, concluded a Concordat with the Holy See. This was a highly political document, which automatically removed the bishops of the *ancien régime* and excluded the constitutional bishops pledged to the revolutionary regime. It also recognised Catholicism as the religion of 'the vast majority of the French' and no longer the state religion, thus guaranteeing freedom of conscience and allowing other religious communities to exist legally.

Just as Paris was well worth a mass for Henri IV when he renounced Protestantism in order to reunify France, the stability of power was well worth a Concordat for Napoleon, because in exchange for the restoration of religion, he got his regime sanctioned by Rome, which thus broke with the Bourbons. This was no small victory and it elicited from the pretender himself, the brother of Louis XVI, a heartrending declaration: 'If, like Saint

Louis, I had my barons assembled, I would post a protest on the doors of the Vatican. But I am without troops, without money, without refuge!'

As a normal consequence of this religious reform, Napoleon wanted the Church to crown him and bless him as it had blessed the preceding emperors of the West, Charlemagne in 800, and Otto I in 962. A realist, the new master of France considered questions of faith from a liberal point of view and expected his legislators to do the same. 'There are many paths to Heaven, and the honest man has always been able to find his own, from Socrates to the Quaker,' he declared at a session of the Council of State. 'That is my profession of faith.' He also said: 'In religion I see not the mystery of the Incarnation but the mystery of social order. Religion connects with heaven a concept of equality that prevents the rich from being massacred by the poor ... Only religion allows men to bear inequalities of rank, because it offers consolation for everything.'

Catholicism was not the only religion to receive Napoleon's attention. With regard to the Protestants, he only regularised the Edicts of 1787 and 1789, which had made them full citizens, grouping them into 'consistories' and making the pastors civil servants paid by the State. But the Jews benefited from his special protection. Their problems were familiar to him. In Ancona, which he conquered from the Papal States in 1797, he had been struck by the spectacle of Jews forced to wear a cap and yellow star and live in a ghetto that was closed at night. He had immediately given the order to free them in the name of equality of civil and religious rights which France recognised for the populations of countries it liberated, regardless of their origin or religion. And after taking Malta in 1798, when he learned that Jews could not practise their religion outside their homes, he had ordered the construction of a synagogue. But it was during the Syria campaign, after the occupation of Egypt, that he showed a special solicitude towards the Jewish people that could be considered revolutionary.

One event that is not well known occurred the night after Passover, the major Jewish spring holiday, during the siege of Acre, when he wrote a proclamation making Palestine a Jewish State. He expected to occupy Acre in the following days and then go on to Jerusalem and make the proclamation there, but he was not able to carry out that plan because the English rushed to the aid of the Turks and he never took Acre. Palestine had to continue on its tumultuous course. The following is the text of the proclamation, which was originally written in Hebrew and has lost some of its flavour in multiple translations:

'Proclamation to the Jewish Nation, Headquarters, Jerusalem, Floréal 1 [20 April 1799], Year VII of the French Republic.

'Bonaparte, commander in chief of the armies of the French Republic in Africa and Asia, to the legitimate heirs of Palestine:

'Israelites, unique nation which conquests and tyranny have for thousands of years deprived of its ancestral lands but not of its name or its national existence! Attentive and impartial observers of the fate of nations, while they do not have the prophetic gifts of Israel and of Joel, have realised the accuracy of the predictions of the great prophets who, on the eve of the destruction of Zion, foresaw that the children of the Lord would return to their homeland with songs and joy, and that sorrow and sighing would flee (*Isaiah* 35:10).

'Stand up in joy, exiles! This war, without precedent in history, was undertaken in self-defence by a nation whose hereditary lands were considered prey to be dismembered by its enemies.

'Now this nation also avenges itself for two thousand years of ignominy. Although the time and the circumstances do not seem very favourable to the affirmation or even the expression of your demands, this war today, contrary to all expectations, offers you the birthright of Israel.

'Providence has sent me here with a young army guided by justice and accompanied by victory. My headquarters is in Jerusalem, and in a few days I will be in Damascus, whose proximity to the city of David is no longer to be feared.

'Legitimate heirs of Palestine!

'The great nation that does not traffic in men and countries in the manner of those that sold your ancestors to all peoples does not call on you to conquer your birthright. No, it asks you only to take what it has already conquered, with its support and authorisation to remain masters of this land and to keep it in spite of all opposition.

'Rise up! Show that all the power of your oppressors has not been able to destroy the courage of the descendants of those heroes that would have been a credit to Sparta and Rome.

'Show that two thousand years of slavery have not succeeded in stifling that courage.

'Make haste! The hour is come! This moment that may not come again for a thousand years is the time to demand the restoration of your civil rights and your place among the peoples of the world.

'You will have the right to a political existence as a nation among the other nations. You have the right to worship the Lord freely according to your religion (*Joel* 4:20).'

Thus Napoleon was the first conqueror since the destruction of Jerusalem and the dispersion of the Jewish people in AD 72 to conceive of a Jewish homeland. As such he was, a century and half before others, a distant forerunner of the modern state of Israel, and this should earn him the eternal gratitude of the Jews, very few of whom know that he dared, while Palestine was under the yoke of the Turks, formally to declare himself in favour of their independence.

During the Revolution the Jewish population of France included some 7,000 in the south and about 30,000 in Alsace and Lorraine. The problem of their citizenship had been the subject of much discussion in the legislative assemblies, and they had finally obtained French nationality in 1792 – at least on paper, for it was only in 1806 that a decree, issued on the initiative of the Emperor, allowed them to enjoy all the rights of French nationality and made them the equals of other citizens. In 1807, to the great indignation of the government in London, which would wait another half-century to adopt the same liberal policy and accept Jews in the Parliament of Westminster, he called a meeting of the Great Sanhedrin that would lead to the integration into European life of half a million Jews who had lived without rights. Of this initiative, the famous Jewish lawyer Bédarrides wrote: 'The Sanhedrin was an immense and meritorious achievement accomplished by the will of the Emperor. It was the beginning of the complete regeneration of my brothers and their obtaining civil rights. For them, the name Napoleon symbolises the start of a new era.' And the elected rapporteur, Furtado, summed up in his closing speech the importance of this assembly initiated by the sovereign: 'Blessed be the God of Israel, who placed on the throne of France and Italy a prince according to his heart. He chose the great Napoleon to be the instrument of his mercy . . . The anointed of the Lord has allowed every man to worship God according to his belief and his faith . . . In the shadow of his name, our brothers now can build, sow and harvest in equality with all human beings and serve the great family of the State.'

The precepts defined by the sages of the Sanhedrin were welcomed by Napoleon, who wrote to his minister of the interior: 'They have successfully fulfilled the goal I set in spite of the obstacles they had to overcome. Tell them of my satisfaction.'

The concluding declaration of the assembly underlined the scope of the results: 'The French who practise the religion of Moses, wishing to make themselves worthy of the benevolence of His Majesty the Emperor and King, intend fully to comply with his paternal will. Their religion orders them henceforth to consider the law of the French State the supreme law in civil and political matters. In cases where their religious customs may contain civil provisions in conflict with the French Civil Code, those provisions would immediately cease to govern them.'

For the Jews, this was freedom at last; for Napoleon, it was a victory of order in a new domain. On St Helena, in November 1816, Dr O'Meara, his doctor, asked him point-blank why he had given the Jews so much support. He answered: 'I hoped, by making them free and granting them equal rights with Catholics and Protestants, to make them good citizens . . . Being like my other subjects, they should, to my mind, treat them like brothers, as if we were all of the tribe of Judah. In addition, I thought it would attract great wealth to France, because the Jews are very numerous and they would flock in large numbers to a country where they would enjoy greater privileges than in any other nation. Had it not been for the events of 1814, all the Jews of Europe would have come and settled in France, where their equality was assured and the door to honours was open to them.' As early as 1808, in fact, a Jewish student had been admitted to the prestigious military school in Saint-Cyr.

Those who accuse Napoleon of antisemitism – and what has he not been accused of? – invoke a restrictive decree of 1808 concerning the suppression of usury and of Jewish immigration into France. It must be pointed out that this legislation was adopted only reluctantly, that it was intended to satisfy complaints by the Alsatians about the rights that had been granted to the Jews – which some of them were abusing – and finally, that it was temporary and that exemptions could be granted, and were granted almost immediately throughout the country.

Like his other political achievements, Napoleon's regulations concerning the Jews outlasted the Empire, not only in France but in the territories where Napoleonic law was in effect. By 1840 there would be Jews in the French government. In England it took until 1858, and the fifth consecutive election of Lionel de Rothschild to the House of Commons – the four preceding ones having been annulled – for the Parliament of London to accept the children of Israel within its ranks, this Parliament of a nation that called itself liberal and accused 'Buonaparte' of tyranny and absolutism!

Napoleon also took an interest in Masonic lodges, discussion groups and spiritual associations. He encouraged the fusion of the two French Masonic groups, the Grande Loge and the Grand-Orient, and had his brother Joseph named grand master and his brother Louis assistant grand master. The Masonic Council included the best of his generals and associates: Murat,Soult, Masséna, Lannes, Kellermann, Junot, Macdonald, Fouché, Maret, Cambacérès and Regnault de Saint-Jean d'Angély. During the Empire, it was commonly acknowledged that the Emperor himself had 'seen the light', but there is no conclusive proof of his ever having joined the Freemasons, and the praise of the brothers was addressed to the head of state, protector of freedom of conscience, rather than to a 'brother'. In protecting the lodges and reorganising their structure, Napoleon was only exercising his love of order while reinforcing his power. 'The Freemasons do some good things,' he explained on St Helena. 'They helped the Revolution, and just recently they have diminished the power of the pope and the influence of the clergy.'

Napoleon not only resolved the delicate problem of national reconciliation of all religions and philosophical beliefs; ahead of his time, he also formulated a revolutionary position on religious freedom. What he described to Dr O'Meara on St Helena was carried out by subsequent leaders of France and almost all countries in the world: 'I wanted to establish a universal system of belief. My system was to have no dominant religion but to tolerate all. I wanted everyone to believe and think in his own way, and all men, Protestants, Catholics, Jews, Moslems, etc. to be equal . . . My intention was to make everything belonging to the State and the Constitution purely secular, without consideration for any religion. I did not want to give the priests any influence or power over civil affairs.'

This was the man who is accused of intolerance.

Education

In royalist France, education was a privilege of the religious orders. The Revolution, imbued with the philosophical theories of the Enlightenment, decreed that public education was the right and duty of the State, and defined three levels – primary, secondary and higher education. However, it was the laws of the Consulate and the Empire that truly founded the university and guaranteed its monopolies. It took a great deal of courage for the First Consul to take on this superhuman task when the schools had been emptied of their teachers by the exile of the clergy and the youth of 1800, the youth of the new century, was appallingly ignorant. 'Of all institutions, the most important one is public education,' Napoleon declared to the Council of State. 'Everything depends on it, the present and the future . . . Public education must above all be sensible and classical.'

Napoleon's detractors never fail to interpret his words as meaning that he founded the imperial university to prepare young people for sacrifice on the battlefield. This is a total misunderstanding. He liked to repeat, 'True conquests, the only ones that leave us with no regrets, are those we make over ignorance.' He felt the true sorrow of a cultivated mind realising that France, whose literary glory had spread throughout Europe, whose language was that of the European élite, had been deprived for ten years of all education worthy of the name. This man of learning remembered his own education with righteous indignation: 'We were very poorly taught at Brienne. I was fifteen years old. All they gave us were insipid excerpts! Excerpts, what a pitiful method! Young people have the time to read at length and the imagination to grasp big things. Later, I corrected this deficiency by reading prodigiously but not very selectively in a garrison library. In Valence, my soul was still asleep. The day I came across Bossuet and read his *Discourse on Universal History* on the sequence of empires . . . it seemed to me that the veil was torn from my eyes and I saw the gods walking.'

The Act of 1 May 1802 gave the communes responsibility for primary instruction and provided for the creation of thirty *lycées*, where some three thousand 'national students' were boarded and educated at government expense. The curriculum – from Latin to transcendental mathematics – the schedules, the discipline and the uniform were set by consular orders. 'We must see,' declared the head of state, 'that the morals and political ideas of the coming generation no longer depend on the news of the day or the circumstances of the moment. We must above all achieve unity and ensure that a whole generation is cast in the same mould.' He said this in 1806, and it was the signal for a review of the system, which in four years had shown its strengths and weaknesses.

The review lasted two years and required nine drafts, and it led to the law of 1808 which granted the imperial university a monopoly on public education throughout the Empire. The university was placed under the authority of a principal, whose powers were as extensive as those of a minister and included granting some 6,500 state bursaries, appointing teachers and awarding degrees with the help of a university council. In the departments, teaching institutions were grouped into academies run by rectors. Some thirty inspectors visited every faculty, lycée and college annually. Institutions of higher learning, which had been eliminated by the Revolution in 1793, resumed their role as faculties and were given responsibility for awarding doctorates and bachelor degrees in the major disciplines – medicine, law, theology, letters and science.

The numbers alone give some idea of the immensity of this enterprise carried out by Napoleon as First Consul and then as Emperor. The number of *lycées* went from nine to forty-six in fifteen years; private secondary schools, which were overseen by the State, went from 300 to 1,200; the number of colleges, which were a completely new institution, reached 370 in 1815. In 1814 France had thirty-seven academies, thirteen faculties of theology, seventeen faculties of law, nine faculties of medicine, thirty-one faculties of letters and seventeen faculties of science.

In 1810 the Emperor sent the great scholar Cuvier on a mission to Holland and Germany to study their systems of primary education, and in 1811 a decree was issued to the effect that the methods used in those countries would be applied in the departments of the Empire. In December 1812, in the sleigh that brought him back from the disastrous campaign in Russia, Napoleon was still discussing education with Caulaincourt: 'I will concern myself again with public education. With peace this will be my primary concern, for it is the guarantee of the future. I want education to be public for everyone, even for part of my son's education. I have a great plan for it.' Since he was not the kind of man who only defined the broad outlines of an undertaking, he provided precise details.

On the need for education: 'This country can no more do without thinking and the mind than it can do without air ... Consider the effect of the example of an élite group of young people selected from among forty million souls! What a reward for talent, and what an incentive for that talent to be born! ... Human reason, its development and the development of our faculties – there lie all the keys to society, all the secrets of the legislator. Only those who want to cheat the people and govern for their own profit could want to keep them in ignorance, because the more enlightened they are, the more people will be convinced of the necessity of laws and the need to defend them, and the more stable, happy and prosperous the society will be.'

On the spirit of teaching: 'Young people can only properly judge facts according to how they are presented. To deceive them by retracing memories is to prepare them for errors in the future.'

On the training of teachers: 'In general, I have organised the university as a body because a body never dies and it enables the transmission of the organisation, administration and spirit . . . The members of the teaching body will embrace education as their predecessors embraced the Church ... I want this taking of the habit, while called by another name, to be something solemn.'

And what about women, we might ask, because all this was intended for young men. The century, alas, was not open to women's liberation, and Napoleon hated blue stockings: 'All girls have the same goal in life and that is marriage, and public education almost always makes bad women, women who are frivolous, vain and of loose morals ... A common education, which is so good for men, teaching them to help each other and preparing them for adult life through camaraderie, is a school of corruption for women. Women are made for private life and the family and inner life.'

In keeping with these remarks, he founded schools for the

daughters of members of the Légion d'honneur whose purpose was to make them good mothers and devoted wives. 'I want the school to turn out not pleasing women, but virtuous women, whose attainments are those of morals and the heart rather than of the mind and amusement . . . I would want a girl who came out of the school and found herself at the head of a little household to know how to make a dress, mend her husband's clothing and make baby clothes for her children.' What marvellous common sense! And these institutions still exist; their superintendents, wearing a red ribbon across their chests, have educated generations of girls in this same spirit. On a frosty day in December 1840 their graduates had the honour of lining up along the banks of the Seine to witness the passing of the sarcophagus, with its six nested coffins, of the last conqueror in history, who had not disdained to concern himself with their problems of sewing, dance and mending.

Is it necessary to say that Napoleon's university structure as a whole is still in place and still bears his mark? Changes made in the twentieth century have essentially concerned administrative matters or teaching methods. Is it necessary to recall that when the First Consul came to power, there were no classrooms or school teachers in public education?

The economy

Napoleon summarised the objectives of his economic policy as follows: 'Agriculture: the soul, the main basis of the Empire. Industry: the prosperity and happiness of the people. Foreign trade: the abundance and proper employment of the other two.' This was good thinking on the part of a man who did not claim to be an economic theorist but who never strayed far from common sense and the bourgeois concept of good management, and whose genius supplied the rest. His vigilance as an honest administrator naturally made him recoil in horror from two scourges of the Revolution, speculators and paper money, and to eliminate them from his own administration. He also had an implacable hatred for the disorder, the 'poorly clothed, poorly fed soldiers', the 'ridiculous, shameless behaviour' of the war commissioners, which had stunned him when he took command of the army of Italy. He often told his staff he would not fall into that trap, and blamed the fall of the Directory on bad financial administration. He also said, 'Louis XIV would not have been ruined if he had known how to count and make a budget.' To him, good finances were a prerequisite of good policy.

During the early years of the Consulate, he had to work wonders to restore financial order, using methods that were not to his liking; he borrowed from the banks and sold off state property. This left him with bad memories and he did not do it again.

What boldness he demonstrated in his struggle against bankruptcy and financial panic – and it was successful! The numbers speak for themselves. At the end of 1799 five per cent bonds were trading at a little over eleven francs, the interest rate was between three and four per cent a month, the deficit had reached 250 million francs, one third of the budget, and the state coffers contained only 167,000 francs, the balance of an advance made by the banks a few days earlier. In 1804 the bond was at sixty francs, the discount rate had come down to four per cent a year and the budget was balanced. To achieve this, Napoleon made one decision after another at an alarming speed: the sale of national lands, payment of old debts in bond coupons, the creation of departments of direct and indirect taxation, setting of the legal exchange rate in relation to silver, deep spending cuts in every area and, finally, the crowning achievement by this 30-year-old general rich in military victories but without political or economic experience, the founding of the Bank of France, in February 1800.

'The Bank does not belong only to the shareholders; it also belongs to the State, since the State gives it the privilege of minting money,' Napoleon said. 'I want the Bank to be under enough government control, but not too much.' These words would have the force of law for 132 years, until 1936; a governor and two sub-governors appointed by the government served with fifteen directors chosen from among the shareholders, thus guaranteeing an intelligent balance between the general interest and special interests.

The existence of two ministries 'in opposition' ensured the proper functioning of the government's financial operations. 'My budget is designed to keep the minister of finance and the minister of the treasury at war with one another,' joked the

Emperor. 'One says, "I've promised this much, we must receive this much." The other says, "We've only received so much." Their opposition is my security.' The two 'feuding brothers' were both officials of great talent. Gaudin, 'a rigid man', according to Napoleon, 'a fortress against corruption . . . a man of clear ideas and strict integrity', was minister of finance from 1799 to 1814, and Mollien, minister of the treasury from 1806 to 1815, was 'one of the best financiers of Europe'.

Studying a budget is an ideal activity for a man of numbers and statistics, and Gaudin has left an account of a night when Napoleon spent from eight o'clock in the evening to dawn with him, going through the nation's accounts with a fine-tooth comb, chapter by chapter, item by item. For the minister of finance, on the other hand, the one responsible for filling the public coffers, the task was difficult, because the Emperor did not want to hear about the wonderful solutions proposed by the experts, financiers and bankers he called ideologues, who reminded him of paper money and loans. For Napoleon, taxes, direct or indirect, had to be the only source of revenue.

Once the revenues were guaranteed and collected, the role of the minister of the treasury began. The Emperor demanded meticulous accounting, checked by an audit office, the *Cour des comptes*, his last great creation, which consisted of a hundred senior officials who were responsible for auditing the expenditures of the nation, but not for judging the legality of those expenditures.

There was no more paper money, of course; the law of 28 March 1803 instituted the franc, divided into 100 centimes, as the monetary unity; it had the value of a five-gram piece of silver and was struck in coins of one, five, ten, twenty and forty francs in silver and gold, and coins of one, five, ten and twenty-five centimes in bronze.

From 1806 on war disrupted the Emperor's plans and compromised the financial situation that had at last been put in order. Against coalitions that were generously financed by London, France had to dig deep into its resources to assemble its armies. The breathtaking growth in the budget beginning with the fourth coalition (England, Russia and Prussia) is evidence of the extraordinary contribution by taxpayers: the budget went from between 700 and 800 million francs in 1806 to 955 million in

1811, 1.3 blllion in 1812 and 1.15 billion in 1813, with military spending swallowing up about half of it. Ten years of war imposed by a rich and implacable enemy, England, destroyed both Napoleon's civil power and the imposing economic structure that had made France the first nation in Europe.

The terrible financial effort required for defence, for the maintenance of France's armies, fleets and fortifications, did not cause Napoleon to abandon his magnificent economic projects, in particular the public works that were so important during his reign, but the time the military leader spent in the field was sorely missed by the statesman. He stated, 'I suffer because of the way I live, which takes my attention away from the first object of my concern and of my heart: the solid organisation of everything related to banks, factories and commerce.'

The economic situation inherited from the Revolution and the Directory would have discouraged anyone but the young First Consul. Agricultural production, after a period of prosperity following the sale of the rural property of the émigrés, was at its lowest level, because the peasants justifiably lacked confidence in the depreciated paper money. Industry was in crisis for lack of export markets, and the capital traditionally invested in production had been diverted to trade, because considerable profit could be made very quickly through speculation, particularly on colonial products. Exports had declined because business was severely handicapped by the interventionist laws of the Convention, and then prices had risen dramatically as a result of the economic liberalism of the Directory; after all this, business had trouble regaining its balance for lack of funds and the poor state of the lines of communication, roads and canals, which had been neglected. Peasants, manufacturers and merchants therefore had every reason to welcome a government, or rather a man, who asserted, 'The first interest of France is agriculture and the second is industry; trade, insofar as it is necessary for the development of the other two, is in the same rank.'

Like the famous Sully of old France, Napoleon had a high regard for 'ploughing and pasturing', the livelihood of the majority of the French. To him agriculture was still 'in the first rank of the useful arts', which shows his profound knowledge of the rural mentality of the peasants attached to their land and his great political realism, because this was what enabled France to withstand the economic aggression of England. The land produced beets, which enabled the country to get along without colonial sugar, whose transport was blocked by English vessels. To make the most of this fact, Napoleon personally presented the coveted cross of the Légion d'honneur to Delessert, the 'inventor' of beet sugar, and ordered the planting of 100,000 hectares of this valuable root. In the same spirit, he made Parmentier, who introduced potato growing to France, a baron.

The land also sustained horse farms, without which there would have been neither ploughing nor artillery and cavalry, and sheep farms, which supplied wool for industry. The veterinary schools were reorganised to offer free admission to the sons of rural society, already attached to the land by a kind of instinct, and six stud farms and thirty stallion registries were set up. All kinds of experiments were encouraged. Since cotton fabrics were fashionable, cotton was planted in the south and in Corsica. Since there was no coffee to be had from the colonies, the cultivation of chicory was promoted. Since dyes were being seized by English ships, attempts were made to grow madder. Close to two million grapevines were planted, and the production of wine, which was traditional in France, reached thirty-five million hectolitres in 1814.

A land register was drawn up, which in 1814 surveyed more than thirty-seven million parcels of land and guaranteed their owners full title. Agricultural societies were created that dealt with technical problems and organised competitions. By the end of the Empire, agricultural production reached five times the levels of 1800, and the prosperity of the countryside dazzled foreign visitors. It was not surprising, then, that in spite of conscription, which took so many young men away from work in the fields, the peasants venerated the Emperor. 'They are his most ardent supporters,' wrote Chaptal, a senator and former minister of the interior, 'because he reassured them that there would be no return to tithing, restitution of the émigrés' property or oppression by the nobility.' This was a very patronising judgement. Napoleon had won the support of the rural population through a profoundly humane policy of sympathy and encouragement. Farming was their livelihood, of course, but thanks to him the landowners had access to the general councils and town councils, they received tokens of appreciation from the government and they at last had a feeling of working undisturbed for themselves and their children.

'Industry and foreign trade made enormous progress under me,' Napoleon recalled on St Helena. 'The application of chemistry in the factories allowed them to take a giant step forward. I started the momentum that spread throughout Europe.' This had not been easy, given that there had been a slowdown in technological progress during the revolutionary period. The big problem had been in mechanisation, an area in which England was quite far ahead.

Just as Napoleon had used the magic of his presence as a catalyst on the battlefield, he was seen in person in almost all the major factories. Visiting the Jouy plant in 1806, he admired the magnificent printed fabrics made by the brilliant Oberkampf and asked if he was a member of the Légion d'honneur. 'When Oberkampf answered that he was not, the Emperor removed the Eagle pinned to his own lapel and presented it to him,' reported the *Journal de l'Empire*.

This gesture was intended to support ongoing activities. The Emperor created the *Société d'encouragement de l'Industrie*, an organisation that held exhibitions and competitions of modern machinery. He opened the magnificent *École des arts et metiers*, a training school for technicians, which is still in existence today, and schools for training in mining. He allocated substantial sums of money to start new industrial facilities and to save those that were in difficulty. He had laws drafted on manpower, fiscal and customs protection, trade names and unsafe working conditions. He allocated the huge sum of six million francs to the *Caisse d'amortissement*, a sort of pawnshop for industrialists in difficulty, for loans on merchandise. Was it possible to be more imaginative and more liberal? And the results were appreciable. The production of coal went from 250,000 tonnes in 1794 to 800,000 in 1814; iron, from 60,000 tonnes to 112,000; rock salt, from 40,000 tonnes to 150,000.

When the economic crisis of 1806 came, he made available to the companies that were most affected a sum of three million francs and, the following year, another six million, a measure that was not merely political since it maintained full employment. 'My goal is not to prevent such-and-such a factory from going bankrupt – the finances of the State would not suffice – but to prevent such-and-such a factory from closing ... I am using money from the Treasury only to keep the workers from being without work.' Eighteen million francs were finally distributed in this way. At the same time the government was making massive purchases to increase the money supply, while always arranging to resell the stocks acquired without losing a penny.

It has been said that Napoleon succeeded in reconciling liberalism and interventionism. This is true. But the industrialists, unlike the rural people, never gave him their confidence in spite of all his efforts. Perhaps because his views on the welfare of the working class were revolutionary, they considered Napoleon's positions inconsistent. This was essentially the view of the economist J.B. Say, who felt that it was ignorance of political economy that led Napoleon to St Helena. However, this underestimates the importance of England's economic aggression towards France. There was no time for the Emperor to solve the political problems caused by it. Though justified by the necessities of the hour, that is, by the pressure of the coalitions, his actions in the industrial world appeared more tyrannical than paternal to the capitalists of the era. With the perspective of hindsight we can imagine them being too eager to consolidate the fortunes they had managed to amass in brighter days to be willing to support a system whose future, based on the genius of a single man, seemed uncertain.

The great public works

'I based the glory of my reign on changing the face of the territory of my Empire. These great works are as necessary to the interests of my peoples as to my own satisfaction,' wrote Napoleon to his minister of the interior in 1807. This was a remarkably pithy statement, like everything said by this man of action. Like the Roman emperors, he left reminders of his power and his glory for posterity, but these works – prestigious monuments and roads, harbours, canals and tunnels – benefited the people.

First of all, he transformed Paris, the capital of an Empire rivalling that of the Romans, with its irregular network of narrow streets dating from the Middle Ages. At a cost of five hundred million francs of the time, some twenty-five million pounds sterling, he made it into a monumental city. The Arc de Triomphe, the Vendôme Column, the Madeleine and the Cour du Carrousel which forms the harmonious completion of the old palace of the kings of France built by the Capetians are only a few of Napoleon's contributions to imperial Paris. 'I want to sustain sculpture in France for ten years,' stated the Emperor when he visited the construction sites, speaking to the workers with the same familiarity and warmth as to his soldiers.

All the major projects of modernisation were started simultaneously: the five new bridges; the eight kilometres of quays that would protect the banks of the Seine from flooding; the creation of the Rue de Rivoli, the Rue de la Paix and the Rue de Castiglione; the system of sewers and canals; the building of fountains; the numbering of houses; and the creation of cemeteries, slaughter-houses, marketplaces, the wine market, granaries and *lycées*. All this activity, which turned the capital into one vast construction site, astounded contemporaries. 'History tells us that Augustus found Rome built in brick and left it built in marble,' wrote a newspaper in 1806. 'It could be said that Napoleon found Paris obstructed, unadorned, cluttered with the ruins of its former splendour. He has already opened it up, cleaned it up and supplied it with water, and soon he will have decorated it, enriched it, and embellished it with all the splendour of the fine arts.'

Anyone other than this 35-year-old Emperor would have shied away from a task that one writer summarised as follows: 'It is easy to imagine Paris in 1800 after ten years of anarchy, sedition and weakness during which no useful work was done, no street cleaned, no residence repaired, nothing maintained, nothing embellished and nothing cleaned up.' Imagine, then, the wonderment of the Parisians as they saw the thousands of workers busy building sidewalks and waterways channelling the water of the canals and the Beuvron river.

The same feverish activity went on in the provinces. Between 1802 and 1807 roads were opened up linking France and Italy: the Corniche along the coast, Mount Geneva, Mount Cenis and the Simplon Pass, gigantic endeavours; in all, 52,000 kilometres of roads were restored or constructed. Bridges were built in river cities. Harbours were created and marshes were drained. Let us read the Emperor's own words when his jailers on St Helena demanded he hand over the secret of his treasure, which was believed to be fabulous:

'You want to know about the treasures of Napoleon? They are immense, it is true; but they are displayed in broad daylight. Here they are: the fine port facilities in Antwerp; those in Vlissingen, which can accommodate the most numerous squadrons and protect them from the sea ice; the hydraulic works in Dunkirk, Le Havre and Nice; the huge port facilities in Cherbourg; the maritime works in Venice, the good roads from Antwerp to Amsterdam, from Mainz to Metz and from Bordeaux to Bayonne; the Simplon, Mount Cenis and Mount Geneva roads and the Corniche, which open the Alps in four directions; that alone cost more than eight hundred million. The roads from the Pyrenees to the Alps, from Parma to La Spezia and from Savona to Piedmont; the Jena, Austerlitz and Arts bridges and those in Sèvres, Tours, Roanne, Lyon, Turin, Bordeaux, Rouen and over the Isère and Durance rivers surpass all the works of the Romans in boldness, magnitude and workmanship. The canal connecting the Rhine to the Rhône by way of the Doubs, joining the North Sea with the Mediterranean; the canal between the Schelde and the Somme, linking Amsterdam and Paris; the one that joins the Rance to the Vilaine; the Arles canal, the Pavia canal, the Rhine canal; the draining of the marshes of Bourgoing, Cotent and Rochefort; the restoration of most of the churches demolished during the Revolution and the construction of new ones; the construction of a large number of workhouses to eradicate begging; the construction of the Louvre, public granaries, the Bank of France, the Ourcq canal; the water system in the city of Paris; the many sewers, the quays, the embellishments and monuments in Paris; works for the beautification of Rome; the restoration of the factories of Lyon, the creation of several hundred cotton spinning and weaving mills employing millions of workers; the creation of more than four hundred factories producing beet sugar for part of France's consumption, which would have provided sugar for the same price as the Indies if they had continued to be encouraged for only four more years; the replacement of the indigo plant with woad, which has been grown in France of the same quality and as inexpensively as in the colonies; the number of plants making all kinds of art objects, etc.; fifty million francs used to repair and decorate the palaces of the Crown, sixty million pieces of furniture in the palaces of the Crown, in France, in Holland, in Turin, in Rome; sixty million diamonds of the Crown, all bought with Napoleon's money, the Regent diamond itself, the only one that remained of the old diamonds of the Crown of France, which he himself brought back from the Jews of Berlin, with whom it had been left in pawn for three million; the Napoleon museum valued at more than four hundred million and containing only objects legitimately acquired either with money or as a condition of peace treaties known to everyone, by virtue of which these masterpieces were given in exchange for territories or instead of taxes; several million spent to encourage agriculture, which is the primary interest of France; the introduction of horse races; the introduction of merino sheep, etc.'

All this constitutes a treasure trove worth billions, which will endure for centuries! These are the monuments that give the lie to the slanders. History tells us that all this was accomplished in the midst of continuous wars, without loans, and with the public debt even decreasing daily and taxes being reduced by fifty million francs. Throughout Europe, there are monuments that still provide a lesson in energy and order from this man who asserted with determination, 'I am a Roman Emperor; I am of the great race of Caesars, the race of founders.'

The pinnacle of Napoleonic memory is the Arc de Triomphe, with Jena, Friedland, Wagram, Grande Armée and Kléber Avenues linked by Presbourg and Tilsit Streets, surrounded by the mansions of the marshals. It witnessed the procession for his marriage to Marie-Louise and, in December 1840, the return of his ashes, when the sumptuous catafalque of the last god of war entered Paris surrounded by the survivors of the Napoleonic epic.

The Arc de Triomphe du Carrousel recalls the entrance to the Tuileries and the troop review ceremonies such as the one attended one day in 1813 by the heroine of Balzac's story 'A Woman of Thirty': 'Napoleon was riding a horse. This movement lent life to those silent masses, voice to the instruments, buoyancy to the eagles and the flags, and emotion to all. The walls of the high galleries of that old palace also seem to shout "Vive l'Empereur!" This was not something human, this was magic, a semblance of divine power, or better, a fleeting image of this fleeting reign.'

Today, at the top of the forty-two-metre Vendôme Column, the Emperor, in Roman garb, still dominates the Paris that owes him so much. In the Père Lachaise Cemetery, which he opened in 1804, rest his marshals and many of those who served him; he himself at one time wished to rest there. In Cherbourg there is a bronze statue of him, his outstretched arm showing the harbour, his work. The first dock in Antwerp is still called the Bonaparte Dock. In the Piazza Napoleone Bonaparte in Rome, one can still dream of this man who commissioned an architect to design the wonderful entrance to Pincio Hill leading to a terrace looking out over the Eternal City. And a Napoleon road from Ljubljana to Dubrovnik and Kotor commemorates the work of the soldiers of the Empire.

Wherever one looks in what was Napoleon's Empire, there is something great, something unequalled, that bears his mark.

The arts

'Napoleot,' Talleyrand liked to say, 'had a feeling for the great but not for the beautiful.' The renowned diplomat never missed an opportunity for a gibe at the man who more than once had made him very afraid. While it is true that Napoleon did not have a particular taste for the arts – although he was a very good writer – the fact remains that he had too much common sense and too much concern for his legend not to grant protection to artists, whose mission is to commemorate events.

Did he follow the tastes of the day, or was the public enamoured of the sculptors, painters, engravers and cabinet-makers who enjoyed imperial favour? We do not know, but the fact is that the salons and galleries made fabulous amounts of money during the Empire. Napoleon's natural preferences leaned towards the more classical forms in the visual arts, and so he patronised and admired those artists who recorded the great moments of his life in marble or on canvas in the ancient style. The master of Europe made no secret of the fact that, as the faithful heir of those who had preceded him as heads of State, 'from Clovis to the Committee of Public Safety', he was conservative, and so was in favour of looking back to the Greek and Roman world which spoke of triumph, sacrifice and heroism, but as a man of the nineteenth century who had to respect modern trends, he was also in favour of certain new ideas and avant-garde methods, such as the use of iron in architecture.

Fontaine, the Emperor's first architect, has provided in his diary an interesting account of his relationship with Napoleon and the heated discussions during which the Emperor expounded on his great dreams while never losing sight of a penny. But this is mere anecdote. The truth is that the sound of the work being carried out echoed in all the envious ears of the Empire. As Bausset, a witness, wrote, 'The great and beautiful constructions Napoleon is building in the capital of France are having such an effect throughout Europe that the czar of Russia wants the plans and drawings for those monuments.' Thus was born *Le journal des mouvements de Paris*, dedicated to Alexander, which aroused the envy of the latter and led him to create in Russia a style similar to that of Paris, a style the Russians named after Alexander but which was a mere copy of the Empire style.

Napoleon had simple but precise views on architecture. For example, when the question arose of linking the old palace of the Louvre to the Tuileries, he immediately dictated a note to be used as a guideline for the plans: 'The new gallery should be of uniform architecture. We will not insist that it be absolutely identical to the one opposite, which is of a different type. The large space will hide not only this difference in architecture but also the different directions of the galleries and the different openings of the corners of the square. The Piazza San Marco in Venice is greatly admired, and it is completely irregular in its dimensions and architecture.' And later he said: 'Subdivision destroys grandeur. It matters little if a large building is not completely regular: only people in the field see such defects. They are trifles that strike the smallest minority of people. What is true is always beautiful. The monuments of the centuries have the colour and form of time.'

He therefore conserved and protected the great French tradition of classical architecture, from the Renaissance to Louis XVI. The peristyle of the Chambre des Députés, in the form of a Greek temple, matched that of the Madeleine, which was at that time the Temple of Glory. The Empire style was an ostentatious revival of the classical, whose sense of proportion, power, balance and solidity exemplified the taste of the sovereign. The Emperor's favourite architects, Percier and Fontaine, were instructed to spread this style throughout Europe, to all the cities and palaces of the Empire; thus it is found in Brussels, Antwerp, Rome, Florence and Venice. We need only look at the plans of these two architects to have an idea of what Paris, the imperial capital, would have been if fate had granted the Emperor a little more time.

The Empire style also produced superb furniture, which still has a place of honour in many official and private residences. The style began as a happy marriage of the richness of Roman classicism and the influence of Egyptian art, and was later refined into its final form, in which the powerful beauty of the lines sets off the splendour of woods, gilded bronzes and dark marbles. Chairs were solid, with square backs and sabre legs; desks and pedestal tables were decorated with caryatids, lions, eagles or sphinxes; seats were covered in Beauvais tapestry or costly silks from Lyon, in red, green or yellow; curtains were Empire green embroidered with bees, eagles, crowns of laurels, helmets, swords and other motifs.

Inspired by Roman culture, Napoleon was very fond of statues, and sculptors, like painters, enjoyed his special patronage. All the great monuments of his reign were adorned with columns and paintings by renowned artists such as Houdon, Chaudet, Bosio and Chinard. Although he had little patience, Napoleon submitted to long sittings for portraits and statues by them. In their works, the Consul was a Byronic hero and the Emperor was Caesar. In 1802 he sent for the great Canova, the sculptor of popes, a master of harmony and form, whom one contemporary – apparently forgetting Michelangelo! – called the greatest sculptor since Phidias and another described as 'the Italian Praxiteles'. From Canova's studio came the colossal nude Napoleon for the facade of the Doges' Palace in Venice. Appointed director of the Accademia di San Luca in Rome, Canova was in charge of all art projects in the Eternal City; he produced a statue of Pauline Bonaparte as Venus which is the jewel of the Borghese Palace and a bust of Madame Mère in which she resembles a Roman Empress.

For the great David, whom he made a knight and then, during the Hundred Days, a commander of the Légion d'honneur, Napoleon revived the position of painter to His Majesty, because he liked the artist's richly coloured paintings of antique marbles. When he greeted David publicly, somewhat theatrically, by recreating Charles V's gesture in Titian's studio, he gave a kind of official patronage to that painting, a portrait of such nobility that it still makes us shiver. The portrait of the First Consul, the best

one there is, gave rise to the following revealing dialogue between
the painter and his model:

'What will you paint now?' asked Bonaparte brusquely.

'Leonidas at Thermopylae.'

'Too bad! You are wrong, David, to tire yourself painting the
vanquished.'

'Then, general, I want to paint you with sword in hand.'

'No, David, it is not with the sword that one wins battles.'

David painted him 'calm, on a spirited horse' in the admirable
Napoleon at St Bernard, an allegorical painting of a man sure of his
destiny, who is pointing towards the future with a great swing of
his arm. Aware of the honour that was given him in associating
his talent with the glory of the most formidable figure of the
century, David rejoiced, 'I will slip into posterity in the shadow of
my hero.'

Soon David had the opportunity, unique in an artist's life, to do
a painting of the coronation of his sovereign, a painting that
Napoleon came to see in 1808, accompanied by Josephine. 'This is
good, David,' he murmured, 'you have read my thoughts; you
made me a French knight.' He examined the picture without
saying a word, pacing slowly, his hands behind his back as usual,
perhaps reliving that extraordinary day when, clothed in satin
and gold, he had restored the ancient imperial dignity, or perhaps
thinking of the moment that would pass into history. His
respectful retinue followed him with their eyes. He stopped
abruptly before leaving, raising his famous bicorn hat and saying
loudly, 'David, I salute you!'

Napoleon can be credited with taking the great painter away
from his cold studies of antiquity and making him the head of the
French school, a chronicler of his time, and thus for giving
painting an honourable place in the field of information and
education. 'Let us be true first and beautiful after,' David would
say, conscious of his mission. It was in this spirit that he painted
the grandiose picture of the coronation, a historical work of
genuine reporting, a celebration of the accession of a man of the
people to the throne of the sovereigns who for a thousand years
had made France. As a critic stated, 'Rendering what he saw
before him was his true calling, and that is why he has so ably and
without sycophancy shown the contrast between the plebeian
faces of the onlookers and their fancy costumes, the ostentation,

the quantities of velvet, damask, embroidery, ostrich feathers.' A true reporter, and one possessed of genius – and recognised and encouraged by his sovereign.

The second painter of the regime, Prud'hon, has left us an admirable portrait of Josephine, and the third, Isabey, who was the main painter of the Empress, has given us some striking portraits. The last of the great artists who maintained the tradition of the seventeenth century while initiating new trends was Gros, a precursor of the Romantics. He was the favourite painter of the Emperor, whose excellent taste must be acknowledged. Gros, who painted *The Victims of the Plague in Jaffa*, *The Battle of Aboukir* and *Napoleon on the Battlefield of Eylau*, rejected the Academy's constraints which David had merely attacked, and ably portrayed the teeming activity of the battlefield and the solemnity of the sovereign who dominated his century. 'Only Gros could paint a character as poetic as Achilles, the greatest of all the heroes created by the poetic imagination,' Delacroix said of him.

Géricault became famous in 1812 when he exhibited his portrait *The Charging Chasseur*, and his paintings of battles are anthems to courage and glory rather than mere records. Finally, Ingres, who came from David's studio, painted the surprising portrait of First Consul Bonaparte in a crimson velvet suit. There was no lack of work for all these artists, young and old, because from 1798 to 1814 Napoleon allocated some five million francs for official commissions, paying up to 12,000 francs for a large painting, provided that it met his well defined requirements. The exhibitions were splendid, since the French school, the most famous in Europe, was at the peak of its renown, and the number of participating artists went from 282 in 1800 to 550 in 1812.

Artists like David and Gros drew inspiration from Napoleon's rise and his role in the dizzying events in Europe, an inspiration that ended when he left the political arena. Napoleon on St Helena, cruelly reduced to impotence, and David exiled to Brussels as a Napoleon supporter, living on his past glory, followed similar paths – indeed, the same path, for just as a comet is followed by a tail of light, Napoleon carried in his wake those who had identified with him and had shone with his reflected light. It was Napoleon who supplied these painters with the great themes which were so dear to him – sacrifice, heroism, exalted feelings and the constant presence of death – and which became themes of the Romantic school.

Music

According to Cherubini, Napoleon liked only music which did not distract him from thinking about affairs of state. He himself described his true feelings about music in a letter to the inspectors at the Paris Conservatory of Music dated 26 July 1797: 'Of all the fine arts, music is the one that has the most influence on the passions, the one legislators should encourage most. A moral piece of music created by the hand of a master is inevitably touching and has much more influence than a good book on morality, which convinces our reason without influencing our habits.'

Revolutionary music had obeyed the popular taste for hymns and cantatas that were sung loudly on civic holidays, culminating in works such as 'The Song of 25 Messidor Year I' and 'The Song of 1 Vendémiaire Year IX', but in time the heroic and brutal inspiration diminished, and the composers had to wait for the advent of the Empire to find subjects worthy of their talents. Napoleon's favourite musicians, Paisiello and Spontini, were Italian, but his influence on music can most readily be discovered not at the Opéra but in the camps, on the parade ground, or at official celebrations such as the triumphal entry of his armies into Berlin or Venice, where the imperial music, lively, martial and lyrical, revived the revolutionary tradition. The composers of the Revolution, who were only too happy to become composers for the Empire, vied with each other to celebrate its glories, and Napoleon, conscious of their influence on the people and on the soldiers who hummed the popular tunes on the roads of Europe, held them in high esteem and granted them his patronage.

Méhul, who composed a hymn to the return of peace after the victorious Italian campaign as well as the famous 'Chant du départ' ['Song of departure'], which is still well known in France today, received a commission for the 'Marche de la Grande Armée' ['March of the Grande Armée'] in 1808, after Tilsit. Grétry, a charming creator of operas, was also the composer of 'La victoire est à nous' ['Victory is ours'], which was played at night when the enemy had been routed. Cherubini, a composer of masses, operas and cantatas, had to write a march for the orphans of the Guard, and Dalayrac heard a melody from his comic opera turned into an anthem in praise of the Empire.

All this pleased the Emperor, but what he liked best were the melodies created by military men like David Bühl and Michel Gebauer, who were in charge of music for the Consular Guard and the First Regiment of Foot Grenadiers, and who composed pieces with such titles as 'L'extinction des feux' ['Lights out'], 'Aux étendards' ['To the standards'] and 'La Marche des éclopés' ['The march of the wounded soldiers'], pieces that could still make any army march.

Compared with the clarion calls, marches and fanfares played on the roads of victory, the vocal music of the Empire was mediocre. But was that the Emperor's fault, or was music simply at a turning point just before the birth of the Romantic movement? Napoleon often went to the Opéra, which he required to present eight productions a year. He encouraged renowned composers such as Lesueur and Paër, choirmasters who were paid as marshals, but their creations were few and of mediocre quality. What was he to do if these composers born under Louis XV had run out of inspiration and it would still be a few years before the tumultuous Berlioz would sound the first notes of the French Romantic school? He did not fail in his task as sovereign patron of the arts. He did everything possible to guarantee the independence of the composers and even to see that the Opéra was properly administered. But the Opéra, with a mind of its own and a house which was a bit noisy, failed to reward his efforts, and he was enraged: 'If this doesn't stop, I'll give them a good military man who will make them march to the beat of the drum!'

The Opéra-Comique, with its lighter repertoire, was favoured by the public, and the Emperor himself often hummed its popular melodies. The Opéra-Italien brought the public such charming works as Cimarosa's *Secret Marriage* and Mozart's *Marriage of Figaro*. At the same time, the Conservatory of Music was created, and became the concert society of the Conservatory in 1828, presenting the complete cycle of Beethoven's symphonies.

Sentimental ballads, which were very popular with bourgeois families, expressed the new spirit; in addition to the famous 'Plaisir d'amour', which is still sung today, the best-known melody is 'Partant pour la Syrie' ['Leaving for Syria'] by Queen

Hortense, in which love, obeying the Emperor's wishes, is put at the service of the army. Although the musicians of the Empire did not rival the famous Germans and Italians of the time, at least they had an indelible impact on military traditions. 'La Marche de la garde des consuls' ['The march of the Consular Guard'] better known as 'La Marche de Marengo' ['The march of Marengo'], is still used in military parades, and as cultivated and artistic a man as the former president of France, Valéry Giscard d'Estaing, used to introduce his appearances on radio and television with Méhul's 'Chant du départ'.

Literature

The uneasy position of French writers during the Consulate and the Empire is explained by some of Napoleon's comments. Speaking about Chateaubriand, he told Metternich, 'If he wanted to use his talent the way we would like him to, he could be useful! But he would not agree to this, and so he is of no use.' And in a letter to Cambacérès on 21 November 1808, he said, 'They complain that we have no literature; it's the minister of the interior's fault.' Then, finally, he admitted that he was powerless in this situation: 'I have the popular literature for me and the great against me.'

A tireless reader and a talented writer, Napoleon would have liked to control literature as he controlled public administration. Even the greatest genius could not be without faults, and this attempt to place compliant writers on the right hand of the throne and independent thinkers in purgatory was his greatest error, since it meant that the two most prolific writers of the era, Chateaubriand and Mme de Staël, were penalised, while the mediocre ones monopolised the jobs and pensions. In Napoleon's defence, it must be said that the weakness of the literature can be attributed to the fashion for abstract science in the schools, which took students away from classical studies, and to the emigration of France's intellectual elite. It must also be admitted that the readers of the Empire delighted in the execrable literature born of the Revolution, whose sentimentality and bad taste provide a painful contrast with the splendours of the classical period and the supremely intelligent philosophers of the *Encyclopédie*.

Napoleon wanted the great achievements of the Revolution

and his own accomplishments to inspire heroic works – and he made this known. As one witness reported, 'He wants his reign to be marked by great public works projects and great literary works.' An attentive reader who appreciated ideas more than form – 'I am sensitive', he said, 'only to the power of thought' – he despaired at the mediocrity of the writers of the time. But, unfortunately, he failed to realise that his administration, which was sometimes overly punctilious at its lower levels, prohibited any publication that did not follow his line, so that while the poets of the provinces happily sang the praises of the Civil Code, there was no Homer capable of celebrating Marengo and Austerlitz. This was a cruel blow for him when he thought of how zealously Roman literature had celebrated the works of the twelve Caesars.

The truth is that literature, like music, was undergoing a major crisis. And if there had been persecuted geniuses, they would have been free to publish abroad as did some philosophers of the eighteenth century. But, alas, such was not the case. The novels of the Consulate and the Empire were mainly sentimental romances, which were published at the rate of four or five a day; they came from the pens of women novelists who unscrupulously exploited the fashion for easy emotion and tears. The poetry is hardly more engaging, and it is alarming to discover that twenty thousand works in verse were published from 1800 to 1815 – more sentimental and bucolic pieces, and nothing on the great deeds of the greatest conqueror in history! As for the philosophers and historians, they were also second-rate, and Napoleon had every reason to lament the fact that his throne, which was the beacon of Europe, was surrounded by bad writers: 'What is there in France today for the future of letters and the honour of the human spirit?'

While it is obvious that he cannot bear responsibility for the decline of French literature in the years preceding his taking power, what about this talk of tyranny that always comes up when the names of Germaine de Staël and Chateaubriand are mentioned? Did Napoleon really commit the greatest crime of all, a crime against the mind? Did he persecute literary genius and stifle freedom of thought?

Germaine de Staël, born of Genevan parents and Swedish by marriage, only became French when Geneva was annexed to France in 1791. Intelligent, ambitious and brilliant, this woman was totally lacking in moral sense, and her love life would make a racy novel. She was a tireless and dazzling writer, but one who often showed poor judgement. Unfortunately lacking in physical charm, with a rather mannish appearance, she initially felt an ardent passion for the young General Bonaparte, the conqueror of Italy, and she wrote that he was 'the most intrepid warrior, the most reflective thinker, the most extraordinary genius'. She even took it into her head to become an Egeria to her hero, after having dreamed of playing that role for Mirabeau and then Robespierre.

Through Talleyrand, Mme de Staël finally managed to get herself introduced to Napoleon. Slipping into the circle of people gathered around him, she called out to the First Consul, asking him who was in his eyes 'the greatest woman in the world, living or dead'. 'The one who has the most children, madame,' he answered. The interloper made a face but was not flustered, and pointed out to her unwilling conversational partner that he had a reputation 'of not liking women much'. He replied, 'Pardon me, madame, I like my own very much.'

Mme de Staël was unrelenting, and she laid siege to her idol, a siege Napoleon on St Helena recalled with amusement: 'She almost took me by the pants in my little house on rue Chanteraine. She followed me one day as I went into my dressing room. "But madame, I'm going to my dressing room," I said. "It's all the same to me," she answered, "I'm an old woman." She said the Empress Josephine was a silly woman who was not worthy to be my wife and that only she, Mme de Staël, was right for me. She was crazy about me.'

The crazy woman wept with vexation after the coup d'état of 18 Brumaire, which gave France a leader but which also, through the favour of the First Consul, gave her lover, Benjamin Constant, a position. She pushed Constant to make a speech against the Consulate regime 'of servitude and silence'. She was a fierce Calvinist in spite of her life of debauchery, and when the Concordat was signed with the Holy See she went over to the opposition and began dreaming of the overthrow of the regime with all the determination and malice of a wronged woman. As if to open hostilities, she published *Delphine*, a defence of divorce, Protestantism and England. She chose her time well! 'I hope her friends have warned her not to come to Paris,' exclaimed Bonaparte, 'I would have to have her taken back to the border by the police.' He did not need to say this twice. She was seen in Germany, spreading invective against the man who was to become Emperor and plotting against him in all the courts, even with the Bourbons. But she continued to reside at Coppet, near Geneva, where the prefect of the Emperor, the 'tyrant', turned a blind eye to her activities. She was even seen in some regions of France, still trying to get close to Paris. She soon published *Corinna*, a novel in praise of the emancipation of women, in which the French hero is a good-looking fool and the English hero a beautiful, deep, generous spirit. This further enraged Napoleon, and on St Helena he said, 'I cannot forgive Mme de Staël for having made fun of the French in her novel.'

Fallen under the influence of a German who was carrying on anti-French propaganda activity in Austria, the novelist finally brought down on herself the official wrath of the Emperor, who in 1808 wrote to his minister of police: 'Mme de Staël has an ongoing correspondence with a certain Gentz and has become involved with the clique of low characters in London . . . This relationship with this individual can only be to the detriment of France. You will make it known that until now she has been regarded only as a crazy woman, but that today she has begun to get involved in a clique that is contrary to the public peace.'

The guilty woman returned to Coppet, still without suffering any 'persecution' by the authorities of the department, and started to write her major work, *Germany*, which gave her an excellent opportunity to exercise her bias against French literature, supposedly mired in classicism, and praise German genius in all its forms. She took a notion to have this volume published in France and went there, but the police seized the manuscript and ordered her to leave the territory. The minister Savary sent her a rather stern letter: 'It appears the air of this country does not suit you at all. Your last book is not French; I have stopped it from being printed. I regret the loss to the booksellers, but it is not possible for me to allow it to be published.' Can Napoleon really be blamed for approving this measure and refusing to permit the publication of a French book that was offensively pro-German, a book that would lead to a reawakening of the desire for dominance in Austria, only a few years after the end of the Holy Roman Empire, and cause the greatest damage to a precarious peace?

At the same time, Germaine de Staël, who was now taking opium, secretly married a friend of her son twenty-one years her junior and, fleeing the discreet surveillance that had been established around her château in Coppet, set off on the roads of Europe. She was next seen in the Russian court when Napoleon entered Moscow as a conqueror; she pushed the czar to make an alliance with Sweden, which she took it upon herself to drag into the war by exerting pressure on crown prince Bernadotte, who was her friend. She dared to write, 'The good of France required that it suffer a reversal.' Then she was in London, where she was given a triumphal reception, since she was the embodiment of resistance to Napoleon's 'tyranny'. During the Hundred Days, assuming that Napoleon would relax his surveillance, she rushed to Paris to claim payment of a debt of two million francs loaned by her father, Necker, to King Louis XVI. Could it be that she had changed camps? One might believe this when reading what she wrote to Joseph Bonaparte: 'The return of your brother is extraordinary and surpasses all imagination.' But this was nothing but an act to gain a position for her son and obtain payment of her two million francs, because she maintained contact with the enemies of the 'tyrant'. One can easily get lost trying to follow the intricacies of her schemes.

Was Napoleon wrong to check the torrent of words from a woman who worked to set Sweden, Prussia and Austria against France? And could Mme de Staël, who hated Napoleon and her adoptive country with equal force, complain because she was not allowed to publish her book in France? This is the objective perspective from which the issue must be looked at.

'Bonaparte and I, unknown second lieutenants,' wrote Chateaubriand, drawing a parallel between his rise to fame as a writer of genius and Napoleon's rise to power. Like Mme de Staël but in a different way, he too had a passionate relationship with Napoleon. A royalist émigré who was allowed to return to France by the First Consul, Chateaubriand published *The Genius of Christianity*, which praised religion as the source of all morality, at the very time when Bonaparte was negotiating the Concordat. The able and ambitious young man had shown excellent timing, and thanks to Elisa Bonaparte, who honoured him with her patronage, he was allowed to dedicate the second edition of the book to the new leader of France. And in what terms he framed his dedication! 'The people are watching you. France, expanded by your victories, has placed its hopes in you.'

Devoted as he claimed to be to the cause of the Bourbons, Chateaubriand accepted a post as embassy secretary in Rome. And then he soon became minister plenipotentiary in Valais, a post he considered beneath him and which he resigned on the pretext of his wife's poor health; the real reason was the execution of the Duc d'Enghien, a relative of the Bourbons. He said: 'If Bonaparte had not killed the Duc d'Enghien, if he had brought me closer (which he was inclined to do), what would have happened to me? My literary career would have been over; having leapt straight into a political career . . . I would have become rich and powerful. France might have gained from my joining with the Emperor; I would have lost.' This is the key to the story: it was a political career that interested this magician of the word, and the little importance accorded to him in this sphere irritated him so much that he joined the opposition.

In 1807 he published a scathing article that would have earned him banishment if Napoleon had been a tyrant, 'a lion that has tasted blood'. In it he said: 'When in the silence of abjection the only sound one hears is the clanking of the slave's chains and the voice of the informer, when all tremble before the tyrant and when it is as dangerous to incur his favour as his displeasure, the historian appears, entrusted with the vengeance of peoples. In vain does Nero prosper; Tacitus has already been born in the Empire.' The comparison with the Roman emperor provided a fine phrase but, as Talleyrand liked to say, everything exaggerated is unimportant. Chateaubriand was not thrown to the lions as the opponents of Nero were; he was simply 'banished' – two leagues from Paris – and moved to his charming estate, 'the Valley of the Wolves', which he often left to visit his friends in the capital. Tyranny? In 1811 Napoleon himself insisted that the greatest writer of his time be admitted to the Academy. And what are we to think of this author who used his comfortable banishment to write an inflammatory pamphlet on Napoleon and the Bourbons? In it the man he had called 'Caesar' in his acceptance speech to the Academy has became 'a tyrant, a foreigner, a false great man'.

Chateaubriand was too intelligent, however, not to make amends when he was cast aside by the Bourbons he had served so well, after the fall of the man whose only wrong was not making him an all-powerful minister. In his *Mémoires d'outre-tombe* [Memoirs from beyond the tomb], one of the great works of French literature, he described how in his entire life he had encountered only one person who was worthy of him, and then, with the always fresh and generous inspiration of a poet, forgetting almost half a century of abuse and sarcasm, forgetting that he had said he was 'persecuted' when he was never more than bothered, he lavished praise on his illustrious contemporary:

'Bonaparte is not at all great for his words, his speeches or his writings, or for his love of liberty, which he never had and never claimed to establish; he is great for creating a regular, powerful government, a code of laws that was adopted in various countries, courts of justice, schools, and a strong, active, intelligent administration, one under which we still live; he is great for reviving and enlightening Italy and managing it in a superior way; he is great for bringing order back to France out of chaos, rebuilding the altars, bringing down furious demagogues, vain scholars, anarchic writers, Voltairian atheists, streetcorner orators, cutthroats from the prisons and the streets, good-for-nothings from assemblies, clubs and scaffolds, and making them serve under him; he is great for . . . forcing soldiers who were his equals and captains who were his leaders or his rivals to bend to his will; he is great especially for being born of himself alone, for being able on no authority other than his genius to command the obedience of thirty-six million subjects at a time when there were no illusions about the throne; he is great for defeating all the kings who were his adversaries and all the armies, whatever their discipline or their ability, for making his name known to savage peoples as to civilised peoples, for surpassing all the conquerors who preceded him, for filling ten years with such deeds as we can hardly understand today.'

The press

No one would deny that the situation of the press was difficult during the Napoleonic era, but the honest historian must reveal the circumstances that necessitated such intransigence on the part of the man who liked to point out that there was abundant freedom wherever his Civil Code had been adopted. To unearth the causes of Napoleon's mistrust of the press, we have to go back to 18 Brumaire, to 1799, to that time when he had, to the great relief of the majority of the French, swept away the ideologues, dreamers and ranters, and when the newspapers, which had been tightly restrained by the Directory, had started to proliferate and had taken over agitation from the parties. It was imperative for domestic peace that provocateurs and agitators be silenced, and on 17 January 1800 a decree reduced the number of newspapers published in Paris from seventy-three to thirteen and prohibited the creation of new ones 'until peace'. It was exactly then that a few tribunes of whom the public was already tired – considering them responsible for the anarchy that had existed for ten years – attempted to challenge the power of the young First Consul. They included Benjamin Constant, urged on by Mme de Staël. Bonaparte was pressed to censor these blowhards, but he replied accurately, 'You want me to prohibit words that can be heard by five hundred people and allow those that could be heard by several million?' And he added, no doubt thinking of the violent revolutionary press: 'What is a newspaper? A dispersed club. A newspaper acts on its subscribers the same way a club ranter acts on his audience . . . In France, where people are gifted with quick thinking, keen imagination and susceptibility to strong impressions, unlimited freedom of the press would have disastrous consequences.'

Of course, there were those who objected that England, alone in Europe, guaranteed freedom of the press, but there again Napoleon raised an intelligent objection: 'The difference is that their government is old and ours is new.' For those who are scandalised by the restriction of written information, which was the practice throughout the continent, it is useful to recall that ninety-six per cent of the French people were illiterate and that the thirteen authorised newspapers had a total of just over eighteen thousand subscribers.

Starting in 1800, therefore, the press was subject to constant administrative supervision and was used to control public opinion, a policy that the man in the street, tired of calls to disorder by overexcited tribunes, greeted with indifference and even satisfaction. 'Newspapers have always provided support for revolutions, which they arm, plan and end up making necessary,' wrote one contemporary. 'With their number diminished, it will be easier to monitor them and to direct them towards a strengthening of the constitutional system.' This was the time when Bonaparte was drawing up the Constitution of the Year VIII, an eternal monument to his glory which, as Albert Vandal has said, 'met the permanent and traditional aspirations of the French, the destiny of their temperament and of their history'.

While this young leader crowned with glory was organising the State to regenerate France, no one thought to quarrel with him over the disappearance of papers whose diatribes could only be an obstacle on the road to the national reconciliation everyone wanted, a road fraught with dangers. The French people had other concerns: they wanted an easier life rid of the tyranny of the Revolution and the harassment of the Directory, and a firm policy to establish a general peace in Europe. And the obstacles to those dreams were the left, which wished for a restoration of the monarchy under the Orléans branch of the house of Bourbon; the military faction, mobilized by a handful of generals who wanted their own 18 Brumaire; the anarchists and the Jacobins, who talked of re-establishing the Committee of Public Safety of dreaded memory; the royalists, who were threatening to set fire to the entire country; the Catholic ultras,who considered Bonaparte too republican; and finally, the party of the philosophers, who considered him as having 'sold out to the clergy'. That made a lot of opponents. The vast majority of the country felt it was not the time to tolerate campaigns for or against the observance of Sunday or the restoration of Mardi Gras, rivalries that dated from the Revolution, or struggles against the suppression of such-and-such a newspaper. Especially because Bonaparte, in order to establish his position, needed a victory over external enemies, which he could only obtain if domestic peace was assured, and this in turn depended entirely on the suppression of discord. Could he have set out for the Marengo Plain, where victory awaited him, while allowing the royalists to work and the politicians and generals to fight over what was to be his own legacy?

The end of hostilities with England in 1802 brought no change in this system, which had been set up 'until peace'. Quite the contrary, because successive decrees prohibited newspapers from mentioning the movements of armies and ships or discussing religious matters, and whether he was in Paris or on campaign,

Napoleon saw to the strict execution of his orders, badgering his minister of police with notes. In 1805 the papers were even appointed censors who had control over 'politics and literature, which could be presented in the wrong political light'.

In 1811 there were only four newspapers left in Paris – *Le Moniteur, Le Journal de l'Empire, La Gazette de France* and *Le Journal de Paris* – and in the provinces one newspaper was allowed in each department. The same year, in a decree issued from Compiègne, Napoleon consolidated his regime's control of the press by confiscating the Parisian newspapers for the state. Was this excessively harsh? A quotation from Napoleon comes immediately to mind: 'The first law is necessity; the first justice is public safety.'

Necessity was the war that was raging, a war that was already being waged psychologically, because the English were flooding Europe with vicious satires that they were distributing in Portugal, Normandy and Brittany and on the coast of Italy. The wartime censorship of the French press – and we have seen the same thing in recent times in other countries – was simply one of the tools of victory. And public safety, for a country that had gone through a revolutionary crisis lasting ten years, a crisis that would have destroyed any other nation, was stability, and so the consolidation of the regime the French had deliberately chosen. The press was used mainly to make known as far as the most isolated hamlet the benefits of the Empire, 'the great things the Emperor is doing with his soldiers'.

Those who condemn Napoleon's authoritarianism with respect to the press should be reminded that the regime that came after the Empire went a good deal further, imposing stringent supervision of journalists, with censorship, posting of bonds and 'special offences' punishable in special courts, and a law passed in 1822 put tight constraints on the 'spirit' of publications. It should also be noted that Prince Charles Augustus of Saxony-Weimar was, in 1816, the first ruler to grant freedom of the press in his States – though he restricted it a few years later – and that the situation of newspapers was more precarious in Russia in 1865 than it was in Paris fifty years earlier under Napoleon.

NOTES

1. Part of the material in this chapter is taken from the *Dictionnaire Napoléon* by Jean Tulard (Editions Fayard, 1987).
2. Caricatures of the period show John Bull at the table, eating greedily, handing a fat purse to the Emperor of Austria, saying, 'Let me eat, and go fight those rabid Frenchmen for me.' On the table, there are two other full purses, marked 'For Russia' and 'For Prussia'.

CHAPTER IV

The Military Leader

*Military Genius is a gift from heaven, but the essential quality of a
commanding general is steadfastness of character and the resolve
to win at all costs.*

Napoleon

Baptism of fire

At the military college of Brienne and then in Paris, Napoleon
received the same training as all the officers of the *ancien régime*.
This does not explain how he became an exceptional military
leader. Not all officers from the great schools prove capable of
leading men in combat; exercises, realistic as they may be, do not
change lambs into lions. It is only under fire, when death looms,
that men distinguish themselves. There are those who face it and
those who shame themselves, and no one can foresee with
certainty what his behaviour will be before he receives his
baptism of fire. This is why those who see this moment
approaching, even if they show impatience, assurance and
enthusiasm on the outside, cannot help feeling a certain anxiety.

For Napoleon, the baptism of fire took place on 22 February
1793, on the Maddalena Islands, north of Sardinia, ten kilometres
south of Bonifacio. The French Republic had been at war with
Victor Amadeus III, the king of Sardinia, Savoy and Piedmont
since 1791. At the end of 1792 it was decided that the Army of the
Alps would invade Piedmont, while an expeditionary force
would attack Sardinia, with the main thrust on Cagliari and a
diversion on the Maddalena Islands. That diversion was
entrusted to Colonel Colonna Cesari, who commanded a force of
600 men, including a very modest artillery force under the
command of Bonaparte. Paoli, who was on the verge of once again
proclaiming the independence of Corsica, had given Cesari, who

was his nephew, instructions to see that the enterprise failed. Bonaparte was unaware of this.

On 22 February the flotilla, made up of the frigate *La Fauvelle* and a few transport boats, came in sight of its objective. Cesari gave Napoleon the order to take the small island of Santo Stefano, which was separated from Maddalena only by a narrow channel. Leading fifty men, at nightfall Napoleon pushed back some thirty Sardinian soldiers, who hardly put up a pretence of resistance before shutting themselves up in a square tower surrounded by a moat.

The next day at four o'clock the Sardinians surrendered, and Santo Stefano was in the hands of the French. It was then that Napoleon had the artillery and munitions unloaded. Setting an example and encouraging his soldiers, in a few hours he succeeded in setting up a mortar and two four-inch pieces on a knoll overlooking the village of La Maddalena, which was much better defended than Santo Stefano. Five hundred men from the Courten regiment were solidly entrenched there. At daybreak on 24 February Napoleon opened fire; thanks to the accurate fire of his cannons he succeeded in silencing the batteries of the two small forts that controlled the entrance to the harbour. The town was on fire and the frightened inhabitants were fleeing to the countryside, soon followed by the garrison. The way was clear for the landing of the bulk of the forces.

But Cesari did not see things this way. He told his officers that with the small number of troops available it was better to abandon the attack. Napoleon and the other officers objected so strenuously that the colonel finally consented to making a landing the next morning at daybreak, but he hoped before then to find a way to cancel the order that had been forced from him. At midnight events took a dramatic turn. *La Fauvette* raised anchor and moved off, after the captain informed Cesari that the crew was demanding an immediate retreat and that he had to give in.Then the colonel himself left with most of the transports, leaving Napoleon on the little island with the two worst tubs in the flotilla.

Was the mutiny spontaneous, or was it provoked? We do not know, but what is certain is that on the morning of 25 February Napoleon found himself abandoned and isolated with fifty men, within reach of an enemy ten times greater in numbers. With a great deal of skill, he brought the mortar and the two cannons back to the shore, but there, in spite of all his efforts, he was unable to load the pieces that had been unloaded using the hoists on *La Fauvette*. Furious, he had to resign himself to spiking them before leaving for Bonifacio, where he landed on the morning of 27 February.

This adventure was decisive for Napoleon's future. As new graduates, young officers blindly carry out their commanders' combat orders. And then one day, usually in a tight situation, they discover that leaders, even the most highly regarded among them, can give stupid orders – orders that lead to losses without any appreciable gains – and that a commander can miss opportunities for success through passivity or indecision. Once they have made this discovery, all those who were later to become great military commanders have changed their behaviour and tried to impose their will when decisions were taken by the higher ranks, and when that was not possible they carried out their missions in the spirit rather than the letter, in order to improve the results with a minimum of losses. This could be described as the moment when they lose their adolescent innocence and become responsible adults. All great military leaders, such as MacArthur, Patton, Rommel, Montgomery and De Lattre, were once brilliant lieutenants and captains in combat, able to impose their views and their character. General Navarre, on the other hand, who was experienced in political life, proved thoroughly mediocre in Vietnam. Without the experience gained at Maddalena, Napoleon would certainly not have behaved as he did at Toulon a few months later.

A young officer also has to show his men his personal courage, his ability to function under enemy fire. He must be capable of leading them to victory in the face of death. Thus, little by little, he creates around himself a legend as a lord of battle with the ability to multiply the effective value of his soldiers in combat. If in addition he can talk to them, understand them, encourage them and love them, they will soon follow him with enthusiasm and pride wherever he leads them – even into hell. Napoleon met all these criteria to the highest degree. His legend as a lord of battles was born in Toulon and blossomed during the Italian campaign of 1796, and it continued to grow. As he stated, 'I had to carry out dramatic actions to win the affection and confidence of the soldiers.'

How could a soldier retreat when he has chatted with the Emperor around a bivouac fire on the eve of a great battle or seen him gallop through the ranks in the heat of battle? How could a soldier not love his Emperor when he sees him, dizzy with fatigue after a hard day of combat, spend the night in the mud, rain and wind organising relief and evacuation for the wounded? The irresistible spirit of his soldiers when he was present on the battlefield counted for a lot in victories which were often won when his troops were outnumbered two or three times by the enemy. As Field Marshal Sir Archibald Wavell stated in a lecture at Cambridge: 'To learn that Napoleon won the campaign of 1796 in Italy by manoeuvres on interior lines or some such phrase is of little value. If you can discover how a young unknown man inspired a ragged, mutinous, half-starved army, and made it fight, how he gave it energy and momentum to march and fight as it did, how he dominated and controlled generals older and more experienced than himself, then you will have learned something.'

In addition to his charisma, which was unprecedented in history, Napoleon had a talent for organising and training his units. In the Grande Armée, all the marshals, general, colonels, captains, warrant officers and sergeants had earned their rank under fire. It was very difficult for men who had nothing but the titles they were born with, as was the case with the majority of officers in the armies of the monarchies, to resist such soldiers. At every echelon, Napoleon established élite units that served as an example to the rest. In the army, the élite division was the Guard. Each division had its élite regiment, each regiment its battalion, each battalion its company, and each company its platoon. All the soldiers tried to earn a place in these units, so great was their prestige in the army and the nation.

With this incomparable tool that he had forged and his extraordinary skill in strategy and tactics, Napoleon had little difficulty winning. He already knew where and when he was going to beat his adversaries of the day while they were still trying to figure out what was going on. We will look at this more closely in the following chapters.

For those who dare to claim that Napoleon showed inordinate ambition, it must be explained that a man who faces death on the battlefield just has the ambition to do his day's work as best he can, because he knows very well he may not see the next sunrise. Even when he had reached the summit of power, wealth and glory, Napoleon never hesitated to risk his own life, his most precious possession. He did this not out of ambition but out of duty.

The art of war

Napoleon's military genius came from his limitless self-confidence – what he called his 'star' – and from a quick and fertile imagination, almost supernatural intuition which allowed him to predict his enemies' reactions, the studious application of strategic methods and formidable willpower in deciding tactics. It is humbling to study these gifts in a man who led more than fifty battles and gave his name to a tactic; it is natural to take refuge behind the opinions of the experts, especially the best one of them, the Prussian Carl von Clausewitz, who in his treatise *On War* described Napoleon as 'the god of war personified'. What is most surprising is that this god remained quite unaffected and took pleasure in explaining his genius in simple language:

'The art of war is a simple art, and it is all in the execution; there is nothing vague; it is all common sense, not ideology . . . It does not require complicated manoeuvres, the simplest ones are preferable; but the most important thing is common sense . . . It is like a fistfight: the more you give, the better . . . The whole art of war consists in a well-reasoned, extremely cautious defence and a bold, quick offence . . . You have to be slow in the planning and quick in the execution.'

This is a complete syllabus for training in warfare. It seems simple today, but at the end of the eighteenth century and the beginning of the nineteenth it represented a total revolution in ideas and methods. It was the end of the slow, majestic warfare of the time of Louis XIV, with long sieges and orderly battles and bowing and hat-tipping: 'After you, gentlemen. You shoot first.'

The young Bonaparte, an artillery lieutenant, got his ideas from the work of a man he admired passionately, Frederick II of Prussia, Frederick the Great, whom he called 'the tactician par excellence', and who had shown how a light army using bold manoeuvres can overcome an enemy that is superior in numbers but does not know how to move. He adapted these theories to his need to develop a tactic which he never gave up: draw the enemy out onto familiar ground; occupy the ground the enemy has left; trap the enemy between your artillery and a natural obstacle such as an elevation or a river; turn back against the enemy and crush them by attacking along the whole front to find a weak point and then breaking through at that key point with your own reserves.

Napoleon's tactics were equal to his strategy. He held that it was not necessary to overcome the enemy all along the front, but simply to strike a strong violent blow against one part of it, the key point. 'Once a breach is created, the equilibrium is destroyed; anything else is unnecessary. This violent blow, which he called 'the decisive attack', was what he had in mind when he wrote that 'the outcome of a battle is the result of an instant'. How did he plan it? How did he choose his target? His answer was succinct: 'You engage everywhere and you see.' In fact, his plan was always prepared in advance. The Emperor would point to a spot on the map and announce quietly to his silent staff: 'I will beat the enemy here.'

An outflanking attack very close to the enemy's line of retreat would throw the enemy into confusion, forcing it to sacrifice reserves and lengthen its front, creating a weak point somewhere, and that was where Napoleon would aim his full exploitation force. This force was assembled unobtrusively and sent into action without delay, with the artillery opening a breach that the infantry would occupy and the cavalry would widen to give chase to the fleeing enemy. It was the cavalry that was given the task of exploiting the victory, chasing down the fleeing troops and accepting the surrender. When he put this tactic into practice, Napoleon usually had an army of two hundred thousand men, divided into seven corps of three divisions, each division numbering 10,000 men and thirty-six to forty artillery pieces. The cavalry was made up of two divisions of cuirassiers, four of dragoons and one of light cavalry.

Since Napoleon was an artillery officer, cannons played a decisive role in his tactics. 'Great battles are won with artillery . . . Artillery today determines the fate of armies and peoples . . . You fight with cannons the way you fight with fists . . . The art consists in concentrating a large number of blows on a single point . . . Once the battle has begun, the one that suddenly brings in an unexpected force of artillery without the enemy's knowledge is

1. General Bonaparte at Arcole (by Antoine-Jean Gros).

2. Letizia Bonaparte (anonymous portrait).

3. The Bonaparte home in Ajaccio where Napoleon was born.

4. Napoleon in his coronation robes (by Ingres).

5. The empress Josephine in her coronation robes (by Gerard).

6. The imperial throne in the Tuileries Palace.

7. Napoleon at the founding of the *Maisons d'Education* (by Bazin).

8. Napoleon with his family at Saint-Cloud (by Durcis).

9. How Napoleon's signature evolved between 1792 and 1816.

10. Napoleon with the architects, Percier and Fontaine, at the Louvre (by Couder).

11. A self-portrait by Jacques-Louis David, Napoleon's favourite painter.

12. The First Consul crossing the Alps, by David.

13. Napoleon's triumphal arrival in Egypt (by Lejeune).

14. An English caricature ridiculing Napoleon.

15. The retreat from Russia (by Raffet).

16. Napoleon on the *Bellerophon* (after Orchardjohn).

17. St Helena from the sea.

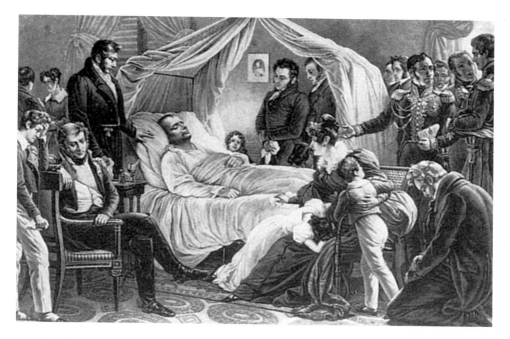

18. The death of Napoleon on 5 May 1821 (by Steuben).

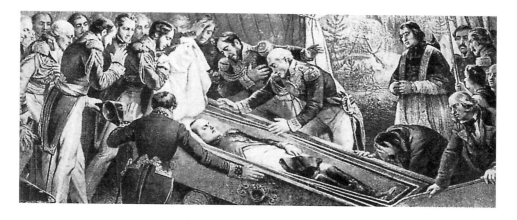

19. The opening of Napoleon's coffin on St Helena on 15 October 1840.

20. Napoleon's tomb in Les Invalides, Paris

21. Ben Weider and his sons in 1975, seated on the steps of the entrance to Longwood House in St Helena. Louis – on the top right, Eric – on the bottom left and Mark – on the bottom right. Note the small tree that they planted near the Tomb of Napoleon.

sure to win.' The artillery therefore had to prepare the attack and win it, opening breaches in the enemy front and following the cavalry in order to lend assistance. This was a precision task requiring substantial means, and as soon as he became First Consul Bonaparte worked to make the French artillery extremely mobile by creating an artillery train and a horse artillery. At the same time, he simplified supply problems by reducing the number of calibres.

The cavalry played a key role in Napoleon's first successes. As he stated, 'Without cavalry, battles are unresolved.' To implement his battle plans, he separated the light cavalry from the line cavalry (dragoons) and created a heavy cavalry (cuirassiers), all grouped in separate divisions. One innovation was that the light cavalry acted as scouts, as an advance guard, a rearguard and on the wings, supported and protected by the line cavalry, while the dragoons and the cuirassiers were responsible for the exploitation of openings at a distance, pursuit and decisive attack during battle. In 1805 Napoleon had at his disposal seventy-eight cavalry regiments numbering 57,000 men, a formidable force.

Finally – and this was an innovation that bore fruit – Napoleon always kept at the ready a mobile force, a general reserve consisting of the élite Imperial Guard, artillery, infantry and cavalry. The presence of this imposing, disciplined and experienced force close to the battlefield constituted a guarantee of success for the troops and a trump card the general would play at the critical or decisive moment.

The infantry, which Napoleon inherited from the Revolution, was an admirable weapon that had learned to function by fighting on all fronts, under deplorable conditions, and that he only needed to shape to his tactics to make it a force almost invincible by conventional means.

There had been little progress in weaponry, however, since France lagged behind England industrially; the rifles from 1777 with their heavy lead bullets did less damage than the bayonets attached to them, and the Gribeauval cannonballs, vintage 1776, were feared mainly for their ricochets. The genius of Napoleon was not attracted by the new weapons – could this be evidence of his basic pacifism? – weapons more deadly than his, which his English enemies would use at Waterloo. He worked on the battlefield like a player at his chessboard, relying only on the training and discipline of his personnel and on what today we call psychological warfare. It was here that he acted on 'the human material'. He demanded a great deal of his men, often asking them to march long distances before a battle. 'They grumbled, but they still marched!'

The marshals, the *grognards* or 'grumblers', the Guard – they are the stuff of legend! Napoleon's impact on his troops was as strong as his influence on strategy and tactics, and the soldier of the Empire entered the museum of history with his Emperor. Never has the relationship between soldiers and their leader been so close. Everyone, from the top to the bottom of the hierarchy, lived and fought only to win his attention or die under his gaze. The marshals were almost all of modest origins and attained the highest positions in the army solely through their bravery; from Ney, 'the bravest of the brave', to Bessières, 'the father of the grenadiers', they were famous in their own time. The generals, so many of whose names are engraved in the stone of the Arc de Triomphe, benefited from the renewal of the officer corps that followed the peace of 1802; they had climbed up through the ranks and, unlike the generals of the *ancien régime*, they lived very close to their men, personally leading them into combat and often paying for their bravery with their lives. The colonels, from whom the marshals were chosen, were all reminiscent of Balzac's Colonel Chabert, ready to die for their Emperor and, when defeat came, distressed that they survived him: 'What do you expect! Our sun has set, and we are all cold now.'

The Emperor's 'children', his family, were his soldiers, those Rostand described as 'the obscure ones of no rank'. There was a fierce attachment, a virile affection, between this leader feared by the powerful of Europe and these simple men; their demonstrations of this feeling were clumsy, bashful and touching.

At nightfall the Emperor, disdaining to set up camp in some château in the area, formed his Guard in a square and set up his table in the midst of his soldiers, who saw him come and go, his hands behind his back, conversing with his officers and eating the simplest repast. Napoleon spoke familiarly to the old soldiers and allowed them to address him in the same way. He often walked through the lines on the eve of battle, exchanging pleasantries with the troops.

'The crop-head is happy,' murmured one old soldier. 'Things will be okay!'

'You won't need to expose yourself tomorrow,' remarked another. 'We'll bring you that army's flags and cannons.'

'We promise you victory,' added a third, 'and that's how we'll celebrate the anniversary of your coronation.'

These nightly walks, this communion in danger, the certainty that the next day, from the top of a knoll, he would be watching them, electrified the soldiers, because he constantly offered himself to their view and shared their sufferings. This elicited from the most humble of the infantrymen the words that flew from one mouth to the next: 'He knows what he's doing!'

The following scene took place at Jena during a review of the reserve cavalry in front of the 13th Chasseurs. The colonel presented to Napoleon an old NCO who deserved to be promoted second lieutenant but who unfortunately did not know how to read. 'Impossible,' said Napoleon, 'we'll make you senior sergeant.' The soldier scowled and rolled his eyes, which Napoleon found amusing. 'Are you clever?' he asked the veteran sardonically. 'Not as clever as you, Sire!' Bursts of laughter. The fellow received his officer's epaulettes. That is the way to win hearts and battles.

Napoleon, whom Thiers liked to call 'the incorrigible warrior', is often blamed for the depopulation of France, and some authors say he was responsible for the deaths of millions of men. Looking at the statistics, it is very easy to answer that. In 1815, within the borders of 1791, France had eight million more inhabitants than in 1800: thirty-five million compared to twenty-seven million, which represents an increase of thirty per cent in fifteen years. This rate of increase has not been equalled either before or since Napoleon.

There are those who see Napoleon as a hard man, insensitive to the suffering and misery of the soldiers, but thousands of statements by contemporaries attest to the opposite. He spoke with his Austrian adversary, the Archduke Charles, of the 'sad laurels of victory'. After the Battle of Jaffa, he wrote to the Directory, 'Never has war been so abhorrent to me.' After Eylau, when someone mentioned to him that the *Bulletin* had been less flattering than it should be to the army, he replied: 'A father who loses his children finds no charm in victory. When the heart speaks, even glory holds no more illusions.' The following letter to the widow of Marshal Lannes, the Duc de Montebello, after the death of his old comrade-in-arms in 1809, is worth rereading:

'Dear cousin,

'The marshal died this morning of wounds he received on the field of honour. My pain equals yours. I have also lost the most distinguished general of my armies, my comrade-in-arms for the past sixteen years, the man I considered my best friend. His family and his children will always have a special right to my protection. It is to give you that assurance that I wanted to write you this letter, for I feel that nothing can alleviate the pain you feel.'

Las Cases, who knew Napoleon so well in the privacy of St Helena, wrote, 'There have been attempts to make Napoleon look like a terrible, implacable man. The truth is that all vengeance was foreign to him and he was incapable of holding a grudge.' In 1803, when England pushed him into taking up arms again, the Russian ambassador heard him say, 'It is with regret and horror that I will go to war.'

And yet some people have criticised him for loving war too much, ignoring the fact that for him it was a matter of defending himself or dying and taking down with him the new regime of France and France itself. He himself energetically answered this criticism: 'I closed the abyss of anarchy and brought order to the chaos. I removed the stain from the Revolution, ennobled the people and reinforced kings. I encouraged all competition, rewarded all merits and pushed back the limits of glory! All that is certainly something! So, then, what accusations could be made against me that a historian could not refute? . . . There is plenty to absolve me. My despotism? But the historian would show that dictatorship was absolutely necessary. Will it be said that I obstructed liberty? He would prove that we were on the verge of licence, anarchy, great disorder. Will I be accused of loving war too much? He would show that I was always attacked.'

The campaigns

In the chapter on Napoleon's diplomacy, we saw that the Emperor was always forced into war. This can further be demonstrated by a brief account of his campaigns, in which he applied the famous maxim that the best defence is a good offence, and by an examination of his bold methods, which revolutionised the art of the war.

It all started in 1793, when the English had just taken Toulon. Bonaparte, a 24-year-old artillery captain, found himself confronting seven thousand Spaniards, six thousand Neapolitans, two thousand Piedmontese and two thousand Englishmen. And what were those Englishmen doing there, who systematically accused Napoleon of always attacking them? This force was supported by considerable artillery and by vessels anchored in the harbour. 'It is the artillery that takes places,' decided this puny young man whose intensity astonished everyone,'and the infantry that enters them'. He therefore set up thirteen batteries close to the harbour and pounded it, then attacked and took a fortification overlooking the roadstead, and two days later the enemy squadrons fled after pusillanimously setting fire to the harbour and the French vessels. The captain was made a brigadier general. 'There history took hold of him, never to let him go,' wrote Las Cases, 'There began his immortality'.

The Italian campaign of 1796-97 was a triumph for Bonaparte's tactics, which involved making up for numerical inferiority with speed of movement and the element of surprise. He arrived in Nice in March and found an army in disarray, which he electrified with one of those proclamations that made him a master of psychological warfare. The circumstances were hardly favourable to this nervous, carelessly dressed little man who had not yet even commanded a division. He had been put in charge of an army that, according to the Directory, was only supposed to provide a diversion to allow the main army from Germany to attack Vienna. Of this secondary mission in a minor zone of operations, the 27-year-old warrior made a battlefield on which every court had its eyes fixed, and soon the names of his victories were on everyone's lips: Montenotte – from which the Emperor Napoleon would date his 'nobility' – Lodi, Castiglione, Bassano, Arcole and Rivoli. In one year he overcame the Austrians and Piedmontese and forced the Sardinians into an armistice. Master of Italy, he imposed on Austria the Treaty of Campo Formio, which gave France the left bank of the Rhine and the Ionian Islands, and which created the Cisalpine Republic (Milan, Modena and Bologna).

The second Italian campaign, in 1800, was even more dazzling. During Bonaparte's absence in Egypt, Europe, pushed by

England, had formed a new coalition which was able to field 360,000 men, as compared to the 170,000 soldiers of the Directory. The national territory was threatened. The English had even landed in Holland – and what were they doing there, these soldiers from a country that claimed it was always being attacked? – and the Russians had entered Switzerland. Bonaparte hurried back, and ensured the success of the coup d'état of 18 Brumaire. Russia and Prussia, frightened, withdrew from the coalition, but Austria, bribed by England, which promised a landing of 20,000 men on the Ligurian coast, persisted in trying to rid Europe of the 'Corsican plague'. Entrusting the troops from Germany to Moreau, Bonaparte led his army over the dangerous roads of the Grand Saint Bernard Pass, a unique exploit, and struck like lightning at the rear of the Austrians. Montebello, Marengo, and the Treaty of Luneville followed.

Thiers describes how, one day before leaving, Bonaparte was writing on his maps, making marks of different colours to represent the positions of French or Austrian troops, and in front of his secretary, who listened with surprise and curiosity, said: 'That poor Monsieur Melas will go through Turin and withdraw to Alessandria. I will cross the Po and join him on the road to Piacenza, on the plains of the Scrivia, and I will beat him there . . . there . . .' And while saying these words, he made one of his marks at San Giuliano, that is, at Marengo.

The Battle of Marengo

Napoleon's detractors always like to use this battle to criticise his military genius. Let us summarise the battle. Not knowing the position of the enemy, Bonaparte formed his army into three columns. His 22,000 men and fourteen cannons unexpectedly encountered the Austrian army, which had 30,000 men and one hundred artillery pieces. Lacking ammunition, the First Consul was forced to retreat, and at three o'clock the battle seemed lost for him, when Desaix arrived, whom he had sent towards Genoa to cut off the enemy's retreat but with orders to march towards the sound of cannon fire. At five o'clock fighting resumed with the help of Kellermann's 800 cavalry, and in the blink of an eye the Austrians were routed and asked for an armistice.

Austria would have entered into negotiations immediately, but

England offered it funds and more funds, and a decisive French offensive towards Vienna was required before it put its signature on a peace treaty.

Is it true that without Desaix's arrival and without Kellermann's cavalry, Bonaparte would have lost the battle and his destiny would have ended at Marengo? 'Had I been beaten,' he later said, 'I would have withdrawn to my entrenched camp at Stadella and crossed the Po on the five bridges protected by my batteries, and the enemy would not have been able to stop me. I would have joined my first division with Moncey's, Lecchi's and Turreau's corps. I would have let one of Melas's corps cross the Po (and that is all he asked for). Then, superior in numbers, I could have attacked with all my forces.' However, the situation had been very perilous, because twenty-one years later, on his deathbed, he murmured, 'Desaix! Desaix! Ah! the victory is decided.'

The Treaty of Luneville was signed on 9 February 1801, supplemented on 25 March by the Treaty of Amiens with England. 'At Amien,' the Emperor said on St Helena, 'I believed in very good faith that the fate of France and mine were set . . . I was going to devote myself solely to the administration of France, and I believe I would have done great things. I would have achieved the moral conquest of Europe as I was to conquer it militarily.'

The Battle of Austerlitz

The peace was extremely precarious, since the motion put before the British Parliament was cynically threatening. It stated that Parliament approved the treaty but at the same time put its full confidence in the wisdom and the vigilance of His Majesty to take any measures that were necessary should matters take a more favourable turn. William Pitt, who had been returned to power in 1803, immediately rejected the Treaty of Amiens and formed a third coalition with Austria and Russia to go back to war against the French Republic. The cabinet in London promised the czar a yearly payment of 250,000 pounds sterling for every hundred thousand men. The First Consul, in the hope of imposing a durable peace, decided to invade England; he assembled an army of 200,000 men at Boulogne.

Since he could not control the Channel for the twenty-four

hours needed to make a landing on the English coast, Napoleon, who had now become Emperor, made an about-face and attacked the Austrians, London's main allies. His plan was ready. 'If my admirals lack character,' he told Talleyrand, 'I will break camp and enter Germany with 200,000 men, and I will not stop until I have reached Vienna . . . I will not let the Austrian and Russian forces join together, I will strike them before they do.' His decision made, he spent several hours dictating the plan for his German campaign. Then, on 25 August 1805, he announced to his minister of foreign affairs, 'My mind is made up. My movement has begun; on the 30th, I will be in Germany with 200,00 men.' All the dispatches, reports and orders from those days provide a picture of the clarity, quickness and range of his military genius.

On 7 September the Austrians opened hostilities, without a declaration of war, by invading Bavaria, and Napoleon began to carry out his plan. He divided his army into seven corps, under the command of Bernadotte, Marmont, Davout, Soult, Lannes, Ney and Augereau. What a stellar group! The reserve cavalry was under Murat, the most daring cavalry officer in Europe. The Guard, as usual, was under Napoleon's direct command. On 30 September, in Strasbourg, he told the army: 'Soldiers, your Emperor is among you. You are only the vanguard of the people; if necessary, the whole people will rise up at my voice to confound and dissolve that new league woven by England of hatred and gold. But, soldiers, we will have to make forced marches and, endure fatigue and privations of all kinds. We will overcome the obstacles they place in front of us, and we will only rest again when we have planted our eagles on the territory of our enemies.'

He crossed the Rhine. An Austrian army was waiting at Ulm, believing that he would cross the Black Forest. He moved on their rear, cut off their retreat and cornered them in the city, where they were forced to surrender. What a spectacle that ceremony was! The Emperor stood on a knoll surrounded by his generals and his army. The Austrian general handed over his weapons to him, followed for six hours by his officers and men. The campaign had lasted fourteen days. Austria had lost 60,000 men, 200 cannons and eighty flags, and in the evening Napoleon wrote to Josephine: 'I carried out my plan. I have destroyed the Austrian army merely by marches. I will now concern myself with the Russians. They are lost.'

'Our Emperor,' said the soldiers, laughing, 'has found a new way to wage war; he no longer does it with our arms but with our legs.'

Vienna surrendered on 13 November, and Napoleon slept in Schönbrunn Palace. But he did not tarry there, because on the plains of Moravia, at Austerlitz, the czar and the Emperor of Austria had mustered some 100,000 men, with whom they thought they could defeat the 80,000 French troops. On 29 November Napoleon, once again seeking peace, tried to avoid battle through negotiation. He sent General Savary to the czar and Savary brought back with him Prince Dolgoruky, one of Alexander's most influential advisors, who told his master that Napoleon was very frightened and that the only purpose of his peace proposal was to avoid imminent disaster.

Austerlitz, 'the Battle of the Three Emperors', was perhaps the military masterpiece of all time. Lacking sufficient forces to use his usual tactics against the Austrian and Russian troops, Napoleon drew them into a trap by ordering Soult, who was occupying the heights above Austerlitz, to retreat as if he were on the defensive. His withdrawal was intended to induce the enemy to try to turn him towards the south and cut him off from Vienna; to do this, the Russians and Austrians would have to withdraw troops from their centre, which was positioned on the Pratzen Plateau, and thus create a break in the line that would be their downfall. Kutuzov fell into the trap, and on 1 December began moving on the plateau. 'The Emperor, looking down from his bivouac, watched with indescribable joy as the Russian army, two cannon shots from his outposts, began a flanking movement to sweep towards his right,' related one witness. 'He then saw how greatly presumption and ignorance of the art of war had misled the advisors of that brave army. Several times he repeated, "Before tomorrow evening, that army is mine".'

At nightfall Napoleon had the proclamation he had dictated in his coach read to his troops: 'Soldiers, the Russian army has come here to avenge the defeat of the Austrian army at Ulm. These are the same battalions that you defeated at Hollabrunn and that you have constantly pursued thus far . . . Soldiers, I will myself lead all your battalions. I will keep myself far from the fire if with your accustomed bravery you cause disorder and confusion in the enemy ranks. But if for one moment victory was uncertain, you would see your Emperor expose himself to the first shots.'

He dined with his staff, cheerful, speaking of Corneille as if he were in a drawing room at the Tuileries. 'You must want to live and know how to die . . . Politics should be the great subject of modern tragedy . . . It is a mistake to believe that the tragic subjects have been exhausted; there are a multitude of them in the necessities of politics, a destiny as imperious, as implacable as the fate of the Ancients.' He also talked about the campaigns in Egypt and Syria, and then rested for a time in a hut. What soldier, what officer, what marshal could lack courage when the leader displayed such certainty and calm?

Around one o'clock in the morning, he went through the camps, regiment by regiment. He was soon recognised and was greeted with great enthusiasm. The camp was suddenly illuminated by thousands of straw torches raised aloft to salute the Emperor and celebrate the anniversary of his coronation. Deeply touched by this spontaneous act of homage, Napoleon expressed his regret that the following day he had to fight a battle which would rob him of a large number of these brave fellows.

At dawn a radiant sun burned off the winter mist, showing the greenery that covered the Pratzen Plateau and lighting the way for the enemy which 'came down like a torrent on the plain'. Napoleon addressed several regiments. 'Soldiers,' he said, 'we must finish this campaign with a thunderclap that will confound our enemies' pride!' Then he asked Soult how long it would take him to reach the Pratzen Plateau with his divisions.

'Less than twenty minutes,' replied the marshal.

'In that case, let's wait another quarter of an hour.'

At about eight-thirty, when he judged that the Russians were sufficiently engaged, he gave the signal and attacked at the centre, on the right and on the left. By one o'clock victory was his, with the Russians fleeing over the frozen ponds as the French artillery broke the ice with cannons. The battle ended at nightfall under falling snow. From the heights the emperors of Austria and Russia watched the total rout of their armies. The Russians were in such disarray that Czar Alexander, separated from his troops, was in danger of falling into French hands. He sent flag of truce after flag of truce to Marshal Davout, asking for a ceasefire. He remained separated from his servants for nearly a week and Prince Czartoryski, his minister, had to act as his valet. The Austrian and Russian losses numbered 23,000 dead and wounded, 20,000 prisoners, and one hundred and eighty cannons and fifty flags.

'The Allies had 100,000 men, and the French 65,000. Of those 65,000 men,' wrote Napoleon, '15,000 élite grenadiers from the reserve did not fire a single shot – so the army of 100,000 Russians and Austrians was defeated effortlessly by much fewer than 50,000 Frenchmen.' Only 50,000 Frenchmen, but led by the greatest tactician of all time, who had prepared his plan and energised his troops as only he knew how.

Napoleon did not withdraw to his tent to celebrate the victory with his marshals. 'I was with him all that night, and he remained on the battlefield until very late,' reported Rovigo, 'and his escort squadron spent the whole night collecting Russian greatcoats from the dead to cover the wounded. He had big fires built and sent soldiers to look for a war commissioner. He did not retire until the commissioner arrived and, leaving him a picket from his own escort, enjoined him not to leave the wounded until they were all in the hospital.' Was he inhuman, this Emperor who had just won an astonishing victory and who thought only of his wounded men? Five days later, he signed two decrees. The widows of all the soldiers who had died at Austerlitz, from the general to the lowliest private, would receive a pension for the rest of their lives. Their children would be adopted by the Emperor and raised at his expense – he would find work for the boys and husbands for the girls – and they would have the right to add the name Napoleon to their names.

The results of the Austerlitz campaign surpassed England's worst fears. By the Treaty of Pressburg, Austria lost Venetia, Istria and Dalmatia, which were reunited with the kingdom of Italy, and the Tirol and Swabia, which were given to the dukes of Bavaria and Wurttemberg, who were made kings. Two weeks after the battle, Napoleon praised Czar Alexander and offered his friendship in order to restore peace in Europe: 'My heart bleeds! May all the blood that has been shed and all the misfortune fall back on the English who are the cause of it all.' On the news of the disaster at Austerlitz, William Pitt, only 46 years old, took to his bed; he died on 23 January 1806, of cirrhosis of the liver.

The Battle of Jena

Marengo had consecrated the First Consul, and Austerlitz consecrated Napoleon Emperor of the West. Joseph Bonaparte was made king of Naples, Louis Bonaparte king of Holland, Murat grand duke of Berg, and Napoleon, already king of Italy and Mediator of Switzerland, proclaimed himself Protector of the Confederation of the Rhine, which consisted of Bavaria, Württemberg, Baden, Hesse, Berg and eleven other states which declared themselves perpetual allies of France. Negotiations with Fox's England and Russia had resumed when Prussia abruptly declared war on France – Prussia which Napoleon liked to consider a natural ally and to which he had just offered Hanover! This was the beginning of the fourth coalition, made up of England, Russia and Prussia, a very dark time.

If England as usual provided the funds, the Russians and Prussians could muster powerful, well-trained armies, and it was feared that Austria, to free itself from the heavy constraints of the Treaty of Pressburg, would side with them. With much ado, Prussia mobilized, buoyed by its reputation and the past victories of the brilliant Frederick, and its king announced that he was going to drive 'those French dogs' out of Germany, where they were still stationed, and cut down 'the disturber of the world'.

Napoleon wrote to King Frederick William, 'This war will be sacrilege. I remain unshaken in my bonds of alliance with Your Majesty.' The Prussians responded with a contemptuous ultimatum, and Napoleon lost no time in sending his Grande Armée into Saxony 170,000 strong, divided into three columns. 'My affairs are going well,' he wrote to Josephine. 'With God's help, in a few days things will take on a very terrible character, I believe, for the poor king of Prussia, whom I pity personally because he is good. The queen is at Erfurt with the king. If she wants to see a battle, she will have that cruel pleasure. I am doing wonderfully well; I have already gained weight since my departure. However, I personally travel twenty and twenty-five leagues a day, by horse, by carriage, by whatever means. I go to bed at eight o'clock and rise at midnight. I think sometimes that you have not yet gone to bed.'

He was 37 years old, his stamina was astonishing and he handled his responsibilities as military leader and as head of state with extraordinary ability. On 5 October he set out from

Würzburg for Bamberg. Knowing that the Prussian forces consisted of a centre of 75,000 men under the command of the king, a left wing of 62,000 men and a right wing of 50,000 men – 187,000 men altogether – he had already decided on his plan. He would provoke the enemy into advancing towards the Rhine, and then, having assembled his own troops in the area of Bayreuth, would drive towards Berlin through Saxony, placing himself at the rear of the Prussians and, better still, at what would be the centre of the action if the Russians and Austrians got involved in the war; the king of Prussia, panicked by this advance towards his capital, would perhaps do a hasty about-face and would place himself in an inferior position, in complete disorder. That is precisely what happened. The Prussians hurried towards Erfurt to protect the road to Berlin through Magdeburg, the only one that was free. 'At last, the veil is torn away!' exclaimed Napoleon.

On the 8th the Prussians were north of the mountainous massif of the Thuringian Forest, and the French south of it. The Prussians moved to cut off his rear, but Napoleon forestalled them by attacking their flank at Jena. The king of Prussia retreated with his 75,000 men, protected by General de Hohenlohe with 46,000 men. In one night, Napoleon set up his artillery on the heights and, with 40,000 Frenchmen, crushed Hohenlohe, while Davout, with only 26,000 men, defeated Brunswick and Blücher at Auerstadt. The French cavalry completed the rout by attacking the fleeing soldiers from behind and taking thousands of prisoners. Of the Prussians that were sent into battle, 25,000 were killed or wounded and 100,000 were taken prisoner, including some twenty generals, Blücher among them. The Duke of Brunswick was mortally wounded.

Not a detail of this campaign escaped the eye of the master. On the night of the battle, holding a lantern, he went with the engineers who were building a road for the artillery up a steep slope and supervised the hoisting of cannons onto the Landgrafenberg Plateau, from which their thunder would rain down on the enemy.

Begun on the 8th, the Saxony campaign ended on 14 October 1806. On the 27th, dressed simply in a grey frock coat, Napoleon entered Berlin at the head of his marshals in full regalia. He wrote to the king again: 'It will be to my everlasting regret if two nations which for so many reasons should be friends are drawn into a conflict with so little justification. I would like to re-establish the old trust that existed between us.' The king and queen of Prussia, who had no more than 8,000 men left, were refugees at Königsberg, and their only hope lay in a victory by the Russian army, which occupied Warsaw and the right bank of the Vistula. Would the Russians allow themselves to be pushed into war? The czar, who was not intimidated by the Prussian rout, tried to get Austria involved in the adventure, but Emperor Francis would not be taken in: 'I will be frank,' he said. 'I will fight as late as possible.'

The Battle of Eylau

To intimidate his adversary, Napoleon marched on Poland. Warsaw was occupied by Murat on 28 November, after the withdrawal of the Russians, and Napoleon established his winter quarters there, welcomed as a saviour by the Poles, who hoped he would give them their independence.

The Russian commander, Bennigsen, thought he could take advantage of the situation to begin a turning manoeuvre along the coast and surround the French in the vicinity of Warsaw. The campaign therefore resumed, during a period of harsh cold, with Napoleon planning to outflank the Russians in their rear, cut them off from their bases and drive them into the sea. The encounter took place at Eylau; there were 54,000 Frenchmen with 200 cannons, against 72,000 Russians with 400 cannons. Using his favourite tactic, Napoleon would launch a frontal attack with three divisions, and an outflanking attack on the Russian left flank, on which he would then launch his exploitation force of two divisions of Murat's cavalry. With 10,000 men, Ney would prevent the approach of the remnants of the Prussian army.

The battle began with cannon fire, and losses were considerable on both sides. Then the three French divisions attacked at the centre and the cavalry of the Russian wing charged them, supported by the infantry. Everything was going as planned, and Napoleon sent Augereau's two divisions in against the disorganised Russian left. But what can genius do against the whims of nature? The snow began blowing so fiercely that it was impossible to see two paces ahead. The French troops strayed and stumbled into a big enemy battery, and were decimated and forced to retreat. Four thousand Russian grenadiers then attacked and took the Eylau cemetery, on a hill where Napoleon's head-quarters was located.

'What boldness! What boldness!' exclaimed Napoleon. 'Murat, will you let us be devoured by these people?' In what was one of the greatest cavalry charges in history, Murat's eighty squadrons began to move, the frozen earth ringing under their horses' hooves, and broke through the Russian lines. Was victory theirs? No, for 8,000 Prussians suddenly appeared and engaged the French centre. But fortunately Ney's 10,000 men were hot on the Prussians' heels, and they forced the Prussians and Russians to flee in disorder at about ten o'clock in the evening.

'The suffering of the enemy has been immense,' announced the *Bulletin* of 9 February, 'and ours has also been considerable.' Twenty-five thousand Russian corpses and 18,000 French ones lay in the snow. The Russian army had not been eliminated, but Napoleon's strategy, a well-organised cavalry and the decision to have Ney neutralise the Prussians, had once again given him the advantage.

Since the weather precluded mobile war, Napoleon decided to establish his winter quarters in order to reorganise his troops of some 80,000 men for the spring campaign of 1807, deal with the rest of the army, which was stationed in Germany, and take care of the affairs of the Empire. From a miserable shack at Osterode, he ran things at the Tuileries, sent reinforcements to Martinique, negotiated with the Ottoman Empire, made regulations regarding work on Sunday, studied the problem of aid for manufacturing, reinforced the defences of Boulogne, Brest and Antwerp, and reformed the recruitment of the Swiss regiments.

He also took up the matter of the kingdom of Naples, where his brother Joseph was playing sovereign, but without the talent for it. It was the perfect opportunity to rebuke this elder brother who was living comfortably off the successes of the French army. 'Staff officers, colonels and officers have not undressed for two months, some for four (I myself have gone two weeks without taking off my boots),' Napoleon wrote to him, 'amid the snow and mud, with no wine, no brandy, no bread, eating potatoes and meat, making long marches and countermarches, without any pleasures, fighting with bayonets, under volleys of grapeshot, very often forced to evacuate the wounded on sleighs exposed to the elements for fifty leagues. It is therefore a bad joke to compare us to the army of Naples, making war in the beautiful countryside of Naples, where there is wine, oil, bread, cloth, bed linens, society and even women. Having destroyed the Prussian monarchy, we are fighting against the rest of the Prussians, the Russians, the Kalmyk, the Cossacks, all those little peoples of the north who once invaded the Roman Empire. We are waging war in all its power and harshness. With all these great strains, everyone has been more or less sick. Personally, I have never been stronger, and I have put on weight.'

The Battle of Friedland

In May 1807 Napoleon tried once more to avoid battle through negotiation. He wrote to Czar Alexander: 'It is time for Europe to live in peace, sheltered from the malignant influence of England. Why this war? What good does it do for us to kill each other when our peoples have so much mutual esteem, so many reasons to be friends?' Alexander's reply, on 5 June, was a massive frontal attack with Bennigsen's 50,000 men, who were contained by Ney's 15,000 men. Russia and Prussia, which had received another million pounds from London and the promise of a British landing of 20,000 men in Pomerania, counted on the isolation of the French in order to beat them. Napoleon first tried to guess the intentions of his enemies. 'It all seems to me like the actions of a scatterbrain,' he wrote to one of his marshals. 'I will try to find the enemy and engage them in a general battle in order to put an end to this. Bennigsen, informed of his approach, withdrew to Heilsberg and entrenched himself there, but Napoleon attacked on 10 June and with 30,000 men dislodged the 90,000 Russians, who withdrew in disorder at about ten o'clock at night.

Then Napoleon decided to march on Königsberg by way of Friedland. But Lannes encountered the Russian army in the process of crossing the bridges over the Alle river in that city and held it off – with 26,000 Frenchmen against 75,000 Russians – and immediately warned the Emperor of the situation. Napoleon was jubilant: 'It is the anniversary of Marengo, and I will beat the Russians as I beat the Austrians.' He established a plan of attack: he would march on Domnau, north-east of Friedland, to wait for the enemy, while Murat and Soult headed towards Königsberg and Lannes cut off the eastward retreat of the troops he had stopped. Then a general realised that Bennigsen was taking his whole army across the bridges in order to establish himself on the left bank of the river and that he could be ready to give battle in an hour. 'Well, I am already ready,' replied Napoleon. 'I therefore have an hour on them, and since they want it, I am going to give it to them.'

He studied the map and examined the terrain through field glasses, and at two-thirty he was convinced that the whole Russian army was there. Expecting a two-day battle, he conveyed an order to Murat to join him with his two divisions of cuirassiers and Davout's corps. The day was drawing to an end, but the number of Russian troops was growing visibly, and some of the French officers, thinking that it would take some time to assemble the reinforcements, advised Napoleon to put off the attack and the battle to the next day. 'No,' replied Napoleon brusquely. 'We will not catch the enemy twice in such a mistake.'

The plan he conceived in a few hours left the enemy no chance. It was to take advantage of the enemy's movement to capture the bridges and cut off their retreat to the left bank of the river. There would be such confusion that, in spite of his numerical superiority, the Russian general would be unable to avoid a rout. In less than an hour, Napoleon arranged his troops as if on a chessboard: Ney on the right, Lannes at the centre, Mortier on the left to make a turning movement on the centre and the left. The orders of battle were summed up in a few words: 'We must always advance on the right and leave the initiative to Marshal Ney, who will wait for my orders to begin.'

Napoleon took Ney by the arm and showed him the city of Friedland and the Russian left that was growing on the shore: 'That is the goal. March without looking around you; penetrate that dense mass, whatever the cost; enter Friedland and take the bridges and do not worry about what may happen on the right, on the left, or in your rear. The army and I are there to take care of that.'

The marshal carried out his orders. At five-thirty in the afternoon, Napoleon gave the signal to neutralise the Russian artillery, which was delaying the advance of his troops, and shell the bridges. Ney entered the city while Mortier and Lannes charged the Russian right, which found itself encircled.

The enemy broke ranks; the soldiers who were not torn to pieces by grapeshot or cut down in the attack were burned to death or drowned. At eight-thirty in the evening, victory was assured, and Napoleon, though suffering from a cold, spent the night among his troops. The Russians had left 25,000 dead in the field.

The victory, Napoleon later wrote, was as decisive as those of Austerlitz and Jena. This is true, since on 19 June, five days later, the French armies were setting up camp on the left bank of the Niemen, on Russia's doorstep. The czar obtained an armistice and requested an interview with the Emperor of the French, which would lead to the Treaty of Tilsit, the peak of Napoleon's power.

The peace was signed on 8 July with Russia and on 9 July with Prussia. The czar joined the Continental System against England and recognised Napoleon's vassal kingdoms of Holland, Saxony and Westphalia as well as the constitution of the Grand Duchy of Warsaw. Not a bad result for a battle that was planned in an hour and won in five hours!

At Tilsit, Alexander expressed his eternal love for Napoleon: 'I have loved no one more than this man. The magic power of his gaze and the smile of his soul, which shows on his lips and in his eyes, have made me completely change direction. The great man of the century, the illustrious captain, is lovable, gentle, magnanimous. He is persuasive because he is sincere.' The czar's last sentence says it all. Napoleon was sincere. He had always been sincere in his desire for a universal and lasting peace. The bloodthirsty tyrants were on the other side, in England, Austria, Prussia and Russia.

At Tilsit, Napoleon, Alexander and Frederick drew up an agreement 'on the conduct which we must maintain so as to finally make England understand all the advantages that it would gain from peace'. England responded to the offers of peace and friendship in two ways. First, on 2 September 1807, the Royal Navy with its heavy guns destroyed Copenhagen, even though Denmark was a neutral country. Hundreds of men, women and children were crushed under the rubble while the officers of the Royal Navy toasted their king each time a shell fell on the defenceless population. Then, on 11 November 1807 England decreed that ships from neutral countries had to pay duty and purchase merchandise in British ports. There were soon 4,000 sailors from American merchant ships rotting in British ports, victims of these tyrants of the seas.

The Battle of Somosierra

After a victory by Marshal Bessières at Medina de Ríoseco, Joseph Bonaparte was 'promoted' king of Spain and took possession of his throne protected by a shield of 80,000 French soldiers – most of them conscripts without experience under fire. Then the timorous General Dupont was beaten by the Spanish and forced to surrender at Baylen, in Andalucia. The news resounded throughout Europe, as this was the first setback for the victors of Rivoli and Austerlitz. It was also the signal for a general withdrawal of French forces and the flight of King Joseph. The English, commanded by Wellington, landed in Portugal and drove out the French troops under Junot. Napoleon, who was in Bordeaux, flew into a rage: 'What do a few insurgents matter to me? I will deal with them with my dragoons! In Spain I will find the Pillars of Hercules, not the limits of my power.'

He first had to rush to Erfurt for a conference with the czar, one of the goals of which he described as follows to his minister of external affairs before setting out: 'I want to come back free to do as I wish in Spain.' The resulting treaty, which included peace overtures to England by France and Russia, did in fact leave his hands free in the peninsula. In fifty days, the Grande Armée was present all the way from Poland to the foot of the Pyrenees.

The Emperor himself was also present. On 8 November he went to Vittoria to find Joseph's government threatened from all sides by rebel bands subsidised by England. As always, his arrival changed the situation; in two weeks, the Spaniards were beaten three times. On 29 November the Battle of Somosierra took place, recalling the Great Saint Bernard Pass with the battle added; during the march from the Sierra de Guadarrama, between Old and New Castile, on the high, winding roads, a force of Spaniards fell on the French infantry, and Napoleon only had the 150 men of his escort of Polish light horse guards. 'Remove that on the double!' he cried. The Spaniards fled, leaving the way clear to Madrid, which surrendered at the beginning of December.

From there, Napoleon intended to march on Lisbon, because 30,000 English troops under John Moore, who had replaced

Wellington, were threatening Soult between Salamanca and Valladolid. The plan was good since it would allow him finally to fight the redcoats in a pitched battle. He sent Ney as a scout, and Moore, to avoid being caught between the two French armies, had to withdraw in disorder to La Coruña to re-embark. Napoleon hurried the march to thwart this plan, and he was only twelve hours from the enemy on 1 January 1809, when he received the news that Austria was re-arming and that in Paris his ministers Talleyrand and Fouché were plotting to replace him, in case of his death, with Murat. He had to change his plans abruptly; he could not stay any longer in faraway Spain. He decided to entrust Soult with 'throwing the English into the sea' and finishing a campaign he considered won. But with him gone, the command slowly became more and more disorganised, and the English escaped, though not without losing their general and their equipment.

In political terms this expedition was a disaster, since the war would soon resume and spread throughout the peninsula, with London fanning the flames. But in military terms, it carried the mark of Napoleon's military talent. His presence in the field was worth several divisions. If he did not succeed in destroying the Spanish military potential, it was because for the first time in his life he had found himself facing an enemy that would not fight a pitched battle – and this was because it did not exist as a body. All the cannons of the Grande Armée could do nothing against an army of shadows that was happy to knife soldiers after dark and to chase down wounded men and stragglers and finish them off after mutilating them most cruelly.

The Battle of Wagram

In 1809 Austria, dreaming of avenging its defeats of 1805 and rich with funds provided by England – always England – committed the folly of entering the war, believing it could take advantage of France's difficulties in Spain and the anti-French agitation that was taking shape in Germany. It was able to assemble 500,000 well-trained men, to which Napoleon could oppose only 300,000 of which 200,000 were Frenchmen – and that included the class of 1810, which was conscripted early – since his best troops, about 300,000 men, including the Guard, were held up in Spain.

For the first three months of the year, when all the indications were that Austria was preparing for a campaign, he organised the movements of his army, which would be assembled at Regensburg, an ideal strategic waiting position from which he could launch an attack on the enemy whatever plan it adopted. On 9 April the Austrians crossed the Isar at Braunau without declaring war. In one week, if he was bold, their commander, the Archduke Charles, could cover the 100 kilometres between Braunau and Regensburg and strike the French army while it was still assembling under the command of Major General Berthier, a brilliant chief of staff but a mediocre commander in chief, who did nothing but report to the Emperor: 'The enemy has appeared in force along the Isar, which they have crossed. They seem to have plans on our right and our left. I await Your Majesty impatiently. It is the time for you to decide your campaign plan.'

Napoleon left Paris on the 13th and travelled as quickly as possible, arriving in Donauwörth on the 17th. He took the situation in hand and galvanized his soldiers, announcing, 'I arrive among you with the speed of the eagle.' He found the army divided into two corps, under Davout and Masséna, more than 100 kilometres apart, and hurried to start them marching to converge at a point where they could stop the enemy advance. On the 20th the two corps of the Austrian left were beaten by Lannes at Abensberg and pushed back across the Isar. The next day, Napoleon rushed northward and joined Davout at Eckmühl after having written to the marshal, 'I am determined to exterminate the army of Prince Charles today or at the latest tomorrow.' What was said was done. On the evening of the 22nd, attacked by forty French squadrons and thirty-four from Bavaria and Württemberg, the enemy fled towards Regensburg. In three days, the archduke lost 50,000 men and one hundred cannons. He had to cross the Danube and take refuge in Bohemia, leaving the road to Vienna undefended.

The political consequences were significant, since Bavaria, Württemberg and Saxony, which Austria was trying to take away from Napoleon, remained his allies. But worse was to come for Austria, because on the 13th Vienna was occupied by the French, and the Emperor found himself, as in 1805, at Schönbrunn, the palace of the old and illustrious Habsburg monarchy, issuing a proclamation to his army which took a hard tone towards the vanquished: 'The princes of the house of Lorraine have abandoned their capital, not as honourable soldiers who yield to the circumstances and reverses of war, but as treacherous wretches pursuing their own downfall! . . . Soldiers, let us be good to the poor peasants and to this good people that has so much right to our esteem. Let us not be arrogant in our success; let us see it as proof of that justice which punishes those who are unworthy and false.'

To impose peace on Emperor Francis, Napoleon conceived a bold and effective new plan to prevent the troops of the Archduke Charles from joining up with those of the Archduke John, which were arriving from Italy, and to block the way to Hungary, where the Austrians could regroup. He would soon make Essling and Wagram, the names of towns, titles for his marshals. In order to win a decisive battle against Charles, Napoleon decided, using his reinforcements from Italy, to go along the left bank of the Danube to the island of Lobau, south-east of Vienna. The troops, under the command of Masséna, moved on the night of 20 May and some 30,000 men occupied Aspern and Essling. A sudden swelling of the river carried off their pontoon bridge, which was 700 metres long, and the archduke, forewarned, attacked the French with 90,000 men. But Masséna and Lannes held them off until evening. The bridge was rebuilt during the night, and in the morning of the 22nd Napoleon joined them with another 30,000 men and sent Lannes against the Austrian centre, which the archduke had taken troops from to attack the French wings. At eight o'clock the pontoon bridge was carried away again, and all movement of reinforcements or ammunition became impossible. The combat was fierce. Essling was captured and lost nine times. Marshal Lannes was fatally wounded. 'Lannes, do you recognise me?' asked Napoleon. 'Yes, Sire . . . You are going to lose your best friend . . . But you, live and save the army.'

And that is precisely what happened. For the first time in his career, Napoleon held council with his marshals. They advised him to go back across the Danube and regroup the army near Vienna, but that would have meant admitting failure and he would not hear of it. He decided to retrench on the island of Lobau, wait for reinforcements from Germany and Italy, rebuild the bridges and resume the fight on the same terrain but under better conditions. And this time, the stakes would be high, for Austria had proclaimed victory, Italy and Germany were starting to move, Prussia was becoming emboldened again, and the czar was issuing 'demands' concerning Poland. If the new campaign ended in defeat, there would be war throughout the continent. 'The monarchs have arranged to meet on my grave,' joked Napoleon, 'but they do not dare to meet.'

For a month and half, Lobau was a fortified camp, to which the Emperor went every day from Schönbrunn; three bridges protected by stockades straddled the main branch of the Danube, and five portable bridges, designed by Napoleon himself, were ready to be thrown across the smaller branch, where the landing would take place. At the end of May the army of Italy arrived and was soon joined by a corps stationed in Dalmatia, commanded by Marmont, so that at the beginning of July the French army was about 140,000 strong. The Austrians, on the other shore, had 150,000 men and a reserve of 20,000 at Pressburg.

On 4 July, at night, the bridges were set up and, under cover of a hail storm, Napoleon crossed to the opposite shore of the Danube with his 140,000 men including 25,000 cavalry and 550 cannons, the biggest concentration of forces ever seen on a battlefield. From the river to Wagram, he deployed them in a fan eight kilometres long, and he spent the whole night of the 5th conferring with his marshals. He had not slept for four days, but his mind was as clear as if he had just left his office at the Tuileries. He explained his plan, which was precise and rigorous: there would be a frontal attack by the army of Italy, followed by an outflanking attack on the enemy's left by Davout's four divisions to cut off any retreat. Masséna, facing the archduke's right wing, was to carry out a secondary diversionary action. The reserve would include Marmont's corps and the Guard, which had come back from Spain – about 10,000 men.

The Austrians attacked first, at four o'clock in the morning on 6 July. Masséna was wounded and thrown from his horse, and had to command from his carriage. The situation was uncertain and difficult when Napoleon arrived. He sat close to Masséna and then left by carriage to inspect the enemy positions to try to figure out their intentions. 'The Emperor,' wrote Marmont, 'was perfectly calm, although he read in the faces of his staff the concern caused by the victorious march of the enemy's right flank.' Napoleon was calm because he had made a new plan: Masséna would swing around to his left, march towards the

Danube and attack the Austrian right. To replace him in the field, where his movement would create a gap of about four kilometres, they would set up a battery of a hundred pieces, behind which the army of Italy would be prepared to advance.

At eleven o'clock he gave the signal for the general offensive, after making sure that on his own right Davout had pushed back the enemy left wing. 'Then,' wrote Marmont, 'the Emperor, still impassive, turned to me and said, "Run and tell Masséna to attack everything ahead of him, and the battle is won."' Another witness, General Paulin, heard Napoleon calmly announce the same good news, 'The battle is won!' and he recounted: 'For three quarters of an hour to an hour, I saw with my own eyes a spectacle that filled me with the greatest astonishment. The emperor himself lay down in a furrow on the parched ground, face down in his hands, and in the midst of us all remained motionless as if asleep until the major general, who had gathered all the reports he was waiting for from the various points of the battlefield, told him that the positions of Neusiedl and Wagram, which had been defended most resolutely by the enemy, had been taken.' At three o'clock the Archduke Charles ordered a retreat and withdrew, though in order, towards Prague. 'There has been enough blood shed,' concluded Napoleon. 'Let us make peace.'

The treaty was signed in Vienna on 13 October. It took the Illyrian Provinces, with three and a half million inhabitants, from Austria. Soon Emperor Francis would even be more or less forced to give the victor his daughter's hand, and an archduchess of the Habsburg-Lorraine house, Marie-Antoinette's own niece, would be Empress of the French and wife of the victor of Wagram. This would provide Edmond Rostand, in *L'Aiglon*, with a nice line for the Duke of Reichstadt, the son of the Emperor, to the chancellor of Austria: 'You cannot have anything but hatred for me, since I am Wagram in the flesh.'

The Russian campaign

The star's rise ended above the plain of Wagram. It was circumstances, more than any diminution of talent, that led to setback after setback; during the terrible Russian campaign and the campaign in France, Napoleon again demonstrated his intellectual ability and his mastery of the military art. In 1805, after Austerlitz, he had declared, laughing: 'One has only a certain time for making war. I give myself another six years, and then I will have to stop.' In 1812, when the Russian campaign that would seal his fate was about to begin, he was 43 years old, and his imagination was still lively, his judgement quick, his vision almost infallible.

The confrontation between France and Russia was entirely the doing of the czar, a strange character, mystical yet cynical, timorous and vain, full of duplicity, and both dazzled and antagonised by Napoleon's glory, since he himself dreamed of playing a leading role in Europe. Beaten, he had used persuasion to save himself, and Napoleon, who was such a good judge of character, had let himself be won over by the man he described as 'a very handsome, good young Emperor' – though he would reduce this later, on St Helena, to the less flattering description of 'Greek of the late Byzantine Empire'. In 1811, under the influence of his family and his courtiers, who were anglophiles and violently hostile to France, the czar decided to break with the man they said was working for the ruination of Russia. Napoleon made a last-ditch effort for peace. He wrote, 'I hope to avoid war; I am firm in the sentiments which united us at Tilsit and Erfurt.' But Alexander was deaf to all peace offers. Even after Napoleon, desperate, had to mobilize, he continued to hope until the last moment that his display of force would bring the czar to his senses.

When everything was ready, around the middle of 1812, the army of Italy, commanded by viceroy Eugène de Beauharnais, began moving on its long route. On 9 May Napoleon left Paris. He was at the head of 423,000 men and 1,150 cannons, a huge war machine in which the Guard rubbed shoulders with Dutch lancers, Prussian hussars, Hessian dragoons, Polish light horse guards, Portuguese and Bavarian chasseurs, Italians, Croats, Swiss, Saxons and even Spaniards. Facing them on the other side of the Niemen were Alexander's three armies: that of Barclay de Tolly, 150,000 strong, with 560 cannons, at Vilna; that of Bagration, 60,000 strong, with 200 cannons at Minsk; and that of Tormasov, 40,000 strong, in the Ukraine; there was also a fourth army of 60,000 men in Moldavia. But Alexander's trump card was Russia's immensity and its climate and the proclamation of a holy war, which meant that the peasants retreating before the invader would burn their houses and crops, leaving the land bare.

'Your empire,' said one of his generals to the czar, 'has two powerful defences: its vast size and its climate. The emperor of Russia will be formidable in Moscow, terrible in Kazan, invincible in Tobolsk.' Did Napoleon suspect the existence of this terrible ally, the cold? If he did not think of the fate of Charles XII, who was vanquished more quickly by snow, famine and disease than by Peter the Great's Cossacks, a Russian parliamentarian who had come to negotiate reminded him of it in no uncertain terms. 'Why are there so many churches to Moscow?' asked Napoleon. 'Because our people is devout.' 'Bah! People aren't religious any more. What is the road to Moscow?' 'All roads lead to Rome, Sire. You take whatever road you like to Moscow. Charles XII went by way of Poltava.'

After spending three weeks in Vilna mustering his troops and letting them rest, Napoleon set out and made a sudden attack on Bagration, who was near Minsk, but his brother Jérôme's incompetence let the Russians escape encirclement. On 23 July Davout had similar problems; he sent the Russians into full retreat at Mogilyov, but was unable to prevent them from withdrawing to Smolensk, where Barclay waited. Napoleon, whose plan as always was bold but logical, decided to go back up the Dnieper to Smolensk and attack the two armies, which he was not afraid to confront in a pitched battle, and cut them off from Moscow. This encounter at Smolensk, which cost the lives of 70,000 Frenchmen and 10,000 Russians, did not solve anything, since the Russians burned the city and vanished onto the steppes towards Moscow.

Dismayed by these first setbacks and by the resolute advance of the enemy, the czar replaced Barclay with Kutuzov, who had been defeated at Austerlitz and who, knowing Napoleon's tactics, accepted a pitched battle at Borodino on 7 September, also known as the Battle of the Moskva River. At last! At two o'clock in the morning, Napoleon had a proclamation read to his troops: 'Soldiers, this is the battle you wanted. Henceforth victory depends on you. It will give us abundance, good winter quarters, and a quick return to the homeland! Conduct yourselves as you did at Austerlitz, at Friedland and at Vitebsk and Smolensk, and may the most distant posterity cite your conduct on this day; may it be said of you, "He was at that great battle under the walls of Moscow".'

What the soldiers, tormented by dysentery and typhus, did not know, however, was that their leader had received news of the disaster of Arapiles, in Spain, where Wellington had defeated Marmont, and that he himself was feverish, that he was suffering from a chill, continually taking burning hot drinks and shivering like a sick man, and that an aide-de-camp had found him at dawn, prostrate, his head in his hands, muttering, 'What is war? A trade of barbarians, in which the whole art consists of being stronger at a single point.'

At five o'clock in the morning, though, he was on his horse and taking a position on a hill with his staff. Finally the torture of uncertainty was going to end! He had available 127,000 thousand men and 580 cannons, and the Russians had about the same numbers. In order to carry out the turning manoeuvre that he was so successful with, he would have needed 40,000 more men. He would make do with an outflanking attack, entrusted to Poniatowski and his 10,000 men.

At ten o'clock the army of Italy had overwhelmed the Russians on the left, and Murat and Ney had taken the fortifications on the right. Reinforcements would be needed since the Russian centre was beginning to give way. 'Things are not clear enough,' grumbled Napoleon. 'I want to see more clearly on my chessboard.' Would he hesitate? 'Since *he* no longer wages war himself, since *he* is no longer a general, since he acts the Emperor everywhere, *he* should return to the Tuileries and let us be generals for him!' cried Ney.

The Russians took advantage of Napoleon's wavering to counter-attack. Bagration was killed. Murat charged wildly. Ney followed with the infantry. At three o'clock victory would have been assured if it had been possible to pursue Kutuzov and wipe out his forces. That would have required sending in the Guard. 'I do not want to have my Guard demolished,' protested Napoleon. 'Eight hundred leagues from France, you do not risk your last reserve.' Age had made him cautious, and disease indecisive. There were 30,000 dead Frenchmen and 60,000 dead Russians in the field, but no evidence of victory; no flags and no prisoners; nothing but a field covered with corpses.

The Emperor was sad, despondent even, and still shivering. Was it sickness? Disappointment? His generals muttered that this success was a soldiers' victory' and not 'a general's victory', and

Murat stated that he 'did not recognise the genius of Napoleon'. Eugène de Beauharnais spoke of 'the indecision shown by the Emperor'. The truth is provided in a book by the Comte de Ségur: 'Since the eve of the battle, the Emperor had been suffering from an attack of dysuria.' According to another witness, Napoleon himself had declared to a doctor: 'Well, you see I am getting old; my legs are swollen, and I can barely urinate.' Another witness spoke of a 'constant dry cough, of difficult, uneven breathing'. At the height of the battle, towards noon, he had eaten only a crust of bread and drunk a small glass of Chambertin; he had no appetite. The next day, he had lost his voice, and the man who wanted to dictate to seven people at once was reduced to scribbling his orders. How right he had been fifteen years earlier in Italy when he said, 'Health is essential for war and nothing can replace it.'

On 14 September, however, Napoleon was in Moscow, and his first words upon seeing the city with its multicoloured domes and rich palaces, were: 'So here, finally, is this famous city.' A pause, then, 'It is about time!' The deserted capital, emptied of its 300,000 inhabitants, who had fled to the east, was ablaze for a week, set on fire by its governor. It did not matter. From the Kremlin, which he took over, Napoleon, certain that the campaign was won, went back to administering the Empire, each day receiving letters brought from Paris in fourteen days by exhausted couriers. He even signed a decree to reorganise the Comédie-Française, perhaps to let Parisians know that the eye of the master was still on them.

However, the Cossacks were already attacking the extremely over extended lines of communications, the stores of the Grande Armée, the reinforcements and the depots. And time was passing. Food was becoming short. How could this man, such a shrewd politician, cling to the idea that the loss of the capital would force the czar to negotiate? Russians were already warning the French soldiers, with deliberate cruelty, 'In two weeks, your fingernails will fall off, your weapons will fall from your numb, half-dead hands.'

A decision had to be made, a bold one, and quickly. Should they spend the winter in the city? What would people say in Paris and throughout Europe? What plots and schemes would they cook up in London? The concerns of the head of state still took precedence over those of the commanding general. Who, indeed, could guess the consequences of an absence of six months? What would the Austrians and Prussians do? Should they march north to take St Petersburg? The marshals objected, citing the season, the food shortage, the deserted road. Retreat to Poland? That would be an admission of diplomatic failure and military defeat.

As Ségur wrote: 'His pride, his policies and perhaps his health gave him the worst advice of all, which was to take no one's advice and to try to manoeuvre with the murderous weather.' Daru, too, was surprised not to find in the Emperor 'that power of decision making which was lively, agile and quick as the circumstances: they say that his genius is no longer capable of yielding to circumstances; they are criticising his natural persistence, which led to his rise and which will be his downfall'. He temporised because he had just experienced the greatest disappointment of his career. Accustomed to laying down the law from the very palaces of his enemies after occupying them militarily, he was astonished by the silence of Alexander, to whom he was making pressing offers of peace.

General Winter decided for him. On 13 October the first frost came, and Kutuzov, who had rested his army and dressed it for the cold and received reinforcements, attacked Murat a few kilometres from the capital. Facing the risk of being besieged within the walls of the Kremlin without provisions or ammunition, Napoleon decided on the 19th to retreat. He abandoned his prize to take the road for Poland with most of his troops, followed closely by Kutuzov, who was biding his time and who, when he was urged to go on the offensive, replied, 'Let the snow come.'

In the disaster of the retreat, Napoleon's conduct was exemplary: on foot, holding a baton, in temperatures of minus twenty or thirty degrees, with birds falling frozen from the sky, he walked in silence at the head of his men. A grenadier was saddened to see him struggle in the snow: 'I do not cry because I will leave my bones in this accursed country. I cry to have seen our Emperor walking on foot holding a baton, he who is so great, who has made us so proud!'

With his army of ghosts, he managed to beat Kutuzov again at Maloyaroslavets, but he told one of his close advisors: 'This is becoming serious. I keep beating the Russians, but it does not end things.' It took so many plans, so many sleepless nights to get the remnants of his army away from the Russian winter and the traps set by Kutuzov, who followed like a jackal and who cheerfully announced: 'The end of Napoleon's destiny is irrevocably marked. The meteor will be extinguished in the marshes of the Berezina in the presence of the whole Russian army.' That did not happen. Napoleon pretended to prepare to cross the river near Borisov, but in fact he crossed it at Studianka, twenty-five kilometres to the north. With 20,000 emaciated, dazed soldiers, he managed to win a few more fights. In one day Marshal Victor routed 40,000 Russians.

And then one morning at the beginning of December, close to the Polish border, Napoleon confided to his Master of the Horse: 'In the current state of affairs, I could not impose anything on Europe except from the palace of the Tuileries.' In Paris, a republican general had tried to overthrow the regime and the vanquished powers were ready to take up arms again. It was not by wandering the roads of Poland with the remnants of his army that Napoleon would regain control of the situation. He put Murat in command and set out on the snow-covered roads in a sleigh, and on 13 January 1813 he was back in his capital, where he admitted frankly to his ministers: 'Fortune dazzled me. I let myself be led instead of following the plan I had devised . . . I was in Moscow. I believed I would sign a peace treaty there. I stayed there too long. I thought I would obtain in a year what could only have been done in two campaigns. I made a serious mistake, but I have the means to repair it.'

Lützen and Bautzen

Napoleon resumed the campaign. He assembled a new army by conscripting the class of 1813, mobilizing the National Guard, merging the troops from Germany and Italy and the remnants of the army from Russia, reinforcing the Old Guard and the Young Guard and equipping a force of artillery. 'Imagination is confounded,' wrote one of his ministers, 'when one thinks of all the work that had to be done, and the resources of all kinds that had to be found to raise, clothe, equip and supply such an army with ammunition in the space of five months.' Once ready, the army marched against the Russians and won two or three victories.

But Napoleon had not taken into consideration the defections that would result from his defeat by the snow. Prussia went over to the Russian camp, and England tempted those who were hesitant with its gold. Napoleon's conscripts, 18-year-old kids facing fire, rain and marches through the mud for the first time, found themselves fighting Marshal von Blücher's Prussians as well as the Russians.

On 15 April Napoleon left Saint-Cloud. On the 25th he was in Erfurt and he established his plan, dividing his armies into three groups that would converge on Lützen and Bautzen. On 2 May two armies joined west of Leipzig, the plan being to attack the rear of the coalition forces, which were in Lützen. Unfortunately, Ney, who was supposed to protect this bold movement, was engaged by superior forces, and Napoleon had to rush to join him and quickly devise other tactics. Ney would support the attack on the enemy's left; Macdonald, with 22,000 men, would make a wheeling attack against the Russo-Prussian right; and with his 30,000 men, the Emperor would break through the central front when he judged that the moment had come 'which decides the gain or loss of a battle'. This was done. 'The fire became frightful and the enemy gave ground on all sides. The enemy's cavalry, infantry and artillery were all in retreat.'

The coalition forces withdrew towards Dresden and Messen, perplexed because, while Napoleon's lack of cavalry prevented him from taking prisoners, he had given a dazzling demonstration of his imagination and his possibilities. 'That was probably the day when he took the greatest personal risks of his whole career on the battlefield,' wrote Marmont.

Since the Russians and Prussians were entrenched at Bautzen, he decided to attack them there and engage a classic battle that would force them to surrender or flee. Ney, coming from the north, would advance on the rear of the enemy while he himself attacked the front.

Unfortunately, Ney let himself be drawn into fighting on his right instead of taking the position that had been assigned to him, which would have allowed them to encircle the coalition forces, who fled without leaving any prisoners. On a hill, lost among the Prussians, an English officer named Hudson Lowe saw the Emperor in the distance, surrounded by his marshals.

The Battle of Leipzig

That Battle of Bautzen on 21 May 1813 was a victory still, and one that threw a fright into the chancelleries, since the man they had believed defeated had once again been able to turn the situation in his favour. To gain time, the diplomats appealed for an armistice, which Napoleon granted them, and which was to be followed by peace talks in Prague. But this was only a ploy and the fighting resumed on 11 August, with Austria going on the offensive with its 230,000 men, plus Blücher's 100,000 Russians and Prussians and Bernadotte's 160,000 Russians and Swedes. Bernadotte had been taught everything he knew about strategy and tactics by the man who had made him a marshal of France and crown prince of Sweden – and whom he had betrayed.

To contain these half-million men deployed in an arc opposite him, Napoleon divided his forces, and since he could not personally be everywhere he delegated his powers to Davout, Ney and Oudinot. That prompted this pertinent remark by Marmont: 'With the creation of three distinct armies, Your Majesty is renouncing the advantages provided by his presence on the battlefield, and I fear greatly that the day Your Majesty wins one victory, he will lose two.'

This turned out to be prophetic. While Napoleon defeated the Austrians before Dresden – having made his Guard march 160 kilometres in four days – Oudinot, Macdonald and Ney were beaten by Bernadotte, their former comrade. Then in September, having received reinforcements of 60,000 men, the Russians, Swedes, Prussians and Austrians decided to make a converging march on Leipzig, where Napoleon would only have 150,000 young, tired soldiers against their 300,000 men. But Napoleon had a plan ready. With his back to the city, he would contain Blücher in the north and concentrate his attack on the Austrians in the south.

But this time his numerical inferiority was too great; after very hard fighting the coalition forces launched an offensive with 180,000 men. Then Napoleon's Saxon troops deserted and turned against their former comrades; the Württembergers also deserted. These defections allowed Blücher and Bernadotte to join forces. One hundred and twenty thousand dead lay on the ground, half of them French, half allies. Napoleon, lacking ammunition, had to order the withdrawal of his exhausted, hungry soldiers.

The French campaign

By forced march, Napoleon withdrew to the left bank of the Rhine, along the way punishing the Bavarian troops who had the audacity to try to block his way. He believed that his enemies would not launch a winter campaign, but on 21 December, after some hesitation, they crossed the river. 'The name of Napoleon was still so formidable,' wrote Chateaubriand, 'that the enemy armies crossed the Rhine in terror; they constantly looked behind them to make sure that retreat would still be possible.' Bernadotte invaded Belgium; Blücher, Lorraine; Schwarzenberg, Switzerland and Burgundy; while Wellington, the master of Spain, set up his headquarters at Saint-Jean-de-Luz, just within France's borders.

Napoleon fought one against five during this French campaign, which was perhaps his greatest, and his genius and daring still won him a few victories. But still, he had only the beardless youths known as the 'Marie-Louise', trained in two weeks and clothed with whatever could be found in the depots, against the well-fed, well-trained allies emboldened by their success.

First Blücher and Schwarzenberg made the mistake of separating and planning to meet in Paris, with each choosing his own route. 'The face of things will change,' exclaimed Napoleon. 'I will defeat Blücher tomorrow.' Using forced marches, he separately attacked and beat the two columns that were sweeping through eastern France. He won nine victories in forty-five days – Brienne, Champaubert, Montmirail, Château-Thierry, Vauchamps, Mormant, Montereau, Craonne and Reims. When Blücher stretched his army out along the shores of the Marne as if on parade, Napoleon attacked, destroying one of his corps on 10 February at Champaubert and another on the 11th at Montmirail. On the 14th, at Vauchamps, he forced the old Prussian generalissimo himself to flee and his troops to fall back in disorder towards Châlons, leaving behind 18,000 prisoners, equipment and cannons. Then Napoleon made a sudden about-face to deal with the Austrians and Russians who were making their way along the banks of the Seine. He beat the Russians at Mormant, dispersed the Württembergers at Montereau and drove General Schwarzenberg himself towards Chaumont with such force that he asked for an armistice. Napoleon refused, exclaiming, 'I am closer to Vienna than the Emperor of Austria is to Paris!'

To one of his marshals, Augereau, who tarried in Lyon instead of joining up with him, he wrote, 'I destroyed three armies and three times saved the capital . . . There is no longer any question of acting as we have recently; we have to put our boots on again and regain the resolution we had in 1793.' His victories had emboldened the peasants, who fought back against the invaders as the Spanish had done, by attacking isolated, fleeing or wounded soldiers. The allies wondered if it might be preferable to negotiate, but London again showed the gleam of its gold, promising to pay six million pounds a year until victory.

Blücher, who had reassembled his fleeing forces, headed towards Paris, which was undefended, but Napoleon followed him, forcing him back across the Aisne and trapping him on the plateau of Craonne, where he beat him again with 50,000 men against 100,000. Three days later a Prusso-Russian corps was put to flight near Reims, but Oudinot and Macdonald were outflanked by the Austrians, who had occupied Troyes, and the Emperor was in danger of encirclement. He got out his map, moved the coloured pins representing the armies and devised a last stratagem worthy of the Napoleonic genius. He would march east, get reinforcements from French garrisons, and turn around and attack the rear of the enemy who were marching on Paris, cutting off their retreat. First, at Arcis-sur-Aube, he provoked the Austrians to slow their march and, with 20,000 men against their 90,000, fought a battle with them and then crossed the Aube towards Bar-le-Duc. He was very cheerful and declared to one of his ministers: 'See how these brave peasants rise up and kill the Cossacks from every direction! They are an example to us, let us follow them. You will take part in wonderful things. I will soon have 100,000 men and I will attack Blücher or Schwarzenberg, whichever one is nearer; I will crush him, and the peasants of Burgundy will finish him off . . . If I am mistaken, well, we will die, but we will die with our honour intact.'

In fact, Schwarzenberg wanted to go to meet him, but Blücher preferred to march on Paris. They hesitated. A few weeks later, the czar acknowledged: 'At the gates of Paris all the generals were of the opinion not to attempt to take the capital. They said we had barely enough ammunition for one day, because Emperor Napoleon had outflanked us and separated us from all our armies' equipment.'

Napoleon's plan was discovered when a dispatch rider with his messages fell into enemy hands. The coalition forces marched on the capital, sending only a few troops east to fool the man they still dreaded. Three enemy columns were soon deployed around Paris. Was all lost? No! Napoleon was warned and rushed there with his army. If only the city could hold out for two days, the besiegers, caught between Marmont's corps and Napoleon's soldiers arriving by forced march, would be compelled to fight. Marmont, who had been won over to Talleyrand's betrayal, capitulated, and that campaign was over.

Two weeks later, at Fontainebleau, the Emperor abdicated and with tears in his voice made his farewells to what remained of his men, the conquerors of Europe: 'Soldiers, for twenty years, I have always found you worthy of honour and glory. You have always conducted yourselves with courage and loyalty. Again in these recent times, you have demonstrated this . . . I am leaving . . . I will always follow your destiny and that of France . . . I will write of the great things we have done together.'

And he went away to 'reign' on the island of Elba, where his presence continued to antagonise the monarchs of Europe and from which he had to flee to escape assassination or deportation to some more remote island. His return from the south of France to Paris was not strictly speaking a campaign, but the speed of his march, the dazzling success of the enterprise and the effect of his presence on the soldiers made it a dramatic event that deserves to be described.

The return from Elba

He landed on the coast of Provence in the morning of 1 March 1815, with 1,100 men who had followed him to his short-lived kingdom, and immediately distributed a proclamation that his soldiers had handwritten during the crossing, which was addressed mainly to his former comrades-in-arms: 'Soldiers, we have not been vanquished. In my exile, I heard your voice. Your general has returned to you, come and rejoin him. Display that tricolour cockade you wore during our days of greatness. Victory will be on the march and the eagle and the national flag will fly from every steeple to the towers of Notre-Dame. Then you will be able to boast of what you have done, you will be the liberators of your homeland.'

That whole day, while his troops were landing, he simply sat in a field bordered with olive trees, studying the map and tracing his triumphal route through the Alps, the most difficult route but the safest one politically, since the region was teeming with his supporters, and at about eleven o'clock on the brightly moonlit night he gave the signal for departure. He walked in front, a baton in his hand, sometimes stumbling on a frozen stone or a patch of snow. 'Not a rifle shot,' he ordered his battalion, 'not a drop of blood!'

Victory, as on the battlefield, depended on speed. On the 3rd he was in Castellane, on the 4th in Digne and on the 5th in Gap, having covered close to 200 kilometres without meeting the slightest resistance. The drama took place near Grenoble, where the military commander had sent a battalion of the Fifth Line Regiment to take up a position at Laffrey in order to block his way. Napoleon ordered his men to halt. The two forces were face to face, soldiers who had perhaps fought side by side at Austerlitz or elsewhere and who today were looking at each other challengingly. One mistake, and blood would flow. The silence was heavy. Only an action could break the tension. Napoleon made the decision. He went forward alone, terribly pale, his step firm and calm. When he came within a few metres of the king's troops, he stopped and asked, 'Soldiers of the Fifth, do you recognise me?' He was answered with a few shouts. He unbuttoned his greatcoat, exposing his chest. 'If one of you wants to kill his Emperor, he can do it, here I am.' It was a bold gesture, and one of quiet assurance, but he knew what he was doing. He had a perfect understanding of the soul of the people. It should be remembered that the Fifth Line Regiment had fought under his command during the first Italian campaign.

'Fire!' ordered a royalist officer. In vain. The soldiers threw down their weapons, rushed forward shouting 'Vive l'Empereur!' and fell on their kneels around their former commander. 'It's all over,' Napoleon said to one of his entourage. In ten days, I will be in the Tuileries.' He had invaded France singlehandedly.

At Grenoble he was already at the head of 7,000 men, but there was a moment of anxiety. 'There is no battle,' he said later, 'in which I have run more risks than when entering Grenoble. The soldiers rushed at me with gestures of fury and rage, and I shuddered for an instant; it looked as if I was going to be torn to pieces. But it was only the frenzy of love and joy.

He had covered 400 kilometres in five days. And over what roads! And in what weather! On the 10th he entered Lyon in a carriage and took power again, and issued decrees, including one re-establishing the tricolour flag. He set out again with 14,000 men, and on the evening of the 20th, his son's birthday, he entered the Tuileries, lifted from his carriage and carried to his office by fifty pairs of arms amid an enormous clamour. With victory his only ally, with no plan, no money, no artillery, he had reconquered his throne and driven out the Bourbons. His old enemy, Chateaubriand, observed with a mixture of admiration, alarm and jubilation, 'When he passed the Niemen leading 400,000 infantrymen and 100,000 horses to blow up the palace of the czars in Moscow, it was less astonishing than when, breaking his banishment and throwing his chains in the face of kings, he came alone from Cannes to Paris to sleep peacefully in the Tuileries.'

He was immediately declared an outlaw in Europe by the enemy monarchs – one wonders on the basis of what law – although the first diplomatic act of his government was to make known in all the courts his desire to maintain 'an honourable tranquillity'. Already, the Russian, Austrian, Prussian and British general staffs were preparing their war plans and committing themselves to maintain 50,000 men under their flags. In fact, a total of 1,000,000 soldiers would attack France.

The attack was being prepared in Belgium. Wellington, who had his headquarters in Brussels, commanded the British, Germans and Dutch, and Blücher, who had made his headquarters in Liège, led the Prussians. In all, they had 230,000 men. Pushed into war, Napoleon again had to work miracles to muster close to half a million men to form several armies, including the Army of the North, 124,000 strong, which he himself would command. It was with great sadness that he went to war again: 'I want peace, and I, who would never have consented to sign the Treaty of Paris, promise now that it has been signed, to carry it out faithfully.'

It did not matter. The Austrian forces were gathering on the south-eastern and eastern borders, Blücher and Wellington were ready to act, the Russians were in Austria approaching by forced march, and the Germans were camped on the banks of the Rhine.

The battle would be rough, and on 12 June, before setting out from Paris on the road to Flanders, Napoleon remarked to one of his close advisers: 'You very much need me to win a battle . . . In twenty or thirty days, everything will be decided.'

His plan was precise. Since Wellington and his 104,000 British, Dutch, Belgian and German troops were separated from Blücher and his 120,000 Prussians, he would attack them separately. With Blücher beaten, Wellington would be pushed to the coast, where it would be easy to encircle him and force him into a precipitous re-embarkation. Napoleon could then turn his attention to the Austrians and the Russians who would have arrived. However, this plan did not allow for any failures. 'A singular campaign,' he wrote later, 'in which I saw the assured triumph of France and the establishment of its destiny slip from my grasp three times in less than a week'.

During the night of the 14th he marched on Charleroi and surprised Blücher, who withdrew to Ligny. It was then – the first unforeseen element – that one of his division generals, Bourmont, a royalist, went over to the enemy and revealed his plans. The tables were turned. Blücher held his ground so as not to be separated from his English ally and settled in close to Ligny, before Namur, where he was engaged on the 16th. Napoleon had General Grouchy hold the Prussian left while he concentrated all his efforts on the centre and the right and Ney attacked the rear. 'The Prussian army is lost if you act vigorously,' he wrote to Ney, Prince de la Moskowa.' The fate of France is in your hands.'

Ney, unfortunately, delayed too long in engaging the English at Quatre-Bras, sacrificing 10,000 men in vain, and Napoleon drove back the Prussian force but without being able to catch them in a vice. Blücher, thrown from his mount, was forced to retreat, but because of the late hour and their lack of troops the French forces could not exploit the victory. Forty-eight hours later at Waterloo, those troops which had just tasted defeat would decide the outcome of the campaign.

With Blücher and Wellington temporarily separated, Napoleon attacked the English, who were deployed on the heights of Mont-Saint-Jean, leaving General Grouchy to pursue the Prussians and contain them. His manoeuvre was masterful: break through the enemy's centre and take the Château d'Hougoumont on the left, the La Haye Sainte farm at the centre, and the La Haye and

Papelotte farms on the right in order to outflank the enemy, which would fall back to the forest of Soignes, where they would be routed. At eight o'clock in the evening on 17 June, he confided to Marshal Soult: 'The enemy army is larger than ours by more than a quarter. We still have a ninety per cent chance of winning.' He reviewed the troops, who had slept in the mud, and was greeted as usual with cheers. 'If my orders are carried out properly,' he assured them, 'we will sleep in Brussels tonight.'

It was at this point that the errors began to multiply. Exhausted and sick, he slept for an hour, waiting for the ground to dry and for Grouchy to arrive, thus losing precious time while Blücher's Prussian reinforcements quickly approached the battlefield. General Reille, who had been instructed to take Hougoumont, sacrificed too many soldiers and did not succeed. The arrival of the Prussian Von Bülow made it necessary to send in divisions which were originally part of the exploitation force. Napoleon would have to cancel his outflanking attack on Wellington's left for lack of troops, unless Grouchy arrived soon.

Around one o'clock in the afternoon Ney attacked La Haye Sainte and, though the artillery reserve was bogged down too far from the enemy positions to be of much help, took the position; carried by the momentum, he attacked Mont-Saint-Jean and pushed back the British cavalry, but not without taking heavy losses. 'It is an hour too early!' exclaimed Napoleon, who was following the movement through his field glasses. He did nevertheless support the marshal with 3,000 cuirassiers, but the British divisions, lined up as if on parade, did not budge. Reinforcements were required, but the only reserve left was the 13,000 men of the Guard. And Bülow was advancing, attacking the French rear, at Plancenoit. If only Grouchy would come! 'This morning we had a ninety per cent chance of winning; we still have sixty,' muttered Napoleon. 'And if Grouchy marches quickly, Bülow's corps will be completely destroyed.' Grouchy and his 33,000 men would decide the outcome of the battle.

Blücher soon rejoined Bülow at Plancenoit and was contained by the Guard only with great difficulty. With night approaching, Napoleon decided to get things over with the English without Grouchy. He sent the Old Guard to attack Mont-Saint-Jean, but Wellington, determined to hold out until the arrival of the allies who would assure his victory, gave strict orders to hold the position to the last man in order to give the Prussians time to come up. The Guard was met with fierce fire from the English lines and had to withdraw. Napoleon was about to send in his last six battalions to help them when a Prussian cavalry force appeared at his right rear. It was a rout. Someone shouted, 'Every man for himself!' Ney retreated. Wellington, taking advantage of the confusion, gave the signal to counter-attack. Caught in a pincer movement between the English and Prussians infantries, the Guard formed a square while the remnants of the army fled towards Charleroi.

Napoleon, who for a long time had been hoping that a cannonball or a bullet would put an end to his ordeal, let his horse take him where it would. His officers pushed him out of the battlefield: 'Sire, the enemy would be too happy!' His face was covered with tears and dust. He had trouble staying in the saddle. He suddenly appeared very old and very weary. 'The man of battles, his eyes blank, listened to the last cannon shot he was to hear in his life,' wrote Chateaubriand.

The manoeuvre of demoralising an army by the sudden appearance of a force on its line of retreat, a manoeuvre which Napoleon himself had used so often, had defeated him. Those who had beaten him had learned his lessons. Wellington's victory, which at first could not have been foreseen, was indeed due to the Prussian attack on the French rear.

Often on St Helena, thinking back to this battle in which it had taken 156,000 enemy troops to rout 72,000 exhausted French troops, Napoleon would blame himself rather than credit the winning generals: 'The mistake I made was going to bed at Fleurus on the night of the 16th. The Battle of Waterloo would have taken place twenty-four hours earlier. Wellington and Blücher would not have joined up . . . If it had not been for the desertion of a traitor, I would have annihilated the enemies at the start of the campaign. I would have crushed them at Ligny if my left had done its duty. I would have crushed them again at Waterloo if my right had not failed me . . . Oh! Wellington certainly owes old Blücher a nice candle. Without him, I do not know where His Grace, as they call him, would be, but I very certainly would not be here. His troops were admirable, and his preparations were pitiful, or more precisely, he did not make any. He had put himself in a position where it was impossible for him

to do so and, strangely enough, that is what saved him in the end
. . . Fortune did more for him than he did for it.'

One thing is certain. On the morning of the battle Wellington
had stated that he could hold out until three o'clock and that if the
Prussians did not arrive by then he would be lost. The Prussians
only arrived with fresh troops at six o'clock, and his great
achievement therefore was holding out for three hours in
hopeless conditions. As for Grouchy, his responsibility is heavy.
He was supposed to contain Blücher and he let him pass without
seeing him. He heard the noise of the cannons and should have
moved. He was with a prominent citizen eating strawberries.

That final defeat matters little in the end. In terms of the number
of his campaigns and his victories, the number of troops involved
and his strategy and tactics, Napoleon is certainly the greatest
military genius of all time, far superior to his illustrious
predecessors Hannibal, Caesar and Frederick of Prussia. 'With
my complete Imperial Guard of forty to fifty thousand men, I
would have had the strength to cross all of Europe,' he explained
on St Helena. 'It might be possible to equal my army of Italy or my
army of Austerlitz, but nothing could ever surpass them.'

There was never anything like those battles, which he analysed
for the little court at Longwood during the long evenings of his
exile: 'Marengo, so long undecided, yielded all of Italy . . . Ulm
saw the destruction of an entire army . . . Jena delivered the whole
Prussian monarchy . . . Friedland opened up the Russian empire
. . . Eckmühl decided a whole war . . .' Mme de Montholon, little
interested in his memories, asked politely which were the best
troops. 'The ones that win the battles, madame,' replied the
Emperor sharply. 'The best troops were the Carthaginians under
Hannibal, the Romans under Scipio, the Macedonians under
Alexander and the Prussians under Frederick.' He could have
added his own, under his command.

CHAPTER V
The Writer and Thinker

What a novel my life is!

Napoleon

Thiers said: 'It is acknowledged that Napoleon was the greatest man of his time, but he was also the greatest writer.' Vigny, Hugo and Balzac also admired the Emperor's style and his intellect. Barbey d'Aurevilly maintained that all the writers of the century had been influenced by Napoleon's revolution and marvelled at his 'genius for writing'. Sainte-Beuve compared him to Pascal. Several critics have likened him to Julius Caesar; the two men of war shared a knack for expressing clearly what they conceived so easily. Another described his writing as simplicity itself, and commented that the man who had inspired so many words had expressed himself in so few. On St Helena, re-reading his proclamations and his bulletins, he himself exclaimed with some satisfaction, 'And they dared to say that I could not write!'

Had it not been for his great genius for action that marked his century and the next, he would undoubtedly have been attracted to the prestige of literature. Because his true passion was not war but improving the living conditions of the population, he would certainly have been tempted by the power of the pen. From his first writings, a work on Corsica and a defence of Jean-Jacques Rousseau written when he was about 17 years old, to his will, a literary masterpiece, he demonstrated what his historian, Frédéric Masson, called *imperatoria brevitas* or imperial concision, 'the crafting of clear, incisive, powerful sentences'. His thinking was as clear, lively and swift as his imagination, and in addition to the ability to zero in on the essence of his subject, he possessed a flair for images and a talent for well-aimed barbs. Quite naturally then, this man who had filled the whole world with the sound of his

153

actions as a military leader and statesman found a special place in the literature of the nineteenth century and perhaps even, like Julius Caesar, in the literature of all time.

The important authors of his youth were Voltaire and Rousseau. According to one witness, he read Rousseau's *New Héloïse*, a book described by its author as 'a sensual dream accompanied by moral instruction', an early work of Romanticism, at the age of 9 – unusual reading for a youngster! Actually, the passionate, sensual love story interested this scrawny, unprepossessing kid less than Rousseau's association with Corsican nationalism, of which he himself wrote a history during his stay in Valence. He wrote a study comparing love of country and love of glory, in which he examined 'the motives of the famous patriots who hold a distinguished place in the annals of the Universe'. In an essay on royal authority, dated 1788, when he was a young man of 19 he stated with quiet audacity: 'There have been very few kings who did not deserve to be dethroned.'

He next wrote a series of notes on Frederick I, financial problems during the reign of Louis XV and the East India Company, as well as notebooks on the history of artillery, his own military speciality. From Plato's *Republic*, which he read with pen in hand, he got the idea that 'it is just for subjects to obey their rulers'. He soon became interested in Bernardin de Saint-Pierre and Buffon, and took statistical tables on demographics from the latter. Already fascinated by the East, he filled two whole notebooks while reading a history of the Arabs. But he did not accept all the views of the author; for example, when the author said Muhammad did not know how to read or write, young Bonaparte noted: 'This does not seem likely to me.' From a history of Venice that fascinated him for weeks, he retained details which he still remembered during his Italian campaigns.

The readings and notes that involved so much activity and insatiable curiosity in his youth were followed by a period of personal writing: a short story, 'Le Comte d'Essex' ['The Count of Essex'], his first stylistic exercise, a well executed ghost story, one of those fantastic narratives for which he would have a penchant throughout his life; then a history of Corsica in the form of some very lyrical letters addressed to the Abbé Raynal, the most prominent philosopher of the time. In 1791 he finally had the satisfaction of seeing his name on a pamphlet published in one hundred copies, his *Letter to Buttafuoco*, a Corsican legislator, which Stendhal described as 'a satirical pamphlet absolutely in the style of Plutarch'. His 'Dialogue on Love', of 1792, contains a very bold statement for a young man of 20: 'I believe love to be harmful to society and to the individual happiness of men.'

In 1793 he became quite well known with the publication, at the expense of the Republic, of *Le Souper de Beaucaire*, which was a timely work of propaganda. In September 1795, as a general on half pay, he wrote 'Clisson and Eugénie' after the end of his affair with Desirée Clary, the sister-in-law of his brother Joseph and the future queen of Sweden. In 1796 he married Josephine de Beauharnais and on his way to Italy wrote her letters full of youthful passion which should win him a place in the literature of love: 'I have not spent a day without loving you. I have not spent a night without holding you in my arms. I have not taken a cup of tea without cursing the glory and ambition that keep me away from the soul of my life. In the midst of things, leading troops, visiting the camps, my adorable Josephine reigns in my heart, occupies my mind, absorbs my thoughts. If I rush away from you with the speed of the Rhône, it is only to return to you more quickly. If I get up to work in the middle of the night, it is because that might advance the arrival of my sweet friend by a few days.' And again: 'Love me like your own eyes. But that is not enough. Like yourself. More than yourself, than your thoughts, your mind, your life, your all . . . I will sleep without you. I beg of you, let me sleep. For several days I have been holding you in my arms.' These were fiery words for a young philosopher who not very long before had considered love harmful to society.

Placed in command of the army of Italy, which thanks to him was soon victorious, he lost the habit of writing in his own hand, preferring to dictate, but he continued to aspire to literary work and he sacrificed the verbosity of youth for the concision of a man of action, and sentimentality for forceful eloquence. 'He developed,' wrote Lanson, 'a short, brusque, tense, nervous style that admirably expressed both his true nature and the idea he wanted to present of himself.' His proclamations to the army and to the nation and his bulletins from Italy through to Waterloo are masterpieces of psychological warfare reminiscent of Julius Caesar's *Commentaries*; they have a spellbinding power and consist of short, striking sentences full of images: 'Soldiers, you are naked and poorly fed'; 'Soldiers, I am happy with you'; 'Soldiers of Italy, could it be that you lack courage?' Using everyday words and simple ideas which every soldier as well as the officers could understand, he spoke of honour, homeland, the glory of France, liberty and the great plans that the army and its leader shared. The lecture always ended with the promise of victory, salvation, rest and personal glory: 'You will return to your homes, and your fellow citizens will point to you and say, "He was in the army of Italy"; or you will only have to say "I was at the Battle of Austerlitz" for people to answer, "Here is a brave man"; or people will say, "He was at the great battle before the walls of Moscow."'

The bulletins, which Chateaubriand said had 'the eloquence of victory', are not mere staff reports, but well worked narratives, with tables, figures, dialogues, reflections and comments by the Emperor, and they were sold in the schools, the towns and the countryside. 'Our teacher,' Alfred de Vigny recalled, 'constantly read us the bulletins of the Grande Armée and our cries of "Vive l'Empereur!" interrupted Tacitus and Plato.' Even children went effortlessly from the style of Tacitus to that of Napoleon.

How could we fail to mention Napoleon the journalist? He was quite an unusual journalist, of course, since he published only in *Le Moniteur*, his official organ, but a journalist nevertheless, finding time throughout the period of the Consulate and the Empire to write articles that would serve his policy, and doing so with extraordinary talent. The shortest piece, one which all political journalists should refer to when they are tempted to fill columns, is of uncommon strength. On 17 April 1801, when Czar Paul I had just been assassinated and all the chancelleries thought England might have had something to do with it, Bonaparte wrote in *Le Moniteur*: 'Paul I died on the night of 24 March. The English squadron had crossed the sound on the 21st. History will show us the relationship that may exist between the two events.'

For any journalist worthy of the name, there are no unimportant subjects. In 1802 a priest in Paris refused to allow the body of an actress in his church. He certainly picked a good time – just when the First Consul had his head full of the Concordat! 'The priest of St Roch, in a moment of folly, refused to pray for Mlle Chameroi or admit her into his church,' he wrote. 'One of his colleagues, a reasonable man, learned in the true morality of the gospel, received the procession in the Church of the Daughters of

St Thomas, where the service took place with all the regular ceremonies. The archbishop of Paris ordered a three-month retreat for the priest of St Roch so that he could remember that Jesus Christ told us to pray even for our enemies and so that he would be reminded of his duties and would learn that all superstitious practices born in times of ignorance or created by fevered brains and preserved in some ritual and which degrade religion through their foolishness have been prohibited by the Concordat and by the law of 18 Germinal.'

The military leader could with unfeigned emotion create the phrases that brought a family the most terrible news, that of the death of a husband or a father. His letter to the widow of Admiral Brueys after the Battle of Aboukir deserves to be quoted in its entirety: 'Your husband was killed by a cannonball while fighting aboard his ship. He died without suffering, the sweetest death, the one most desired by military men. I feel your pain intensely. The moment that separates us from the thing we love is terrible; it isolates us from the Earth; it makes the body feel the convulsions of mortal agony. The faculties of the soul are annihilated; it maintains its connection with the Universe only through a nightmare that alters everything. One feels in this situation that, if there was nothing to oblige us to live, it would be much better to die. But when,after this first thought, one presses one's children to one's heart, tears, tender feelings bring nature back to life . . . Yes, madame, you will cry with them, you will raise their childhood and cultivate their youth; you will talk to them of their father, of your pain, of their loss, of the loss to the Republic. After reconnecting your soul to the world through family love and maternal love, realise the friendship and the keen interest I will always feel at the death of my friend. Be persuaded that he is among those men, few in number, who deserve to be the hope of pain, because they feel with warmth the sufferings of the soul.'

The eloquence of the political man sometimes reaches the level of Shakespearean tragedy. Recall this tirade to the members of the legislative corps on 1 January 1814: 'France is in peril, on the verge of being invaded by the enemy, and the deputies are becoming arrogant.' Or: 'I am of the race that is killed but not dishonoured . . . What is the throne, anyway? Four pieces of wood covered with a piece of velvet. Everything depends on who sits in it.'

Defeated, fallen, hunted, when he spoke to the nation, to his soldiers or to the enemy that had seized his person by the most vile of stratagems, he still found sentences that one might believe were written by Plutarch. To the nation, he explained simply: 'I offer myself as a sacrifice to the hatred of the enemies of France. May they be sincere in their declarations that it is only my person they have anything against.' To those who had fought throughout Europe under his command, he promised: 'Soldiers, when I yield to the necessity that forces me to go away from the brave French army, I take with me the happy certainty that the homeland, by the distinguished services it expects, will justify the praise that our enemies themselves cannot refuse it.'

In writing to the prince regent of England after he abdicated, he became the man of letters again, imbued with classical culture: 'Your Royal Highness, pursued by the factions which divide my country and by the enmity of the greatest powers of Europe, I have ended my political career and I come, like Themistocles, to sit at the hearth of the British people. I place myself under the protection of its laws which I claim from Your Royal Highness as the most powerful, constant and generous of my enemies.' We know the answer of that prince, who was perhaps unfamiliar with the story of Themistocles.

When his enemies sent him to St Helena, without judgement, in violation of all laws, he struck a tragic note: 'I protest solemnly here, before heaven and men, against the violence done to me, against the violation of my most sacred rights by the seizure of my person and of my liberty . . . I am not a prisoner; I am the guest of England . . . Once I was aboard the *Bellerophon*, I was at the hearth of the British people. If the government, in ordering the captain of the *Bellerophon* to receive me and my retinue, sought only to lay a trap, it has forfeited honour and sullied its own flag.

'I appeal to history: it will say that an enemy who had made war on the English people for twenty years came freely in his misfortune, seeking refuge under their laws.' What more resounding proof could he give them of his esteem and his trust? But how did England respond to such magnanimity? It pretended to hold out the hand of hospitality to this enemy, and when he had turned himself over in good faith it sacrificed him.'

And then on St Helena, he endured inactivity and constant persecution. The martyr's crown. The legendary antechamber. The statesman fallen from grace, the military leader with nothing to do, returned to literature with all the diligence and rigour he had brought to his former endeavours. His life was no longer anything more than the reflection of his memory. The St Helena writings are many and varied, and may be placed in three categories. The memoirs as such cover the siege of Toulon, the 13 Vendémiaire, the Italian campaign, the 18 Brumaire and the beginning of the Consulate, Elba, the Hundred Days and Waterloo. Also in this category are many notes dictated during conversations, on subjects such as the Convention, political relations with Russia and Spain, and religious affairs. The occasional writings refute or criticise publications on his reign or on him as a person, or discuss the conditions and the principle itself of his exile; they include his response to a speech by Lord Bathurst, his letters from the Cape of Good Hope, and admonitions to Montholon. There are also studies of the campaigns of great military leaders, including Turenne, Frederick of Prussia and Julius Caesar.

All this represents a huge amount of work, especially considering that Longwood's library was practically non-existent in 1815 and was adequately stocked only in 1818. It was urgent work, since the exile counted on being returned to the throne, hoping this would come about through a change of heart on the part of his enemies or, sometimes, through a popular uprising against the Bourbons. Even on the days when he became discouraged and resigned himself to the idea that he would die on that rock, it seemed just as urgent to him, and he would think of his son and say, 'My martyrdom will restore the crown to him.'

In any case, through these writings he was preparing for the future, his own or that of his dynasty, by clarifying his political views and explaining his actions as a statesman. They are therefore quite different from the writings of his youth and the rhetoric of his years in power – they show greater eloquence, but also lucidity, logic, even warmth, which make his account of the Italian campaigns, for example, a true literary work. This exceptional man, treated without generosity by a jailer who carried out his orders to the letter, had lost nothing of his intellectual vigour. His writings have all the freshness and force of the discussions of former years in the Council of State. At the very most, when he surveys the centuries and analyses history, he allows himself a little disillusioned nostalgia. Given that he had occupied, then lost, the greatest throne in the world, suffered all kinds of betrayals and then been condemned to walking up and down in a 'park' the size of a flower bed at Malmaison, it is a wonder that he still had the courage – and what courage! – to review his deeds with such lucidity and that he did not simply consider all human enterprises insignificant. Many of the works he wrote during his exile are exercises in style that many a famous writer would have been happy to put his name to.

What did he have to say of the title 'General Bonaparte' that they tried to impose on him? 'When I boarded the *Northumberland*, I was told that I was a prisoner of war, that I was being transported across the Line and that I was called General Bonaparte. I should have been addressed publicly as Emperor Napoleon and not General Bonaparte.'

His response to being condemned to exile without trial was: 'Fifteen million men are oppressing one man in peacetime because he led armies against them in time of war.'

On the respect due him as a sovereign freely chosen by the people of France: 'When with the passing of the centuries a king of England is brought before the fearsome court of his nation, his defenders will invoke the noble nature of a king, the respect due the throne and any crowned head, the anointed of the Lord, and will not his adversaries be able to reply: "One of his ancestors banished his guest ... He exposed him in the most unhealthy place, on a rock in the middle of the ocean ... That man perished there in painful mortal agony, tormented by the climate, by deprivation, by insults of all kinds. Well, that man was also a great sovereign held in high esteem by thirty-six million citizens, the master of almost all the capitals of Europe, host in his court to the greatest kings. He was generous to all. He was for twenty years the arbiter of nations; his family was allied to all the royal families; he was twice the anointed of the Lord, twice consecrated by religion."'

This is what he had to say of the cowardice of the oligarchs who held him prisoner and killed him with petty annoyances: 'Are your ministers not aware that the spectacle of a great man grappling with adversity is the most sublime spectacle? Do they not see that Napoleon on St Helena facing all kinds of persecutions with serenity is greater, more sacred, more venerable than on the highest throne in the world, where he was for so long the arbiter of kings? Those who thus wrong Napoleon demean only their own character and the nation they represent.'

The chroniclers

We must not fail to mention the chroniclers of St Helena, those to whom Napoleon dictated or with whom he conversed with the ulterior motive of using his immense charisma to win them over and leave an image of himself for legend, an image of the liberal Emperor, heir of the Revolution – an image that the monarchs meeting in a congress at Aix-la-Chapelle had contemptuously defined as 'the power of the Revolution concentrated in one person', not knowing that the terrible new spirit embodied in the man they had exiled would soon be shaking their thrones. When boredom and harassment by his guardian took away his desire to give dictation, he told his story through conversation. Knowing that his conversational partners were taking notes and that not one word would be lost, he spoke with the greatest candour. Like a philosopher, he reviewed his life with calm lucidity, returning often to the Revolution and the Italian campaigns, his first successes. 'What enthusiasm,' he said, 'and what shouts of "Long live the liberator of Italy!" At the age of 25! From that time on, I saw what I could become, I saw the world rushing along beneath me as if I were up in the air.' He judged those who had been around him, who had served him and who had betrayed him.

'Two thousand leagues from France,' wrote Albine de Montholon, 'the Emperor recounted his life to us. I felt as if we were in the next world and I was hearing a dialogue of the dead.' The poor woman, whom Napoleon described as 'a bit of a ninny', did not appreciate the magnitude of the situation. 'Napoleon talking about himself . . . in a small circle . . . It was a little like listening to Tacitus.'

'I found all the elements of the Empire,' Napoleon said. 'People were tired of the disorder, they wanted to be done with it. Had I not come along, another would have done the same. France would have ended up conquering the world! I repeat, a man is only a man. His abilities are nothing if the circumstances and public opinion do not favour him.' He would glance out at Longwood's little garden in the sun or rain and continue his monologue: 'As much as they try to cut out, eliminate or mutilate, it will be difficult to make me disappear completely. Some French historian will be obliged to deal with the Empire, and if he has any heart he will have to restore something to me, to give me my due, and his task will be easy, because the facts speak for themselves, they shine like the sun.'

He was a talented philosopher of history, and he explained with the clarity of a teacher: 'I closed the abyss of anarchy and brought order to the chaos ... I encouraged all competition, rewarded all merits and pushed back the limits of glory ... what accusations could be made against me that a historian could not refute? ... My despotism? But the historian would show that dictatorship was absolutely necessary. Will I be accused of loving war too much? He would show that I was always attacked. Of wanting universal monarchy? He would show that this was not the chance result of circumstances, that it was our enemies themselves who drove me to it step by step.' These were the elements of his story that he provided to those who listened and then ran off to write down his words, with the Comte de Las Cases leading the way. 'What will we be able to do in that godforsaken place?' Napoleon had asked his chamberlain when he sailed for St Helena. 'We will live on the past,' replied the cunning courtier. 'You will re-read yourself, Sire.' 'Well,' sighed Napoleon, 'we will write our memoirs!'

Las Cases's *Mémorial de Sainte-Hélène* would naturally become the bestseller of the nineteenth century, and there are innumerable contemporary editions, because, although compiled by a rather complex, convoluted writer, it contains, like diamonds embedded in rock, sentences whose style carries the stamp of their author, reflections, prophecies and protests with an unmistakable ring: 'The men who have changed the Universe never achieved this by winning over the leaders, but always by stirring the masses.' 'The colonial system we knew is finished for everyone.' 'The irresistible ascendancy of liberal ideas ...' 'England will end up like Venice.' 'Europe will be Cossack or republican.'

Even though Las Cases signed these books with his own name, one need only skim through their pages to discern on the wall of history the formidable silhouette of the man of the century, the man who 'had the future in his mind': 'Nothing could now destroy or erase the great principles of our Revolution ... These great and beautiful truths must endure forever, we have so interwoven them with splendour, with monuments, with wonders. We have drowned the first stains in waves of glory. They are henceforth immortal! Having emerged from the tribunes of France, they have been consolidated with the blood of battles, decorated with the laurels of victory, greeted with the cheers of peoples and sanctioned by treaties and alliances of sovereigns,and they cannot be reversed . . . They will be the faith, the religion, the morality of all peoples and, whatever they have tried to say, this memorable era will be connected to my person because, after all, I made the torch burn and consecrated those principles, and because today persecution has made me the messiah.' This is the image which went down in legend and which led Stendhal's Julien Sorel to call the *Mémorial de Sainte-Hélène* his 'Koran'.

Ironically, it was a book by a British subject, *Napoleon in Exile* by Dr O'Meara, the Emperor's doctor on St Helena, which had the greatest success after Las Cases's book. This smiling young man, who spoke fluent Italian and who conversed freely with his famous patient, had also acquired the habit of rushing to his work table after these conversations and writing down what he had heard as accurately as possible. 'Wherever I found talent and courage, I raised it and put it in its place. My principle was that career was open to talent without asking if someone had degrees of nobility to show.'

One day he talked about his plan to invade England, a plan which was twenty years old but whose every detail was still fresh in his mind: 'I would have gone into England with a flotilla of 200,000 men; I would have landed as near as possible to Chatham; and from there I would have headed towards London, where I could have arrived four days after my landing. I would have proclaimed the Republic . . . the abolition of nobility and the House of Lords . . . liberty, equality and the sovereignty of the people; all that would soon have brought me supporters. I would have let the House of Commons continue to exist, but only after it had been substantially reformed. I would have made a proclamation to announce to England that we had come as friends of the English nation, to deliver it from a perverse and corrupt aristocracy, in order to give a popular form to its government.' O'Meara objected that the residents would have burned London down, but he shook his head and replied, 'No, no, I do not believe it; you are too rich and too much in love with money.'

The *Journal de Sainte-Hélène* [*The St Helena Journal of General Baron Gourgaud, 1815-1818*] also has the ring of truth, especially because the author, who did not want it to be published, did not have the slightest literary ambition. He took down conversations with Napoleon or monologues by him in a jumble every evening, and the journal perfectly reproduces the atmosphere of the moment and the mood of the man who spoke while pacing back and forth in his miserable parlour. In these pages, we find a very familiar Napoleon, extremely candid, even brutally frank, because Gourgaud, argumentative and finicky, often pushed him to the limit – but so incisive! None of it is boring, because it is all brilliant, the fits of rage, the recriminations and the regrets, the energy, the style, even a humour which is quite unexpected and which today would be described as black. What emerges is a portrait of a very human hero, who even in adversity remained in good spirits: 'I get irritated, saying that Montholon thinks only of setting himself up comfortably and of having nice furniture, and the others – nothing,' says Gourgaud. 'I only have two chairs. Napoleon replies: "You're a bachelor, and that's enough." "But, Sire, a woman is a nice piece of furniture." His Majesty gets mad. So do I. He calms down. I sulk. He tells me to be happy. I tell him that only schemers succeed in this world. His Majesty says, "Oh, indeed."'

Talking with this young man, who had been at his side on the battlefield since 1805, allowed Napoleon to relive the past. What a storyteller he was when he talked about the Revolution, the campaigns, religion, God, history, literature, Waterloo. It was as if he was in a waking dream. The shout of a sentry or the sound of the rain on the roof of his miserable house of exile would bring him back to reality, and Gourgaud would hear him say with a sigh, 'Do you believe that when I wake up in the night, I have no bad moments when I remember what I was and where I am now?'

General Bertrand, the grand marshal of the palace, whose *Cahiers de Sainte-Hélène* [*Notebooks from St Helena*] have recently been published, was a veritable stenographer, the clerk of that period. Although he sometimes had to pay for it – Napoleon treated him inconsiderately – he gives us Napoleon's blunt words unedited, because Napoleon spoke with a certain forthrightness which his secretaries had always softened. With this faithful old companion, Napoleon talked about strategy, administration, politics and diplomacy, and played with ideas and words. 'What distinguishes the Emperor's kind of mind,' wrote Bertrand, 'its distinctive characteristic, is his faculty of focusing his attention on an idea, examining its every facet and not abandoning it until it is exhausted, or, to use his characteristic expression, taking it "by the neck, by the tail, by the feet, by the hands, by the head", considering it thoroughly from every point of view; he easily spent ten or twelve hours on a single idea.' Thus we find in Bertrand stylistic touches, turns of phrase, and judgements which are the essence of Napoleon – right to the end, of which the grand marshal was a faithful witness.

The Emperor's days were numbered in that spring of 1821. Three weeks before his death, confined to his room, he wrote his last work, his will, whose well-crafted sentences are engraved in almost everyone's memory:

'I die in the Catholic religion, apostolic and Roman, in which I was born more than fifty years ago.

'I wish my ashes to rest on the banks of the Seine, amid the French people I loved so much.

'I die prematurely, murdered by the English oligarchy and their hired assassin. The English people will not take long to avenge me.

'I had the Duc d'Enghien arrested and tried because this was necessary to the safety, the interests and the honour of the French people when the Comte d'Artois by his own admission had sixty assassins in Paris. Under similar circumstances, I would do the same thing.

'I bequeath to Marchand, my chief valet, 400,000 francs. The services he rendered me are those of a friend. I want him to marry a widow, sister or daughter of an officer or soldier of my Old Guard.

'I recommend to my son that he never forget that he was born a French prince and never let himself be used as an instrument in the hands of the triumvirs who oppress the peoples of Europe. He must never fight against France or harm it in any manner; he must adopt my motto: Everything for the French people.'

It was a political work, of course, which was to direct the conduct of his executors, Bertrand, Montholon and Marchand –

whose actions could promote the accession of Napoleon II. Therefore, no one was forgotten, neither the wounded and amputees of Waterloo nor the ravaged cities and devastated towns, nor any faithful follower or widow or orphan. And fearing that his writings would not get to France or that they would be misunderstood, he left oral instructions to those who would close his eyes, repeating the clauses of the will more emphatically and even more frankly: 'My son must not think of avenging my death, he must take advantage of it. He must be the man of his time . . . He should often read and meditate on history; it is the only true philosophy. But everything you say to him, everything he learns will be of no use to him if he does not have, deep in his heart, that sacred fire, that love of the good, which alone makes it possible to accomplish great things.'

It was an exhausting effort for a dying man and he had to stop often to recover and change position, but he went on. The language is clear, the style strong: 'I had come to sit at the hearth of the British people; I asked for honest hospitality . . . I was answered with irons . . . England saw fit to surprise and to drag down kings and to give the world the unheard-of spectacle of four great powers hounding a single man. You have killed me slowly, in detail, with premeditation. England will end up like the superb Republic of Venice, and I, dying on this horrible rock, deprived of my own family and lacking everything, I bequeath the disgrace and horror of my death to the ruling family of England.'

He still had the strength to write something of an author's flourish, a 'last word' addressed to General de Montholon, when the papers had been signed, the inventories completed, the boxes sealed: 'Well, my son, wouldn't it be a pity not to die after I have put my affairs in such good order!'

It was not all over yet, however, for this man who was so precise, so meticulous, so orderly. On 22, 24 and 26 April, ten days before breathing his last breath, he gave some additional instructions to Bertrand, who immediately made a note of them. 'He said he had made a very popular will, one that left the executors a great deal of latitude and a nice job to do. "I have examined my conscience; I wish to pay all my debts, all those of my childhood."'

Bertrand further recounted: 'He stated that he was dying in the Catholic religion and that he wanted communion and the last rites, but he actually died a theist, believing in a god that rewards virtue and is the principle of all things, and had said he was Catholic because he felt this was "acceptable to public morality". He asked that his French doctor carry out the autopsy alone, but expected that the governor would send a British doctor and cautioned that it would be necessary to make sure that "there were no stupidities added to the report".

'He said his family would have to take over Rome, ally itself with all the princely families, that is, the ones that have had popes ... With the Hercolanis and Gabriellis, of course ... His nieces could wash the feet of the pope but not those of anyone else. Two days later, this idea of a Roman alliance came back to him and he repeated it with the forthrightness of a soldier. His family could live with dignity only in a theocracy like Rome or a republic that had a real stability and independence, like Switzerland; making themselves oligarchs of Switzerland, they would be independent, with obligations to no one, and they would maintain their dignity. There alone could his family be respected: it could kiss the pope's arse – that wasn't kissing just anybody's arse nor any family's – but it could not kiss the arse of the king of England, Sweden or Naples.'

What should be his friends' and supporters' guiding principle? 'The interest of France ... I see no other.'

The thinker

A writer is by definition a thinker, and Napoleon's writings and conversations leave us with the image of an exceptionally complex personality, one which nevertheless may be defined in a few words: a man of the nineteenth century, blessed with all or almost all the talents, consumed by a new spirit and ahead of his time. He was a man of the Enlightenment and he always remained a follower of Rousseau although he sometimes denied it with a joke: 'The future will tell whether it would not have been better for the peace of the world if neither Rousseau nor I had lived.'

He presented himself as the heir of the great and generous principles of the Revolution and spoke often of liberty and equality, stating emphatically, 'Everything that it is possible to give of equality, the French have received from me.' Equality in duties, but also equality in rights: 'I encouraged all competition, rewarded all merits . . . My maxim has always been: career open to talent, without distinction as to birth . . . Whenever I found a man of merit and talent, I promoted him, without asking him how many degrees of nobility he had.' He had experienced the evils of social injustice and the consequences of inequality of opportunity, and he reduced them: 'One of my main goals was to extend public education among all classes of the population. I made the costs of an ordinary education so moderate that a simple farmer could pay them . . . If I had thought only of myself and my power, if I had really had any goal other than the rule of reason, I would have tried to smother its light under a bushel; instead I tried to bring it to everyone.' He saw himself as the embodiment of the French people's love of equality: 'I governed for the whole community, for all of the great French family. I have always thought that sovereignty resides in the people.' A silence, and then, skilful storyteller that he was, he continued: 'I am the man of the people, I come from the people myself . . . I in no way usurped the crown, I found it in the gutter; the people placed it on my head.'

His detractors immediately ask the question: 'And the liberty of the people?' His answer: 'Those who reproach me with not giving enough liberty to the French are unaware that in 1804 ninety-six Frenchmen out of a hundred did not know how to read . . . I gave all I could give of liberty to these masses, intelligent but ignorant and demoralised by the anarchy of the revolution and by war.'

He did indeed give them liberal laws: 'I have sowed liberty with both hands everywhere I introduced my *Civil Code*.'

He granted religious freedom: 'I wanted everyone to believe and think in his own manner, and for all men, Catholics, Protestants, Jews, Muslims, deists, to be equal.'

But his dictatorship? insist his adversaries. How could this 'philosopher' accept that? 'It was necessary, and the proof is that I was always offered more power than I wanted.' It was necessary because reactionary Europe of the absolute monarchs dreamed of annihilating the France of 1789 and its principles embodied in one individual, and necessary because within France there was danger from those who were nostalgic for revolutionary violence: 'From outside they attacked our principles with arms, but it was precisely in the name of those principles that I was attacked from within. If I had released my grip even a little, I would soon have been brought back to the time of the Directory.'

If only he had had the time to disarm the conspiring kings. In 1820, stuck on his rock, he dictated to one of his generals a draft Constitution for his son to use as a model if he was called on to reign:

'The French are equal before the law, whatever their social position.

'Individual liberty is guaranteed to all.

'Freedom of the press is established as a right.

'Freedom of worship is guaranteed.

'All property is inviolable.

'All Frenchmen enjoying civil rights are voters.'

That was the constitutional monarchy he dreamed of and which he would have established if Europe under arms had not provoked him unrelentingly. He was the champion of the new spirit on the scale of Europe. Let us listen to him on a night in February 1818, dictating his continental policy: 'I have always considered general peace to be the first condition for the regeneration of Europe. When I received the mandate to govern from the French nation, I understood the need to put its social organisation in harmony with that of the other nations of Europe in order to close the abyss of revolution and carry out the reorganisation of everything, using the kings to satisfy the legitimate interests of the peoples.' This system would have had the inevitable result of increasing the splendour and the security of royalty while giving full satisfaction to public liberties. Never had a broader vision, at once both royal and popular, been conceived for the conciliation of two great interests made enemies as a result of the French Revolution: the old monarchies and the peoples.

He was a man ahead of his time and his great dream, so timely today, was that of a balance in Europe: a federated Europe governed by the principle of nationalities. 'There are more than thirty million Frenchmen, fifteen million Spaniards, and thirty million Germans in Europe; I would have liked to make each of these peoples a single national body. That would have been a wonderful way to win the benediction of history!'

Whenever he discussed the building of this Europe he was haunted by the Russian peril: 'Russia will one day flood Europe with its Cossacks.' If there was an emperor of Russia who was courageous, forceful, capable, who had backbone – only he used a much more colourful expression – Europe would be his. He could begin his operations on German soil, a hundred leagues from the two capitals, Berlin and Vienna. He could take one by force, and with its aid crush the other one. If circumstances required, he could in passing throw a few firebrands over the Alps into Italy, very ready for an explosion, and then he would march triumphantly towards France, of which he would once again proclaim himself the liberator. The only rampart against this fearful threat was a strong independent Poland, supported by the Western powers: 'Poland is western Europe's natural barrier against Russia.'

With that border guarded, he saw his Europe being built quickly. For the Germans, he laid the foundations for a unity that would only be realised in 1871: 'The unification of the Germans would require more time; all I did was simplify their enormous complexity. Not that they were prepared for centralisation; on the contrary, they could have reacted blindly against us before understanding us. How did it happen that no German prince had considered the inclinations of his nation or knew how to take advantage of them? Assuredly, had heaven had me born a German prince ... I would have governed the thirty million united Germans infallibly.'

For the fifteen million Italians, unification was already well advanced; it only needed time, and each day brought closer the unity of principles and legislation, of thought and feeling, that unfailing bond of human society. The joining of Piedmont, Parma, Tuscany and Rome with France had no goal other than to supervise, guarantee and advance the national education of the Italians.

The smaller countries were not left out of his calculations: 'If I had succeeded in my planned invasion, I would have separated Ireland from England and made it an independent republic ... Greece awaits a liberator ... I was perhaps not far from it ... When I reached the shores of the Adriatic during my Italian campaign, I wrote the Directory to say Alexander's kingdom was within my view.'

His detractors say he failed, that these were nothing but fanciful dreams. Absolutely not! 'Whatever happens, this unity will come about sooner or later of its own necessity; the impetus is there, and I do not think that after my fall and the disappearance of my system there is any great balance possible in Europe but the unification and confederation of the great peoples.' Once, in Paris, he had even stated:

'Perhaps then it would be possible to dream of a designation for the great European family like that of the American Congress or the amphictyonies of Greece . . . What a prospect of strength, grandeur, joy, and prosperity!' To the end, this vision haunted his meditations in exile: 'I wanted to prepare for the merging of the great European interests as I had effected that of the parties among us. Europe would in this way truly become a single people'.

Europe was not the only focus of his speculations on the future. He was convinced that the Spanish colonies of America – Mexico, Venezuela, Chile, Argentina – which were in revolt against the power of Madrid, would emancipate themselves: 'This is a new era,' he announced in 1812. 'It will bring the independence of all the other colonies . . . They will all emulate the United States. One tires of waiting for orders from two thousand leagues away, obeying a government that seems foreign because it is far away and because it necessarily subjects you to local interests that it cannot sacrifice for you. As soon as colonies feel strong enough to resist, they want to shake off the yoke of those who created them.'

While the soldier deplored the fact that he had to do battle on all the plains of Europe, the philosopher always regretted that the goal of a united Europe could not be attained through conferences. He once confided this to his minister of public education: 'Fontanes, do you know what I admire most in the world? It is the inability of force to organise anything. There are only two powers in this world: the sword and the spirit. By the spirit I mean civil and religious institutions. In the long run, the sword is always beaten by the spirit.'

One has to admire him! But one can understand the bewilderment of his contemporaries. Only a scholar like Laplace could exclaim: 'Thanks to the genius of the Emperor, the whole of Europe will soon form a single, huge family united by the same religion and the same code of laws.' But a diplomat of the old school, born under Louis XV, groaned as he left an audience with Napoleon: 'What a man! What great ideas! What dreams! Where is the straitjacket for this genius? It is unbelievable. We are between Bedlam and the Pantheon!'

The material selected from his writings shows why the Emperor is as popular for what he wanted to do as for what he did. He is remembered for his dreams, which subsequent generations have often made reality, as much as for his military glory and his gifts as an administrator. He was as certain that he would endure on that rock of St Helena as he was on his throne 'thinking for ninety-five million people'. One sentence perfectly conveys that assurance. On St Helena Las Cases once asked him why he had not brought with him Frederick of Prussia's sword which he had taken at Potsdam as well as his alarm clock. He smiled, cheerfully pinched his chamberlain's ear and said, 'I had my own!' He indeed had his own! As a man of war he eclipsed Frederick and Alexander, and as a writer he may well be the equal of Julius Caesar.

CHAPTER VI
Assassination on St Helena

More than ten years ago, I wrote a book describing the research I carried out for several years with my Swedish friend and colleague Sten Forshufvud in order to prove that Napoleon was poisoned on St Helena. That book, *The Murder of Napoleon* (New York: Congdon and Lattès, 1982), has been published in eighteen languages and has sold more than a million copies. Not bad for a history book. This proves that there is still very strong interest in everything about Napoleon. More books have been written about Napoleon than any other person in history. The *Encyclopaedia Britannica* states that two hundred thousand books have been written on his period; some French historians claim the number is closer to four hundred thousand.

This is astounding. People often ask me how I can be so certain that Napoleon was poisoned. After all, he died almost two hundred years ago. The answer is relatively easy. Eight eyewitnesses have told me so – through their books, of course – and the information they provided has been confirmed by nuclear science. These eight eyewitnesses, who were Napoleon's companions on St Helena, were:

- the Marquis de Las Cases, who, with Napoleon, worked on what would become his book, *Memorial de Sainte-Hélène*;
- Baron Gourgaud, a general in the Grande Armée, who had insisted on sharing the Emperor's exile;
- Dr O'Meara, an English doctor of Irish descent, appointed by the English to act as the Emperor's physician;
- Dr Francesco Antommarchi, a Corsican doctor sent by Napoleon's family to replace O'Meara when he was sent away from St Helena by the English governor, Hudson Lowe;
- Grand Marshal Bertrand, who lived close to Napoleon for more than fifteen years;

- Louis Marchand, the Emperor's loyal servant for ten years;
- Dr Henry and Dr Stokoe, two English doctors who examined Napoleon several times.

It does not take a genius to understand what is stated explicitly. You just have to be receptive and alert, have a little common sense and pay close attention to the facts. However, these facts, as they were reported by the eight witnesses, have been ignored by historians, or at least their meaning was not understood.

The key that put us on the track of the poisoning was provided by Louis Marchand, Napoleon's faithful servant. He was attentive, discreet, educated (he often tidied up drafts of letters written by Napoleon and Montholon), perceptive and absolutely loyal. All the historians are in agreement on this assessment. He was also a very good artist. Napoleon treated Marchand like a son and left him 400,000 francs in his will. He wished to honour him with the title of count, and this wish was carried out when Napoleon III came to power. Unlike Napoleon's other companions in exile, who wrote books to make money, Marchand kept a journal because he wanted his family to know what actually happened on St Helena. He asked that his family and descendants never publish it. However, when his belongings were finally sold in the early 1950s, the journal was purchased by Commander Henri Lachouque of the French army, and it was published for the first time in 1955. It was like a bombshell, shedding new light on the mystery of Napoleon's death.

In this chapter I will often speak of Longwood House, the house where Napoleon lived on St Helena, and that is where he was poisoned. Marchand's painstakingly accurate record of daily events at Longwood House is like a doctor's case file of careful notes detailing the decline of a terminally ill patient. His information was vital in 'blowing the cover' on what would otherwise have been the perfect crime.

On 6 May 1821, the day after his death, Marchand brought home to France a lock of hair cut from Napoleon's head and carefully placed it in an envelope on which he wrote, 'The Emperor's hair'. That lock of hair in its original envelope was carefully preserved by his descendants. Neither he nor any other of Napoleon's companions in exile could have suspected that one day, long after they were gone, the contents of this envelope would tell more about the years at Longwood House than the total of all the correspondence, books and manuscripts published on the Emperor's exile on St Helena.

Anyone who examines the evidence I present here and in my book *Assassination at St Helena Revisited* will have to agree that Napoleon was murdered. He was murdered to prevent him from ever returning to France and reclaiming his throne as he had done after his first exile on Elba. The facts reported by the eyewitnesses are irrefutable. Napoleon was poisoned on St Helena; there is absolutely no doubt about it. He was poisoned in the way most often used in the nineteenth century. To this day, no pathologist or toxicologist has seriously opposed my thesis. I call it a thesis for lack of a better word, because the poisoning is a fact. Of the thirty-four known symptoms of arsenic poisoning, thirty were reported by the eight witnesses. Furthermore, the presence of a high concentration of arsenic in Napoleon's hair has been confirmed by the most modern methods of forensic medicine and nuclear science.

For the past hundred years, doctors and historians have attributed Napoleon's illness and death to more than thirty causes ranging from gonorrhoea and syphilis to scurvy, hepatitis and cancer. Official history claims that Napoleon died of stomach cancer, although he was very fat when he died. How could this be possible, since stomach cancer is a wasting disease and emaciates the patient? Furthermore, Napoleon never showed any symptoms of cancer. How can a person die of a disease without showing any symptoms of it?

More than thirty years ago, my colleague Sten Forshufvud had tests made of the hair cut from Napoleon's head. Hair grows at a rate of about 2.5 centimetres every two months. Since the hair was cut close to the scalp and was 7.5 centimetres long, it had grown during the last six months of Napoleon's life. By analysing the hair in sections, we were able to determine the exact days on which he was given large doses of arsenic. The analyses showed highs and lows in the levels. The lowest was 2.8 parts per million, and the highest was 51.2 parts per million. In each section of hair tested, the level went up and down, proving that Napoleon ingested a lot of arsenic on some days. The normal arsenic level at the time was about 0.08 parts per million. The following is an example of the results obtained on different sections of Napoleon's hair: 51.2; 45.2; 24.5; 18.8; 2.8; 7.1; 20.4; 24.1.These results, which are very much higher than normal, prove that Napoleon ingested arsenic at different times. There is absolutely no doubt about this.

Some people have attributed the high levels of arsenic in Napoleon's hair to various sources such as the wallpaper in Longwood, the water the Emperor drank, the medicines he took or the hair cream he used. Such causes cannot in any way explain the high densities measured or the substantial variations recorded from one section to the next of each hair. These theories must therefore be dismissed.

In 1974 Sten Forshufvud and I established two chronological lists. The first consisted of Napoleon's symptoms as reported by eyewitnesses on specific dates in the last six months of his life, the period corresponding to the growth period of the hair sample we had had analysed. On the second list we recorded the arsenic levels obtained in the analysis, specifying the dates of the variations. The two lists matched perfectly. For the days when Napoleon showed symptoms of arsenic poisoning, the analysis by the Harwell laboratory indicated spikes in the level of arsenic in the hair.

The reports of the witnesses cannot be questioned. The renowned Harwell laboratory, which did the research for the creation of the British atomic bombs, is one of the most advanced laboratories in the world. The results of its tests cannot be questioned. Therefore, it must be admitted that Napoleon periodically ingested doses of arsenic. The most modern scientific methods have shown that the symptoms reported by the witnesses more than 170 years ago were caused by arsenic poisoning.

In 1821, and even today, it is rare that a doctor doing an autopsy is able to detect arsenic poisoning without carrying out scientific tests. I asked Professor Henri Griffon, the chief of toxicology of the Paris police, to explain the difficulties encountered in detecting arsenic poisoning. He replied that he had never met a doctor who had correctly diagnosed arsenic poisoning as the cause of his patient's illness. Arsenic is tasteless and odourless; it is a first-class poison.

In September 1967 Mrs Esther Castellani died in Vancouver, Canada, after being sick for nine months. Long after her burial, a woman contacted the Canadian minister of justice to say that Mrs

Castellani had been murdered and that if she were given immunity she would reveal the identity of the guilty party and how the crime had been committed. The autopsy report had concluded that the cause of death was a viral infection and a heart attack but, since the woman insisted, the minister finally granted her immunity. She then described in detail how, in complicity with the victim's husband, René Castellani, she had poisoned the victim with arsenic. René Castellani had promised to marry her as soon as he collected the insurance money, but when the money was in his pocket he changed his mind. The body was exhumed and the hair tested, exactly as we did for Napoleon. The result showed that the arsenic level was high enough to cause death. Mr Castellani was arrested, tried and convicted, and sentenced to twenty-five years in prison. On 26 September 1967, the day of the verdict, Dr Moscovitch, who had treated the victim, said neither he nor the many specialists he had asked to examine the patient had ever thought of poisoning. He stated, 'The possibility of arsenic never occurred to us at all.' During Mrs Castellani's illness, 125 tests had been performed without detecting the presence of arsenic.

Dr Moscovitch also said that arsenic poisoning has many guises and that the symptoms are very often misleading. This is exactly what led Dr O'Meara to believe, in turn, that Napoleon had dysentery, scurvy, gout, ulcers or other illnesses. If a doctor considers two or three symptoms of arsenic poisoning separately, it is not possible to determine their true cause. To diagnose arsenic poisoning, a doctor would have to consider 'all the symptoms together' and realise that they 'are specific to arsenic poisoning'. Unless the doctor were informed in advance, there would be no reason to suspect arsenic, since the symptoms, taken separately, resemble those of many other diseases. It is only when they are all considered together that the pattern becomes clear.

Let us look at some of the symptoms described by one witness, Dr Francesco Antommarchi, who was Napoleon's personal physician. In his diary entry for 26 February 1821, he wrote: 'The Emperor, who has been quite well since the 21st, had a sudden relapse, with a dry cough, vomiting, an almost unbearable burning in the intestines, general agitation, anxiety and a burning thirst.' On 27 February: 'The Emperor is worse still than yesterday. The cough has become more violent and the painful nausea did not stop until seven o'clock this morning.' The analysis of the hair section corresponding to this period shows a spike in the arsenic level, indicating that Napoleon ingested a dose of arsenic at that time.

It is important to realise that Napoleon did not die of arsenic poisoning, but rather that he was actually poisoned to death in two phases, by a method used by professional poisoners of the period. The classic method of killing a person without leaving any trace consisted of a latent phase (arsenic) followed by a lethal phase (the *coup de grâce*). The latent phase of the poisoning of Napoleon began in June 1816 with arsenic poisoning. Arsenic is colourless, odourless and tasteless and can be mixed with food or drink without risk of detection. A quantity that can be contained in a small envelope is enough to murder someone. Napoleon was given arsenic gradually and periodically in order to break down his health and make it appear that he was declining in a normal way from disease. Killing him outright would have sparked a new revolution in France, where he was still deeply loved by the vast majority of the population and the army. To succeed in this first phase of the process, the murderer had to have access to the food and drink the Emperor consumed, but he had to be careful not to poison anyone else. The food eaten at Longwood House was shared by all those living there, but Napoleon had his own wine supply, which was Vin de Constance, a wine imported from Cape Town especially for him. He was the only one who drank it. The others drank whatever wines were available.

In their diaries and notes, the eight eyewitnesses reported more than thirty symptoms of arsenic poisoning, just as they are described in the most modern books on toxicology. To ignore what these eyewitnesses say is to ignore history. If Napoleon had not ingested arsenic during the latent phase of the poisoning, then how could the eight witnesses, independently of each other, have reported symptoms of arsenic poisoning? If Napoleon died of stomach cancer, why did he never show any symptoms of it, and how could he have died fat? It is obvious that he simply did not die of cancer.

The lethal phase

This phase began at the end of March 1821 and, were it not for modern methods of forensic medicine and our painstaking investigation, it would never have been discovered. The crime would have been a perfect crime. It was carried out by means of the introduction of toxic chemicals such as tartar emetic, a salt of antimony, followed by orgeat and calomel (sweet mercury). Dr Antommarchi wrote on 21 March 1821: 'I felt the emetic would be very useful and I pleaded with Napoleon not to neglect himself . . . but he expressed his repugnance at the very mention of the medicine.' This might lead one to think that Antommarchi was the author of the poisoning or an accomplice, but that was not the case; all he did was prescribe what was the classic treatment of that time.

In Louis Marchand's diary, the following entry appears for 22 March 1821: 'The Emperor ended up accepting the medication at the insistence of the Comte de Montholon, who supported Antommarchi's efforts to persuade him to take it. The emetic was administered to him in two doses, taken some time apart; the resulting efforts (to vomit) were extremely violent . . . but he only brought up some mucus.'

The treatment was repeated several times in the following days. The emetic was antimony potassium tartrate. Its symptoms resemble those of arsenic poisoning. It is no longer used today because of its high toxicity. Given the limitations of medical knowledge at the time, it was quite common for doctors to prescribe the emetic in the hope that, by vomiting, the body would rid itself of illnesses for which they had no other treatment. Antimony potassium tartrate corrodes the mucous lining of the stomach. This eventually inhibits the normal vomiting reflex by which the stomach protects itself, and the patient becomes unable to expel poisons. Before administering the *coup de grâce* with mercury cyanide, it was necessary to make Napoleon's stomach incapable of expelling that poison. Mercury cyanide is obtained by mixing orgeat and calomel.

On 22 April a new drink was served to the Emperor for the first time. It was orgeat. Orgeat is an orange-flavoured drink which usually contains the oil of bitter almonds. It was served to Napoleon on the pretext of quenching his overpowering thirst. Thirst, incidentally, is one of the symptoms of arsenic poisoning. On 25 April Lutyens told Gorrequer (both were officers on governor Hudson Lowe's staff): 'The Comte de Montholon asked

179

for bitter almonds, because he cannot find any in Jamestown [the port of the island].' That same day, 25 April, Grand Marshal Bertrand reported, 'Hudson Lowe sent a case of bitter almonds.' The orgeat that Napoleon had been drinking for three days was for the time being harmless. With the addition of bitter almonds, which contain prussic acid, it could become deadly. Before that date, there were no bitter almonds at Longwood. Apparently the poisoner began to worry about being able find any, because Grand Marshal Bertrand noted, without mentioning the name, 'Someone asked my son Arthur to go out and gather peaches and put them in the pantry.' Peach stones can have the same effect as bitter almonds, since they also contain prussic acid. As we shall see, these bitter almonds made it possible for Napoleon to be killed without leaving any evidence of a criminal act.

The book *Toxicologie clinique* states that oil of bitter almond rapidly becomes a poison when ingested, and death occurs quickly in an adult who ingests a quantity of 7.5 cubic centimetres. Grand Marshal Bertrand tell us in his journal that a few days before his death Napoleon was very thirsty (a symptom of arsenic poisoning) and he drank a lot of orgeat. Antommarchi's journal mentions that he was concerned about Napoleon's constipation (another symptom of arsenic poisoning). The remedy for this ailment at that time was calomel. In the book *Clinical Toxicology of Commercial Products*, we read that calomel contains mercurous chloride.

Now – and this is particularly important – Louis Marchand says that on 3 May at 5:30 p.m., he administered to Napoleon, without his knowledge, ten grains of calomel in powder form mixed with sweetened water. This dose may be called heroic – or insane. The normal dose for constipation was a quarter of a grain, and so ten grains was forty times the normal dose. Grand Marshal Bertrand stated, 'This [the 10 grains of calomel] was the direct cause of Napoleon's death.' Let us see how the decision was made to give Napoleon ten grains of calomel.

On 3 May Grand Marshal Bertrand wrote: 'At 2:30 p.m., Hudson Lowe arrived at Montholon's with the English doctors Shortt and Mitchell.'

Dr Antommarchi: 'I have been summoned to Montholon's where I had to list the symptoms of the Emperor's illness . . . The English doctors recommended a purgative of ten grains of

180

calomel. I protested against this prescription; the patient is too weak.'

The Marquis de Montchenu: 'The disagreement between the doctors was then submitted to Montholon, who sided with the English doctors, and the medicine was therefore administered.'

Louis Marchand: 'When I received the order to administer the calomel, I said that the Emperor had clearly told me he wanted no drink or potion that he had not approved . . . They answered that the Emperor was lost and every effort had to be made to save him . . . So I finally agreed to mix the powder [the grains of calomel] with water and a little sugar . . . When the Emperor asked me for something to drink, I presented it to him as sweetened water. He opened his mouth, swallowed with difficulty and even tried unsuccessfully to throw it up. Turning to me, he said with a tone of reproach so affectionate and so difficult to convey: "Are you too deceiving me?"'

Calomel contains mercurous chloride, and orgeat with bitter almonds contains prussic acid. The combination of these two substances in the stomach forms mercury cyanide, which is immediately expelled by a healthy stomach. But Napoleon had already ingested large quantities of emetic, which had inhibited his vomiting reflex. Consequently, the highly toxic mercury cyanide was retained.

What happened next?

Grand Marshal Bertrand: 'Shortly afterwards, Napoleon lost consciousness. He became completely paralysed. He could not even swallow.' It is well known that mercury cyanide paralyses the voluntary motor muscles.

Antommarchi, 10 p.m.: 'The ten grains of calomel have not yet produced any result.'

Grand Marshal Bertrand: 'At 11:30, the Emperor produced a black stool.'

Saint-Denis: 'The potion had an effect; it produced the evacuation of a thick blackish substance, partly hard, that looked like pitch or tar.'

Comment by Forshufvud: Stools from a stomach that is corroded and bleeding are very dark brown. Metallic mercury, produced by the calomel-orgeat reaction, is black as ink.

Louis Marchand, 4 May: 'About 10 p.m., the Emperor tried to

vomit. I gave him a small basin in which he threw up a blackish substance.

Comment by Forshufvud: Again, this colour is characteristic of metallic mercury. Napoleon's stomach made a last effort to save the poisoned organism, but it was too late. The poison had done its work.

Napoleon died on 5 May 1821, at 5:49 p.m., that is, forty-eight hours after taking the ten grains of calomel.

What does mercury cyanide do to the stomach? It corrodes the stomach wall and causes an annular swelling of the pylorus muscle. The *Larousse médical illustré* explains the very toxic effects of orgeat and calomel in combination and warns against combining them in any treatment.

The autopsy performed by Antommarchi in the presence of many others, including the English doctors, revealed that the stomach lining had been heavily corroded and there was swelling around the pylorus. The doctors concluded that Napoleon had died of a condition leading to cancer. In fact, he died of cyanide poisoning following a long period of arsenic poisoning. People do not die of a condition leading to cancer – they die of cancer.

Dr Henry, after the autopsy, noted how effeminate Napoleon appeared, because he had no body hair. He should have realised that the loss of body hair is a symptom of arsenic poisoning. The Marquis Henri de Montchenu was Louis XVIII's representative on St Helena. He reported: 'Of the five doctors present at the autopsy, not one knew the exact cause of death.'

Was there a poisoner on the island? Yes, beyond the shadow of a doubt. On 24 February 1818 Cipriani, Longwood's majordomo, suddenly fell sick, though he had always been in perfect health; he died two days later. He had violent stomach pains and chills. These are signs of acute arsenic poisoning, which can be detected by autopsy, as we saw in the Castellani affair.

Cipriani had been in the service of the Bonapartes since his early childhood. He was an orphan who considered Letizia, Napoleon's mother, his second mother. He was very intelligent and clear-sighted, and nothing escaped his attention. Montholon did not hide his aversion to him, and once remarked: 'The Emperor prefers Cipriani to all of us. Majordomo is a very lowly position for someone who possesses all the qualities of a minister of the police.'

Cipriani was buried the day after his death, in the cemetery of Plantation House, that is, very close to the residence of Hudson Lowe. However, William Balcombe, who had been host to Napoleon at his property 'The Briars' at the beginning of his exile, was convinced that Cipriani had been poisoned. The decision was made to do an autopsy, but when they went to the grave to exhume the body, they discovered that it had recently been desecrated and the body had disappeared. Did the poisoner panic when he found out an autopsy was to be performed? The investigation that would have followed the proof of poisoning would probably have led to his discovery or, at the very least, would have created a climate of suspicion at Longwood which would have considerably hindered the continuation of his criminal activity. Who could have taken the body from the grave and transported it to a place where no one would find it? The poisoner could not have done so alone. Nor could he have asked for help from the French at Longwood, for he would have risked being immediately denounced.

It must therefore be acknowledged that this heinous crime was committed by the English, acting under the orders of Hudson Lowe, since nothing that happened on the island, and *a fortiori* at Plantation House, escaped his attention. The body was probably weighed down and thrown in the ocean. No one other than the English could have taken the body from the grave and made it disappear forever.

Now, we must ask the key question: since Napoleon was poisoned, who was the guilty party?

We must review certain facts to find the answer to this question. Whoever poisoned Napoleon had to have lived at Longwood House from the summer of 1816, the period during which Napoleon began suffering from arsenic poisoning, until 5 May 1821, the date of his death. This immediately rules out everyone who left St Helena before his death as well as those who arrived after the summer of 1816. There remain only Louis Marchand, Grand Marshal Bertrand and the Comte de Montholon. The person responsible for the poisoning would have had to be in regular contact with Napoleon, and therefore had to live in Longwood. This rules out Grand Marshal Bertrand, who lived elsewhere because his English wife wanted more privacy than Longwood afforded.

The only ones left are Louis Marchand and the Comte de Montholon. Louis Marchand is recognised by all historians, as he was by the St Helena exiles, as a loyal and devoted servant who served Napoleon like a son. He had no possible motive to harm Napoleon.

The Comte de Montholon, on the other hand, had no reason to admire or serve the Emperor on St Helena, although he had volunteered to go with him. Napoleon was only 46 years old when he arrived on the island, and he was in excellent health. He could have lived at least twenty years more. That would have meant that Montholon would have to spend a good part of his life on a rock in the middle of the ocean. Unless he was an agent of the Bourbons and knew in advance that his stay would be short, there can be no logical explanation for his presence.

It is even possible to find a good reason for Montholon to hold a grudge against Napoleon. He had been discharged from his post as ambassador of France to Würzburg because he had disobeyed the Emperor's express orders by marrying Albine Roger, who was already twice divorced.

The Comte de Montholon had strong ties with the royalists. His father-in-law, the Comte (later Marquis) de Sémonville, was a friend of Louis XVIII and the Comte d'Artois. The Comte de Sémonville was known as a schemer and a very crafty individual. He had held high positions in successive French regimes from Louis XVI to Louis-Philippe, including the Revolution, the Consulate and the Empire, almost a unique feat in those turbulent times. It has been established that he was always an agent of Louis XVIII's brother, the Comte d'Artois, who would himself become king under the name of Charles X. For outstanding services rendered to the Bourbons, on 4 June 1814 (when Napoleon was exiled on Elba), King Louis XVIII named him a peer in the French House of Lords and a Grand Referendary. He therefore occupied one of the highest positions in the court of France. It was he who insisted that his son-in-law, the Comte de Montholon, go with Napoleon to St Helena.

The Comte de Montholon had used the name Montholon-Sémonville. However, when he left for St Helena, he dropped Sémonville to become simply the Comte de Montholon. He was known as a Don Juan, he enjoyed the fast life and he was always short of money. Louis XVIII had appointed him a general in the royal army in 1814, during Napoleon's exile on Elba. At that time, he had embezzled military funds amounting to six thousand francs. He was never punished for this crime, thanks to the intervention of the Comte d'Artois. Why would a man like this have wanted to spend twenty years of his life on St Helena? Quite simply because he was there on a mission, a mission of the greatest importance: to see that Napoleon had no chance of returning to power in France.

After the death of Cipriani, Montholon got himself assigned to the position of Longwood's wine steward. He thus had exclusive control of the wine served to the Emperor, and it was with this wine that Napoleon was poisoned. Indeed, Baron Gourgaud in his memoirs reports that he warned Napoleon of the possibility of his being poisoned through the wine. Napoleon did not take this warning seriously. What had got Gourgaud thinking about this was that on 11 July 1816 he had surprised Albine de Montholon while she was reading the book *Histoire de la marquise de Brinvilliers* [*The Story of the Marquise de Brinvilliers*]. Marie Madeleine d'Aubray, the Marquise de Brinvilliers, was the most famous criminal of the century of Louis XIV. Convicted for poisoning a large number of people with arsenic, including her father and her two brothers, she was beheaded and burned in the Place de Grève on 16 July 1676. Before dying, the marquise made a detailed confession of her crimes. Her confessions and those of two of her accomplices provide the material for the book, which describes in detail how to kill someone slowly without risking discovery. In fact, the marquise would never have been suspected, in spite of the deaths occurring repeatedly around her, if thirty-four incriminating letters had not been discovered after the sudden death – natural in this case! – of her lover Sainte-Croix. The Montholons had thus brought to St Helena what was in a sense a *poisoner's manual*.

It is also interesting to note that Grand Marshal Bertrand, in a letter to Cardinal Fesch, wrote that a few days after the death of Cipriani, a servant of Montholon also died with the same symptoms. Could she have drunk some leftover wine that Montholon had prepared for Cipriani? We will never know, but it is still a bizarre coincidence.

Montholon was alone with Napoleon, who was semi-conscious, when a whole series of codicils were added to his will.

It should therefore not be surprising that he received the lion's share. He was named one of the three executors and he received 2.2 million francs, a huge sum at a time when the average annual income of a household was in the order of two thousand francs. It should also be noted that in 1829 he had to flee to Belgium to escape his creditors. All the historians agree that Montholon was an unscrupulous schemer who lied easily on any occasion. All the companions of Napoleon's exile kept diaries or wrote memoirs. All recorded Napoleon's symptoms in more or less similar terms, with the exception of Montholon. For example, Montholon wrote that Napoleon was emaciated when he died, while all the others, including the English doctors who were present, said that Napoleon was excessively fat. To prop up the cancer version, Montholon had to lie and say that Napoleon died emaciated. Louis Marchand was still alive when Montholon's book was published in 1848. He declared that either Montholon was a liar or his memory had betrayed him.

When Napoleon's body was exhumed, nineteen years after his death, to be brought back to France, it was in an excellent state of preservation. This is typical of arsenic poisoning. Arsenic kills, but it also slows down the decomposition of the tissues. The Harwell nuclear research laboratories, which are among the most advanced in the world, could not have been wrong in detecting levels of arsenic as high as 51.2 p.p.m. in their analyses of Napoleon's hair.

I asked Roger Martz, the head of the FBI toxicology unit, who directed the blood and hair analysis for the O.J. Simpson trial, to measure the quantities of arsenic contained in two of Napoleon's hairs. His answer was as follows:

U.S. Department of Justice
Federal Bureau of Investigation
Washington, D.C. 20535
August 28, 1995

Dear Dr. Weider,
    The FBI laboratory examined two of Napoleon's hairs that you had submitted for arsenic analysis.
Listed below are the arsenic results which were analysed by Graphite Furnace Atomic Absorption Spectroscopy:

Hair Number	Length (cm)	Weight (ug)	Arsenic (ppm)
1	1.75	45.0	33.3
2	1.40	35.8	16.8

The amount of arsenic present in the submitted hairs is consistent with arsenic poisoning.

If you should have any further questions, please contact me by phone or fax . . .

Sincerely yours,
Roger M. Martz
Unit Chief
Chemistry / Toxicology

Thus the FBI confirmed the results from Harwell without the least ambiguity. This should put an end to any controversy. Napoleon was indeed murdered on St Helena. In this account, we have detailed the means and method used by the murderer. We have also, by determining the facts and the motives, identified that murderer. The case is perfectly clear. Napoleon was killed by Montholon, who used, in succession, arsenic to weaken his body and a high dose of cyanide for the death blow.

In committing the crime, Montholon certainly acted alone at Longwood House, but it seems obvious that he received outside support from Hudson Lowe. Already, on 15 November 1816, in his diary, Dr O'Meara noted that Hudson Lowe had asked him to write a report on Bonaparte's health and had instructed him to keep in mind that the life of one man could not outweigh the adverse consequences if Napoleon were to escape, that General Bonaparte had caused millions of deaths and could cause more, that the life of one person was of little significance and that his position as Napoleon's physician was of very great political importance. In 1818, after his dismissal from St Helena, O'Meara confided in the surgeon of the *Favourite*, that if he had followed Hudson Lowe's instructions, Napoleon would already be dead. For repeating this allegation in London, he was discharged from the Navy.

In May 1962 in London, Sten Forshufvud met Mabel Brookes, an elegant old lady who was the great-granddaughter of William Balcombe. 'I am delighted that you are presenting the evidence

187

that the Emperor was poisoned,' she said. 'You know, it is a tradition in our family that great-grandfather believed the very same thing.' And Cipriani? 'Great-grandfather was always suspicious about Cipriani's sudden death.' How can we explain the disappearance of Cipriani's body the day before the scheduled autopsy without thinking of Hudson Lowe, who tightly controlled everything that happened on the island?

Finally, the most important element: Hudson Lowe was the one who provided Montholon with the bitter almonds for the *coup de grâce*, and he was also the person who went to Montholon's on 3 May to impose the ten grains of calomel.

Major Gorrequer noted in his diary on 17 May 1821: 'Hudson Lowe, through passion and insistence, forced Doctors Shortt and Arnott to modify the conclusions of the autopsy report, because he did not want them to describe the changes they had noted in the liver.'

As Hudson Lowe was not the kind of man to take such an important initiative as the assassination of Napoleon, it is certain he was ordered to do it by the cabinet in London, with the full agreement of the French court.

Thus the plot to murder First Consul Bonaparte, which had begun in 1803 when William Pitt returned to power and, in league with the Comte d'Artois, had the Royal Navy transport some killers – Georges Gadoudal on 23 August 1803, and then General Pichegru on 16 January 1804 – to the Normandy coast, finally reached its conclusion when Napoleon was without protection on St Helena. Montholon had been sent to St Helena by the Comte d'Artois to see that Napoleon would not have the least chance of returning to France and regaining power as he had done after his first exile on Elba. He carried out his mission as an agent of the Bourbons perfectly.

CHAPTER VII

The Judgement of History

It is better not to have lived than to have left no trace of one's existence.

Napoleon

'I have no fear for my fame; posterity will do me justice,' Napoleon said. He added: 'Once the first fury has passed, people of intellect and judgement will come back to me; I will keep as enemies only the foolish or the wicked . . . And what is the end result, after all, of the huge sums spent to ridicule me? Soon there will be no trace of the ridicule, while my monuments and my institutions will commend me to the most distant posterity. Once again he was right, and he deserves credit for keeping a cool head after being showered with so much flattery and so many insults.

It was Napoleon's fate to be practically deified on his throne – in the Ingres portrait, he looks like thundering Jupiter – and then vilified after his fall, and in both cases with extreme exaggeration. Already during the Consulate, a prefect declared in a speech, 'God made Bonaparte and then he rested.' The bishop of Mainz expressed the wish in the pulpit, 'May the Earth be quiet, so that it may listen in silence to the voice of Napoleon.' A preacher stated, 'What good fortune for God that so great a homage should be given him by such a powerful genius.' The contagion spread to the highest dignitaries, and the idol himself had to throw a little cold water on this ardent worship. He rebuked his minister of the navy, Decrès, without mincing his words: 'I will thank you for not comparing me to God. There is so much singularity, and so much disrespect for me, in those words that I prefer to believe that you did not think about what you were writing. I pity your judgement.'

But the hyperbole continued nevertheless. A woman of letters wrote that he made history pale, and a famous scientist stated,

'His head is the source of great ideas as the Sun is the source of light.' It makes one believe the words of Alfred de Musset: 'A single man was alive then in Europe; the other creatures tried to fill their lungs with the air he had breathed.' As he had done with Decrès, the Emperor at the height of his power rebuked the sycophants unsparingly and complained about the platitudes heaped upon him. 'There is too much flattery around me,' he grumbled. 'I have lost all patience with it.'

But what could he do about it? Even the czar and the kings besieged him with messages saying they admired and were indebted to him, to the point that after his defeat they had to use all kinds of trickery and spend a great deal of money to recover their correspondence, which had become compromising. They had written to 'the illustrious first consul' of the 'veneration and wonder' with which Europe regarded its 'hero', the 'brightness' of his 'virtues' and the 'salutary purpose' of his policy. Such adulation could only encourage an almost excessive pride in the Emperor of Europe of the years 1808 to 1812 – in the Emperor more than in the man, for it was the person and the majesty of the sovereign, 'always alone on one side with the world on the other', an actor always on stage, who let himself get carried away and surrounded himself with pomp, protocol and etiquette; the man, on the other hand, did not lose his bearings and, as observed by his soldiers, valets and doctors, remained simple, frugal and thrifty, like a country gentleman, 'obliging, good, pleasant and kind to everyone.'

In 1814, when Czar Alexander entered Paris as a conqueror and discovered the Vendôme Column, topped with a statue of his 'friend', the Emperor of the French, he said, making a witticism, no doubt, but also explaining a phenomenon that amazed him: 'How could one's head not be turned when one is placed so high?' And yet, while the head of the Emperor was sometimes bothered by excessive compliments, Napoleon the philosopher never allowed his head to be turned. The wise man never allowed himself to be crushed by the weight of his statue. Nor did the man who would accept only praise addressed to the first sovereign of Europe allow himself to be disturbed by the hatred of his enemies outside France or that of the royalists within it, for whom he was the Antichrist, the evil genius, the ungodly one, the son of the satanic Revolution, the beast of the Apocalypse, the monster of iniquity . . . The man himself, a fine psychologist and a coolly lucid person, familiar with what Goethe called the use of mirrors, was well aware that neither the praise nor the insults had any substance, that none of it came from very deep in the heart, that those who praised him would be the first to criticise him and that his most stubborn enemies would be won over in time. There were people such as his minister Fontanes, who owed everything to him, and who proclaimed in 1806 that the Emperor 'obliterated all the greatness of the three preceding dynasties,' and who ten years later eased his conscience for having betrayed him by saying that after all 'he was not even French'.

To those who wanted to place him in bronze or marble on all the monuments, Napoleon merely replied, 'It is not for me to make monuments to myself.' Not for him, no, but for history.' The truth will be known,' he said, 'and the good that I did will be judged with my failings. If I had succeeded, I would have died with a reputation as the greatest man of all time. And even without having succeeded, I will be considered an extraordinary man. I fought fifty pitched battles, almost all of which I won . . . I created a code of laws that will bear my name for centuries. I rose from nothing to become the greatest monarch of the world. Europe was at my feet.'

While he was still buried in an unmarked grave in Geranium Valley, there was one printing after another of the *Mémorial de Sainte-Hélène*, the gospel of the prophet, an apologia for the man who had wanted to give the peoples of Europe a new era of liberty, order and peace. And more than one young head was disturbed by a familiar voice that was believed extinguished and ideas thought buried under the stones guarded by a sentry, as Béranger sang:
'Tell us about him, grandmother,
'Tell us about him.'
And Byron, another victim of British ostracism, issued a challenge:
How low, how little was this middle state,
Between a prison and a palace, where
How few could feel for what he had to hear!
Vain his complaint – my lord presents his bill,
His food and wine were doled out duly still:
Vain was his sickness, never was a clime

So free from homicide – to doubt's a crime.

Heinrich Heine, the most French of German writers, attacked eternal England: 'To you belongs the sea; but the sea does not have enough water to wash away the shame this illustrious man has bequeathed to you in dying ... Even to the most distant future, the children of France will sing and tell of the terrible hospitality of the *Bellerophon*, and when these songs of irony and tears resound beyond the channel, the cheeks of every honest Englishman will be red. But a day will come when this song will be heard, and then there will no longer be an England. It will lie in the dust, the people of vanity ... And St Helena will be the Holy Sepulchre where the peoples of East and West will come in pilgrimage on flag-bedecked boats.'

His poem 'The Grenadiers', set to music by Schumann, was soon being sung by Romantic youth, for whom Napoleon was a hero: 'Then the Emperor will ride over my grave on horseback to the beat of drums and the clash of sabres; and I will emerge fully armed from the grave to defend him, the Emperor.'

As for Goethe, confined in illustrious solitude and an old age rich in memories, he silenced detractors of the great man with his 'Leave my Emperor in peace!'

Heine spoke of a 'pilgrimage' and the word was not too strong, because the deification of this personage who had been martyred on St Helena was well under way. How right he had been once again, the prisoner tormented by his guardians, killed, as he said, by 'pinpricks', petty annoyances: 'Adversity was all my fame lacked. I have worn the imperial crown of France and the iron crown of Italy; and now England has given me another, greater still and more glorious – the one worn by the Saviour of the world – a crown of thorns.'

By deporting him to a remote barren rock, by quibbling over the title he would be called by history – because when one says 'Emperor', it always means him – by rationing his supplies, by treating him like an outlaw, England really made this prophet a martyr. As for those who tried to humiliate him, we need only recall the words he threw in the face of Hudson Lowe in 1816: 'In a few years, your Lord Castlereagh, your Lord Bathurst and all the others, you will be buried in the dust of oblivion; or if your names are known, it will be for the indignities you subjected me to!'

Hudson Lowe, demoted from lieutenant general to colonel, was offered the command of a regiment somewhere in the Far East by ministers who wished him to be far away so they could forget him like a bad dream. A petit-bourgeois who was eager to push himself into fashionable society and who believed that he had on St Helena acquired the right to a kind of celebrity, he knocked on many doors, but without success. Lady Holland, whose salon at Holland House was the most elegant in London, was instructed by her husband, a nephew of the great Fox and a Whig leader, not to receive him, because with Lowe present it would be difficult for him to maintain any restraint when speaking of the treatment Napoleon had received from the English government and its consequences for his health and his life, and it would be equally difficult for his wife to hear the language he might use.

Lord Castlereagh, who had heaped hatred and sarcasm on Napoleon, slit his throat in 1822. And Louis XVIII, in Heine's apt words, was rotting on his throne. Meanwhile, the poets of Europe were celebrating the man who, as Victor Hugo said, 'dominated the horizon of his era as Vesuvius dominates the Bay of Naples'. But the peoples of the continent were still oppressed, and the unfortunate continent was carved up, to the great indignation of Musset, by moribund powers 'who had made themselves from the purple of Caesar a harlequin's cloak'. Those peoples were beginning to throw off the yoke, and the young people of Rome, Milan and Berlin were shouting, 'Long live the Emperor!' and 'Long live liberty!', which to them meant the same thing. The exile himself had predicted this on his death bed: 'You will again hear Paris shout, "Vive l'Empereur!"'

In 1833 his statue was restored to the Vendôme Column, and in 1840, amid unprecedented popular fervour, his remains were returned to the capital to be placed under the gilded dome of Les Invalides. And in literature his conquest ended, as always, in victory. Balzac, who considered Napoleon 'a great example transposed and reflected in literature', filled his *Human Comedy* with 'the pale and terrible "Caesarian" figure spoken of by Duchess d'Abrantès': 'This woman saw Napoleon as a child, she saw him as a young man, she saw him busy with the ordinary things of life and then she saw him rise and cover the world with his name. She is to me like a blessed person who had come to sit at my side after having lived in heaven, very close to God.'

Before the Chambre des Pairs, the French House of Lords, Victor Hugo exclaimed:

'Seeing the degradation of conscience, the rule of money, the spread of corruption . . . I think of the great things of the past and I am at times tempted to say to the Chambre, to the press, to all of France, "Look, let us speak a little of the Emperor, it will do us good."'

Napoleon's nephew, Prince Louis, the future Napoleon III, stated in a manifesto published in 1839: 'It is not only the ashes, it is the ideals of the Emperor that must be stirred . . . The Napoleonic ideal is not at all an ideal of war, but a social, industrial, commercial and humanitarian ideal. The Napoleonic cause is the cause of the people, it is European, and sooner or later it will triumph.'

Stendhal, who had been in the armies of the Empire, wrote some dazzling pages on Napoleon, a 'teacher of energy'. He stated: 'The more the entire truth is known, the greater Napoleon will be.' Everything done under the reactionary monarchies of Europe after the regime of this iron man, this logician of action, was, he said, doomed to oblivion.

Thus the Emperor became the idol of the Romantic movement, whose ideal was freedom, freedom of ideas and freedom of language. All these concerned young men in a world in ruins deplored the silence that had followed the end of the epic. Musset was one of them; he said:' Napoleon had shaken up everything by passing through the world; kings had felt their crowns shake and, lifting their hands to their heads, had found only their hair standing on end in terror.' The children of this century lamented the destruction of a society that they bitterly missed and naturally mourned those who had won glory by following Napoleon from Italy to Russia to the ring of 'La liberté, fille de nos pères' [Liberty, daughter of our fathers]. It was thus that an era of glory became legend.

With what exultation the Romantics recalled the achievements of a poor young man, a follower of Rousseau, born of a patriarchal family from Corsica, who had begun his career by breaking the chains of the Italian people, who had spoken of liberty and equality, and who had paid for his sins by dying in exile on a remote island. The St Helena grave shaded by weeping willows suddenly became the counterpart of Rousseau's at Ermenonville.

How drab the restored world of absolute kings suddenly seemed! As Heine fiercely proclaimed, 'With Napoleon has died the last hero of the old style, and the new world of money-grubbers breathes easy, as if rid of a glaring nightmare.'

A Romantic hero, Napoleon also became a historical pheno- menon studied by the thinkers of history. Some of his critics wrote some impressive pages! Jules Darni, who called himself a 'martyr to freedom of thought', considered Napoleon devoid of all moral value. Edgar Quinet accused Napoleon of using his capital of glory for low political ends. Taine tried to present Napoleon as a *condottiere* or a kind of Borgia, but by trying to prove too much, he failed to prove anything. In contrast to these, there were many who praised Napoleon. Arsène Houssave wrote precise, impartial studies which won the admiration of Anatole France. Arthur Lévy painted a portrait of a very human Napoleon. Frédéric Masson became a hagiographer without realising it. Albert Sorel showed Napoleon as 'propelled by circumstances, that is, by Europe, its princes, its peoples, their claims, their traditions, their lust for the world, their designs for supremacy' – the man of a turning point in history. Albert Vandal praised Napoleon for restoring the greatness of France and acknowledged the role of fate in the hero's achievements. Louis Pasteur, after conquering anthrax and rabies, sang the Emperor's praises. Finally in the modern era, Madelin, Aubry and Dunan carried out detailed studies of Napoleon's genius which justified the popular fervour.

The passion for Napoleon spread throughout the world. Even in Britain, where Napoleon was so hated, there were countless collections devoted to him. Among them were John Sainsbury's Napoleon Museum in Red Lion Square, the catalogue of which was published in 1845 with a sentence from Fox describing Napoleon as the greatest of all men; the collections of the United Service Museum; the wax figures of Mme Tussaud; and famous private collections belonging to A. M. Broadley, Lord Rosebery and C. K. Shorter. Lord Curzon left a moving narrative of his visit to St Helena and bequeathed to the Bodleian Library a valuable collection of Napoleonic documents, and Field Marshal John French, the victor of Ypres, a fervent admirer of the Emperor, was proud to display his collection of imperial relics at Deal Castle.

Many writers have been led by feelings of indignation, compassion or curiosity to study Napoleon and finally to admire him. Colonel Napier, who fought Napoleon in Spain, made no secret of his admiration for him in his *History of the War in the Peninsula*. Lady Stanhope, receiving a French traveller in her tent in what today is Lebanon, told him bluntly that, having left Europe eight years before with no intention of returning, she missed nothing there, that the nations of Europe were debased and their kings imbeciles, and that there was only one man worthy to command the Arabs and the world but the kings of Europe had exiled him! During the same period, people in London were repeating with delight Lady Granville's description of Hudson Lowe as having the face of a devil.

The books came one after the other. The old Wordsworth grumbled, in very bad verse:

Never may from our souls one truth depart –
That an accursed thing it is to gaze
On prosperous tyrants with a dazzled eye.

In contrast, there were Shelley, Byron, Hobhouse, Landor and Hazlitt, for whom Napoleon was 'a mortal man beyond all mortal praise', and Browning, Ruskin, Meredith, Conan Doyle and Bernard Shaw. And even those, such as Thomas Hardy, who ranted and raved, had trouble hiding their attraction: 'Spirit sinister . . . My argument is that war makes rattling good history; but Peace is poor reading. So I back Bonaparte, for the reason that he will give pleasure to Posterity.'

In 1886 *A Short History of Napoleon*, by the eminent Sir John Seeley, was published. Then in 1900 Lord Rosebery, the former foreign secretary, published *Napoleon, The Last Phase*, a brilliant plea in favour of the exile of St Helena, in which he stated: 'Till he had lived, no one could realise that there could be so stupendous a combination of military and civil genius, such comprehension of view united to such grasp of detail, such prodigious vitality of body and mind.' This judgement set the tone for the book, about which C. K. Shorter wrote: 'The primary service that Lord Rosebery has achieved by this book is that he, a statesman, a man of letters who has held the highest position in the political life of our country, should have offered, on behalf of Great Britain, a protest and apology that the statesmen of another era had treated Napoleon with an entire lack of magnanimity, and degraded this country by their ungenerous treatment of a fallen enemy.'

J. Holland-Rose placed Napoleon 'in the very foreground of the immortals of human history'. His books *The Personality of Napoleon, Pitt and Napoleon, Napoleonic Studies* and *Life of Napoleon* rejected anecdote to focus on the warrior and statesman who had himself acknowledged, 'I do not have much love for women, or for sport; I am completely a political being.'

Then Napoleon had the honour of a volume in *The Cambridge Modern History*. It was edited by Lord Acton, who stated that 'Las Cases' *Mémorial* is one of the best hundred books in the world.' Sir Walter Runciman, a liberal statesman, began his book *Tragedy of St Helena* by observing that 'there is no public figure who lived before or since his time who is surrounded with anything approaching the colossal amount of literature which is centred on this man whose dazzling achievements amazed the world.' He ended it by rejoicing in the fact that 'each day the dead Emperor is canonised and his prophetic words that posterity would do him justice are being amply fulfilled.'

In 1912 G. L. de St M. Watson published *A Polish Exile with Napoleon*, questioning the opinions and conclusions of W. Forsyth, the biographer of Hudson Lowe, concerning the actions of the British government in the years 1815-21. In 1915 two very well documented historical chronicles by Norwood Young were published, *Napoleon in Exile, Elba* and *St Helena*; Young calls Napoleon 'the great Emperor' and Hudson Lowe 'the wicked jailer', which is indicative of the tone of the books. In 1919 the famous *St Helena Who's Who*, an admiring account by Dr Arnold Chaplin, was published. In 1925 the Count of Kerry, a descendant of Lord Keith, the admiral who welcomed Napoleon to England in 1815, published a respectful collection of previously unpublished letters from the family archives. In 1958, finally, there appeared *Napoleon Bonaparte, His Rise and Fall*, by J. M. Thompson, which portrays Napoleon as the creator of 'laws and institutions in which he adapted the ideas of 1789 to the traditions of the Monarchy and enabled France to survive three invasions and a century and a half of political unrest'.

Vox populi, vox dei ... It would take television, a formidable vehicle for ideas, to popularise in Great Britain the man Gladstone called 'the greatest soldier and the greatest administrator in history'. On 25 March 1975 ATV showed a film by Kenneth Griffith called *Man on the Rock*, described by its creator as 'Napoleon's explosion in words'. Nothing is lacking in this popular chronicle of the exile of St Helena, and Napoleon seems greater than ever on the barren rock that was to become his grave. Amazing words pronounced by the Emperor rang in the ears of the viewers: 'I fought for equality . . . Everywhere I planted my Civil Code, I sowed the seeds of liberty . . . I rewarded all merit . . . I wanted to establish universal liberty of conscience . . . I wanted to extend the benefits of education to all classes of the people . . . I wished to establish a European Code, a Court of European Appeal . . . Europe would have soon become the same people . . . A United States of Europe would have been achieved.' At the end of the film, they heard: 'An unknown British soldier entered the room in which the dead Emperor was lying, on the bed of Austerlitz, covered with the greatcoat worn at Marengo. He was holding his young son by the hand. He said: "Look well, my son, this was the greatest man in the world".'

Among the Russians, that formidable figure has fascinated the greatest writers. Pushkin's lyric poem on Napoleon is considered a masterpiece; he damns the English for inflicting 'the torture of rest' on his hero. Lermontov wrote of 'the burning island under the sky of faraway regions, where he had a guard as great as he and like him invincible – the ocean'. Dostoevsky and Tolstoy both wrote about him. Merezhkovsky ended his life of Napoleon with this prayer: 'Receive, O Lord, the soul of your servant Napoleon, and accept him in the City of the Just.'

In Germany, where admiration for Napoleon was ardent, there was a wave of fervour that included Goethe, Hauff, Hebbel, Grabbe and Heine. One critic justifiably spoke of the 'magical' influence of Napoleon on German writers. Goethe, of whom Paul Valéry wrote that his encounter with Napoleon in Erfurt in 1809 was 'his greatest memory and the diamond of his pride', remembered with a lump in his throat that the Emperor had said to him, 'You are a man', that is, a perfect being beside whom other men were only rough sketches. Nietzsche said that seeing Napoleon made Goethe rethink his *Faust* and even the whole German problem. In 1843 a collection of Napoleonic songs appeared. In 1930 a study of Napoleon in German literature was published in which the author pointed out that it was in Germany that the Emperor had the most admirers and especially mentioned Heine, who in his memoirs of his youth, *Reisebilder*, described his own meeting with Napoleon in a humorous vein:

'What did I become, when I saw him myself with my own eyes, him in person, Hosanna! The Emperor . . . My heart beat a call to arms before the man who had tamed anarchy and settled the duel of peoples . . . A warm, calming smile played on his lips and yet one knew that those lips had only to whistle and Prussia would exist no more. They had only to whistle, those lips, and the Vatican would crumble. They had only to whistle and the entire Holy Roman Empire would start to dance.' Heine also wrote, 'At Waterloo, it is not France that lost the battle, it is Mankind.'

We cannot fail to mention Emil Ludwig's book on Napoleon, although it is controversial; to him, Napoleon shows what a man who is conscious of his strength can obtain through courage, passion, imagination, work and willpower, and his life was 'an epic poem'. The Westphalian Friedrich Sieburg wrote a poetic meditation on the Hundred Days and described Napoleon as 'the most intelligent man in the world'.

In Italy, there have been innumerable admirers of Napoleon, starting as early as 1821, when Manzoni, learning of the death of the hero, was seized with a nervous tremor, an attack that gave rise to his famous *Ode of May 5*, which has been translated into many languages:

'He was. As at his last sigh,
When his great soul expired,
His corpse remained inert,
Thus the world at this news,
Stood still, struck dead.'

In Austria, Sedlitz published a poem that included the following lines:

'This is the great review
Which on the Elysian Fields
At the hour of midnight
Dead Caesar held.'

Grillparzer described the day he saw the Emperor on horseback in front of Schönbrunn Palace being cheered by his soldiers.

A list of the works in praise of Napoleon that have been published in Poland, Sweden, Norway, Holland, Belgium, Hungary, Czechoslovakia, Spain, Portugal, Brazil and the United States would fill chapters, as would a list of the five hundred plays about him. We will mention only the most important.

The Dutch writer Bilderdijk, who wrote an ode to Napoleon,

said of the Emperor's career: 'This is the subject of a Pindaric ode. Before such spectacles, no poet, whoever he may be, if he is really a poet, could remain indifferent; in spite of himself, his lyre sings and his breast swells, stirred by unknown transports.'

The great Beethoven confessed, 'I feel shining deep within me the light of his genius, the fascination of the great immortal.'

Europe has produced a handful of great men of action – Charlemagne, Charles V, Cromwell, Gustav II Adolph, Charles XII, Louis XIV and Frederick of Prussia – but none of them has left an impression comparable to that of Napoleon in the annals of the world and in people's imagination. As Stendhal wrote, he was 'the most admirable, talented man to live since Caesar, whom it seems to us he surpassed'.

The path of this meteor did not end on that remote island; from the ashes that grew cold at the point of his fall there rose the 'Napoleon of the people', a ghost which drove out reactionary kings and attracted an army of admirers, just as in his lifetime he had assembled armies of recruits.

'Your masterly lessons, your unrelenting toil are everlasting examples,' said Marshal Foch in 1921 in front of Napoleon's tomb in Les Invalides, and in 1944 Sir Winston Churchill spoke of Napoleon in similarly glowing terms.

In Peking, before Mao, there was a statue of Napoleon, and he was considered a God; sticks of incense were burned religiously in front of the statue.

Over a century and a half, every generation has given testimony before the court of history – many different minds, but all equally demanding in terms of quality. In this court, Napoleon, as strategist, organiser, legislator, founder of great institutions, writer and thinker, has been proved to be among those who have done the most to change the world, build the future and achieve glory, power and greatness.